P9-CBF-141

Edmund Ruffin
and the Crisis of Slavery
in the Old South

Edmund Ruffin

and the Crisis of Slavery

in the Old South

The Failure of Agricultural Reform

William M. Mathew

The University of Georgia Press

Athens and London

© 1988 by the University of Georgia Press

Athens, Georgia 30602

All rights reserved

Designed by Barbara Werden

Set in Linotron Meridien

The paper in this book meets the guidelines for permanence and durability of the
Committee on Production Guidelines for Book Longevity of the Council on
Library Resources

Printed in the United States of America

92 91 90 89 88   5 4 3 2 1

Library of Congress Cataloging in Publication Data

Mathew, William M.

Edmund Ruffin and the crisis of slavery in the Old South.

Bibliography: p.

Includes index.

1. Ruffin, Edmund, 1794–1865. 2. Slavery—Southern States. 3. Agriculture—
Southern States—History—19th century. 4. Southern States—History—
1775–1865. I. Title.

F230.R932M38 1988   306'.362'0924   87-25535

ISBN 0-8203-1011-5 (alk. paper)

British Library Cataloging in Publication Data available

Maps on pages 33 and 80 are drawn from J. H. Colton's General Atlas, 1859 by
Cartographic Services Laboratory, University of Georgia.

For my daughters,
Caitlin and Jenny,
who were Southerners
for a while.

Contents

Preface

————•••◦∞◦•••————

*T*HIS book examines the relationship between slavery and agricultural reform in the old Southern states of Delaware, Maryland,
Virginia, North Carolina, South Carolina, and Georgia over the forty
years preceding the Civil War. The topic has not, thus far, aroused
much interest among historians. Farming advances and slavery are usually
taken to present two discrete sets of issues, with findings in the one only
occasionally undergoing transference to the other. Since the institution had
a largely agrarian base, however, and since its long-run strength depended
heavily on the adaptive capacities manifested in humdrum material affairs,
questions concerning the scale, spirit, and impact of agricultural improvement on slave farms are of central importance to any comprehensive understanding of the antebellum South.

Disaggregation is necessary and opens up a variety of categories within
the broad sphere of reform. Slavery itself is divisible into crops produced,
competitive circumstances, areas worked, sizes of units, degrees of specialization, and interplays with free labor. Attention here will be focused on a
single body of reform ideas: those set before Southern planters by Edmund
Ruffin of Virginia. The selection is based on a combination of intrinsic importance and contemporary accessibility. Another reason lies with Ruffin
himself, since he forcefully underscores the mix of ideological impulses and
ideological constraints affecting reform. His main long-term purpose was to
secure the future of the slave South through economic adaptation. When he
saw that his efforts were failing he gradually moved his emphasis from eco-

nomics to politics, from the quiet arguments for farm improvement to the heady superficialities of disunionism. The failure, as I will argue later, was itself partly a consequence of slavery. There could, however, be no question of dabbling with the institution to enhance the prospects of reform. Agricultural advance, for Ruffin, had usually not been viewed as an end in itself. His proposals were flawed not by any scientific defect or by any irrelevance to a land-abundant United States, but by their subordinate relationship to vital issues of race control and the survival of plantation society and polity in the South. There is, here, a revealing irony: efforts to protect the institution were compromised by the institution itself. It is probable that Ruffin was aware of it, though it is unlikely that he had any confusion over his priorities. The prime purpose of this book is to document the irony and appraise its implications.

The focus throughout is on the Old South, *in its geographical sense*, for that is where Ruffin planted and proselytized. It was also the part of the Union in greatest economic, demographic, and political trouble—thereby bringing slavery itself into the "crisis" referred to in the title.

In the introductory part 1, these and other general issues are set out. Material is also presented on Edmund Ruffin, one chapter setting out professional biography and another analyzing his economic, cultural, and racist arguments for slavery. Part 2 is scientific, demonstrating the significance of calcareous amelioration and establishing its relevance to the soils, produce, and natural endowment of the Southern seaboard states. (Such an unhistorical section must be included at some stage in the study to help illuminate strictly agricultural issues. No other elucidatory historical text can be cited by way of reference.)

Part 3 takes measure of the Ruffin reforms, first by their impact on crop yields and second by the willingness of planters to adopt them. It will show (at the risk of some tedium for the reader) that although the crop-unit boost was often very large, the geographical spread of ameliorative practice was extremely constricted. Part 4 attempts to explain the latter failure through consideration of a number of possible limiting influences: difficult operations, awkward skill requirements, need for major factor diversions, inflexible plantation schedules, high costs, transport deficiencies, and entrepreneurial weakness. The conclusion is that only transport and entrepreneurship posed serious problems, and that inadequacies therein were in notable measure either consequences or components of slavery. Part 5 offers a summary of the main findings on Edmund Ruffin, on agriculture, and on slavery, and attempts a final formulation of the profound irony characterizing Ruffin's defense of slavery in the Old South.

Records from a wide spread of Southeastern plantations have been examined in Washington, D.C.; Richmond, Virginia; Chapel Hill, North Carolina; Columbia, South Carolina; and Athens, Georgia. They are used principally in chapters 6, 8, and 9.

Three major journals have been subjected to exhaustive scrutiny: the *Farmers' Register* (1833–1842), the *Southern Planter* (1842 to the Civil War), and the *Southern Cultivator* (1843 to the Civil War). Other serial publications extensively consulted were the *American Agriculturist*, the *American Farmer*, the *Carolina Cultivator*, *De Bow's Review*, the *Farmer's Journal*, the *Reports of the Commissioner for Agriculture*, the *Reports to the Commissioner of Patents*, the *Soil of the South*, the *Southern Agriculturist*, and the *Southern Field and Fireside*.

Edmund Ruffin's papers at the Library of Congress and the Virginia Historical Society, and in particular the microfilmed material in the Southern Historical Collection at the University of North Carolina at Chapel Hill, have been studied virtually in their totality.

The underlying theme of this book can be conveyed in a sentence of Seneca's from the first century: *Paucos servitus, plures servitutem tenent.* "Slavery enchains a few; more enchain themselves to slavery."

Acknowledgments

A S THIS book was largely researched in the United States and written in England, it has required considerable financial support to meet travel and Xeroxing costs. Funds were provided on a generous scale between 1975 and 1985 by the Social Science Research Council, the Wolfson Foundation, the Nuffield Foundation, and the University of East Anglia. The University of Missouri–St. Louis also employed me in 1979–80, thereby affording further access to valuable source material.

In conducting this work I have received much assistance from staff in a number of academic and other institutions, most notably at the Boston Public Library, the Library of Congress, the Library of the Department of the Interior, the National Agricultural Library, the Virginia Historical Society, the Virginia State Library, the South Carolina Historical Society, the Atlanta Public Library, the John Crerar Library, the Newberry Library, the British Library, the Library of the Royal Agricultural Society of England, and the libraries of Duke University, the University of North Carolina at Chapel Hill, the University of South Carolina, the University of Georgia, the University of Missouri–St. Louis, the University of London, the University of Cambridge, and the University of East Anglia.

My principal personal debts are to William Scarborough and William Albert. The first proved an invaluable correspondent and sympathetic critic over the years; the second sustained a close interest in my changing ideas and uncertainties from the inception of the project. Both have given me much of the confidence and stimulus that I needed, and both have undertaken the tedious labors of reading and advising.

Robert Fogel, Eugene Genovese, and William Parker answered my written queries, invariably with encouragement. Robert Gallman in Chapel Hill gave me a great deal of kind, personal attention in the early days when my ideas were ill formed, and it is fitting that one of his coauthored propositions on slavery is central to my main argument.

Others who gave important assistance include Cam Alexander, Marjorie Bannatyne, Joy Farr, Louis Gerteis, Terry Gourvish, Michael Hoyland, Christine Jope, Nelson Lankford, Robert MacPherson, Angela Mathew, Myrna Mathew, David Moltke-Hansen, Alan Sheldon, Joseph Carlyle Sitterson, Inge Walker Sonuparlak, Judith Sparks, Jacqueline Spray, Valerie Striker, James Rabun, George Rawick, James Roark, Jacquie White, Richard Wilson, and Ann Wood.

I also had the good fortune to discuss my work with members of the Ruffin family. In particular, I was able to enjoy the informed company of one of Edmund's great-great-grandsons, James Skelton Gilliam of Hopewell, Virginia. Much help was also received from David Ruffin, Edmund Saunders Ruffin, and Elizabeth Ruffin.

WILLIAM M. MATHEW

Part One

The Survival of Slavery

Chapter One

The Southern Institution: Viability and

Adaptive Efficiency

———————··❦··———————

*T*HIS is a study of slavery and, specifically, of its capacity for economic adjustment. At its center stands the complex and compelling figure of Edmund Ruffin, the antebellum South's leading agrarian reformer and one of the foremost spokesmen for the slaveholding interest. Improvement for him had to be pursued within the strict confines of slave society, and indeed its main purpose was to rescue the old eastern portion of that society.

Since the defense of slavery was the prime preoccupation, Ruffin's agriculturally progressive ideas were conceived in institutionally conservative terms. Given such intrinsic contradiction, could they work? And what do they reveal about the intellectual base of reform notions in the South?

I

Slavery's viability—by which we mean the existing slave society's capacity for economic and political survival through planter success, diversified development, demographic stability, and sectional influence in Congress—has long fascinated historians.[1] Our findings on Ruffin and his labors can, therefore, be set within a broad historiographical context.

A number of exact, numerative conclusions have recently emerged from refinements in quantitative technique and a scholarly premium on precision. Some of these have been challenging, controversial, and of notable dialectical value. As a result of an excessive preoccupation with statistical evidence, however, there has been an unfortunate tendency to measure economic strength by short-term profitability. This has been narrowing and distorting, and a basic purpose in the pages that follow is to reassert the worth of an alternative, less exact method of analysis. Profitability does, of course, have great *partial* usefulness, the proximate proof of a production system's resilience lying in its ability to strike a favorable balance between costs and earnings. This, though, is to be identified not simply by the realization of profits in particular years or decades but, more tellingly, by a capacity to sustain the circumstances that *allow* profitability.

"No one," write Elizabeth Fox-Genovese and Eugene Genovese, "not even those classical political economists who attacked slavery as an inefficient system, could reasonably deny that it could generate high profits and attendant growth rates under three conditions: fresh land, a steady supply of cheap labor, and a high level of demand on the world market."[2] The emphasis, crucially, is on conditions. Economic viability depends on a dynamic interplay of entrepreneurship, labor, and technique, within a changing context of purchasing power, transport provision, and land and capital availability. This context is, to varying degrees, beyond the control of producers. Their reactions to it are vital, but its elements ought, as far as possible, to lie outside any appraisal of institutional efficiency. Some historians, accordingly, have queried the usefulness of Robert Fogel's and Stanley Engerman's "geometric index of total factor productivity," which is partly constructed around the extrainstitutional variables of land values and market prices.[3]

Brazil is instructive here. In the early seventeenth century its slave-based sugar industry was, in Celso Furtado's words, "perhaps the most profitable colonizing and agricultural business of all time," with spectacular riches accruing to plantation and mill owners. In the 1660s and 1670s, however, there began processes of decline which, by the nineteenth and twentieth centuries, had quite beggared the northeastern portion of the country. Brazilians had been unable to remain competitive and buoyant in the face of growing Caribbean production and falling world prices.[4] Profitability in 1620 held no surety of success in 1720.

Appraisal of institutional viability requires both a strong internal focus and an explicit concern with change and adaptation. A great deal of econometric work, by contrast, derives from the neoclassical tradition, the fundamental concept of which is the static notion of equilibrium. In George Shackle's words, it posits "a state of affairs, not a course of affairs."[5] To come about, equilibrium requires a perfect market in which circulate perfect knowledge and perfect reason. The power of this market, acting through prices and the rationales of cost and utility marginality, is such that no sustained transcendence by individuals is possible. The entrepreneur—or in our case the planter—stands largely functionless: an "automaton maximizer," in William Baumol's term.[6] In studies of the plantation economy it is often loosely and incorrectly assumed that his actions were informed, judicious, consistent, averageable, and without significant periodicity. On occasions, as with Fogel's and Engerman's "capitalist businessmen," he is a mere inference from general economic aggregates. In noneconometric work he often appears, equally chimerically, as an inference from cultural aggregates (for example, the "cavalier fop" and the "pre-bourgeois seigneur").

The central importance of the entrepreneur—defined, unheroically, as "enterpriser" or "undertaker"—will be strongly asserted in this study, not only because he was endogamous to the system, but because he was supposedly in charge of it and because he was the party who carried most responsibility for adaptation to ever-changing patterns of problem and opportunity.[7] "Austrian" economists like Menger, Clark, Schumpeter, Knight, Von Hayek, Von Mises, Shackle, and Kirzner have rejected the neoclassical preoccupation with equilibrium and static analysis, contending that personal perception may matter as much as objective reality, and that timelapses, uncertainty, expectation, and error are key components of economic behavior.[8] The entrepreneur, rehabilitated in a world of complex and often ill-defined optionality, performs a vitally influential role by the way he copes with inadequate or immobile factors of production and noses his way into the mysteries of future production potential and consumer preference.[9] In the last resort, says George Shackle, "Economics is about thoughts."[10] The producer resumes an appearance familiar to historians: that of a sentient, watching, guessing economic agent, at once energized and immobilized by a kaleidoscope of alluring and repelling expectations.

A notable aspect of staticity in slavery analysis has been the tendency to work with period-average or single-year figures. Alfred Conrad and John Meyer argue from averaged findings for a variety of periods; Fogel and Engerman do the same for the single year 1860.[11] Trends are often mentioned, but they are not basic to the analyses. Both sets of authors use their findings to support assertions of slavery's capacity to survive throughout a non-bellum nineteenth century.[12] This is improper. Calculations of average returns for a given year or set of years are logically distinct from calculations of long-term viability into an unknown, counterfactual future. They also tend to ignore the normal complexities of circumstance in which farmers found themselves, and to nudge aside the issue of options and decisions. Not only had the entrepreneur to face a number of powerful short-term climatic and market hazards which, if badly encountered, could cause bankruptcy and emigration; he also had commonly to cope with problems of intensifying indebtedness, land infertility, rigidities of a "fixed capital" labor force, and poor and costly transport.

The single greatest uncertainty for thousands of planters was the demand for cotton and this, as Gavin Wright stresses, was very variable and could have dramatic effects on price levels.[13] The 1820s and the 1840s witnessed much depression; the 1830s and 1850s, a good deal of optimism and expansion. In bad years, according to Lewis Cecil Gray, thoughts turned in a spirit of adaptation to "diversification and retrenchment," with some attention being paid to the prescriptions of reformers (though, of course, low returns and debt obligations at such times could effectively preclude any changes of practice and product).[14] Figures supplied by Ralph Betts Flanders show that the average New York price for upland cotton moved from 29 cents in 1816–18, to 10 cents in 1827–28, 17½ in 1835, 5½ in 1845, and 12 in 1851.[15] Cotton growers, in short, were beset by a host of worries, year by year, and even the most routine-based of them were unable to escape the regular need for at least periodic, modest adaptations in production, marketing, and finance. Problems appeared in good years as well as bad, since an improved market was an invitation to increased output and whatever extra requirements of capital, labor, land, and reorganization that may have entailed.

Fogel and Engerman have recently indicated that they have been studying the "relative technical efficiency of input utilization," with their findings only applicable to staple farmers engaged in the production of cotton, tobacco, sugar, or rice.[16] Wright has suggested "revenue-raising efficiency" as the proper term, and observes that the Fogel and Engerman index is principally "a measure of who happened to be growing cotton during the most extraordinary cotton year of the nineteenth century."[17] This is all much too narrow. The concept of efficiency should be broad enough to embrace *pro-*

cess as well as result. The word *efficiency* and its Latin root *efficere* convey a working towards an objective as well as the achieved objective itself. It implies a compound of directed acts.

These may be *reactive,* in the sense that the institution, through the entrepreneur, is responding to observed difficulty or opportunity; or *creative,* in the sense that the roots of action lie not in expedient response but in random breakthroughs of imagination, intelligence, or will.

We shall work, therefore, with the concept of *"adaptive efficiency."* With clear criteria for judgment, a strong focus on planter entrepreneurship, and a solid and telling case study, we can aim at confident, if partial, evaluation of institutional performance. The exercise will be variably quantitative, though usually falling short of mathematical precision. An institution's adaptive capacities tell us much more about long-term viability than do temporary or averaged profits accruing to producers within it.

We shall look for evidence of adaptability in one sphere of potential and highly rewarding changes in agriculture, and in one part of the antebellum South. The first choice imposes the second. The improvement plans of Edmund Ruffin, deriving from the centuries-old European preoccupation with the correction of soil acidity and the consequent unlocking of soil fertility,[18] were at root a scheme for retrieving the economic, demographic, and political power of the old Southeastern states. Ruffin had no great interest in the lands beyond the Appalachians, or in the fertile, recently settled cotton territories of the Deep South, most of which were in much less need of attention and which in any case often lacked the calcareous resources so central to his program of improvement.

Planters, the key agents, were expected to be informed, innovative, and "nationalist." On them was seen to lie the entire responsibility for success or failure. The slave role was a passive, directed one, and any advances in skill (usually minor) or changes in organization (sometimes major) were, Ruffin considered, managerial issues. This was fair enough, except that the planters were too frequently viewed in isolation, their performance unrelated to slave society as a whole. That society, for Ruffin, performed the absolutely vital function of controlling blacks, and as such lay beyond serious, radical criticism. His political defensiveness did not affect the pattern and sense of his strictly agricultural proposals, but it did provide their impulse and it prevented proper appraisal of their failure. It also turned him into an active and, latterly, extreme secessionist after the 1840s, pulling him off full-time commitment to the cause of farm improvement. His very interest in adaptation was seen to be partial and conditional. Slavery in fact was blocking reform at its very source.

Distinctions between the planter and slavery are unreal inasmuch as the planter was a principal *component* of slavery, but they have some subjective validity, and planters, while integral to the institution, were still influenced by many factors external to it. Such differentiations highlight a general need for specificity in any evaluation of slavery, a variety of conceptual separations being necessary for purposes of analysis. One must try if possible to determine, however roughly, where slavery is, and is not, part of a more general category of "agrarian society"; and the institution itself must be handled at a number of levels ranging from slave culture and the aggregate economy right down through the unit of production, its management, and its schedules to the slave worker with his or her individual bundles of aptitudes and inclinations. This is a necessary part of any effort to escape the intellectual traps of, first, attributing to slavery features that are really those of a preindustrial community, and, second, assuming that revealed characteristics and influences of slavery emanate from the institution as a homogeneous whole, with all parts sharing responsibility.

Even if a separation between "broadly agrarian" and "specifically slave" can be made, a further major difficulty stands in the way of any precise evaluation of the "slave" factor. It concerns the *weighing* of elements attributable to slavery against elements deriving from other influences. This can rarely be done satisfactorily, for social determinants cannot be teased out like strands of wool. Consider, for example, a group of slaveholders who are seen to be engaging in conspicuous consumption of a sort that, for a number of reasons, impedes agricultural reform. How does one isolate the "slave" factors in this complex, imitative behavior from larger "agrarian" factors or different "nonslave" factors, thereby gaining some exact notion of the relative scale of slavery's contribution to the problem? The impossibility is obvious and the historian, accordingly, has to have honest, though not indulgent, resort to imprecision and surmise; to the employment of *prima facie* or theoretical probabilities; and to a focus on opposing extremes of importance and triviality. Often the objective is simply to determine where the *emphasis* of explanation ought to lie. This is done in other historiographical fields without too much anxiety, but it may seem to be unusually defeatist in a study of slavery, given the current prevalence of mathematical exactitude.

Despite the considerable mass of documentary evidence employed in the chapters that follow, we do have to admit this early defeat. Slavery cannot be isolated in a way that suits the requirements of precise analysis, nor can it ever be judged to be the exclusive cause of any ideological, social, or economic phenomenon. There should be nothing shocking about this, for it is only an assertion of the axiom that most major features of society are historically interrelated and interdependent. But it does require stating, lest too much is read into the claims below, and lest the very deliberate caveats and refinements are ignored.

II

There can, as we shall see, be no doubting the potential economic importance of the Ruffin reforms. They provide an excellent basis for a case study on questions of entrepreneurial response and institutional flexibility.

What does need very clear assertion at this stage is the significance of the Old South itself as a region where the idea of adaptive efficiency can be tested. Various lines of deterministic thinking on the Southern economy have generated a loose but widespread notion that by the late antebellum years the Southeastern states really did not matter very much. The issue of reform there, apparently, was of only marginal importance. The area was one of infertile, overworked land whose day had passed. It represented rearguard reaction against the forces of the black-soil revolution. The adaptive efficiency that counted was that of logical economic men abandoning their thin-soiled, gullied fields and making off in search of fresh, rich cotton lands to the west. Fogel and Engerman write of "the extreme flexibility of the slave economy," by which they mean the capacity of the Southern population for sensible interregional migration.[19] Wright remarks that the movement from "inferior to superior soil" was part of "a rational process of geographical expansion and relocation."[20]

One can detect four major and connected determinisms underlying these and similar views: 1) the frontier, both as promised land and as source of dislocative competition (combined with lingering land availability within the old states themselves); 2) the exhausted condition of long-cultivated Southeastern soils; 3) the climatic constraints, manifested especially in excessive summer heat; 4) the overwhelming power of the cotton market, and its selection of the new states as its main providers. All must be queried. It would seem probable that Ruffin's failure was a *social* phenomenon: not a *physical-regional* one.

The open frontier could only have rendered reforms unnecessary in the Old South if a simple pedological rationale had combined with a universal tendency to mobility to bring about a "relocation" of the bulk of the seaboard population in the territories west and south of the Appalachians. Planters, however, did not all behave as good neoclassical agents and follow the simple free-market signals. Many thousands did emigrate, of course, and those who remained were often troubled by competition from their former neighbors, by diminutions of local funds of capital and enterprise, by sales-induced depressions of land values, and by a lot of fatalism and demoralization. They cannot, however, be ignored, and their very difficulties gave a special salvationist note to appeals for reform.[21]

Even without notable attempts at improvement, a great many individuals in the old states would be prepared to make-do with low material rewards in what was, after all, a known and mature environment. Emigration meant upheaval, loss of friends and familiar social props, physical danger, and only the possibility of enhanced income in what Governor James Hammond of South Carolina termed "the savage semi-barbarous West."[22] As a Georgia planter phrased it in 1851: "Here are our good homes, good society, good health, good schools. . . . We can do very well if we husband all our resources."[23] A great many shared such unwillingness to move. The six slave states from Delaware south to Georgia registered a net growth in numbers of well over a million between 1830 and 1860, the figure on the eve of the Civil War representing one-seventh of the total population of the United States.[24] The great majority worked in agriculture and enjoyed a variety of real, if often undramatic, economic options. In Ruffin's view in 1837, amelioration costs could be "about as much as every emigrant from Virginia to the west pays in labor, per acre, for the mere clearing the forest growth from his new land"—and that on top of the original purchase price.[25] "It is certainly a question of some importance," wrote another border-state observer in the same year, "whether the worn-out lands of Delaware, Maryland, and other parts of our country cannot be improved at less expense than to clear off the almost impenetrable forests of the west."[26]

Local options were sometimes elevated into public duties by the political leaders of the Old South, many of them greatly troubled by the reduced congressional power of their states in consequence of economic weakness and relative demographic deterioration. Ruffin himself provides a good example of such concern. "The loss of both political and military strength, to Virginia and South Carolina," he declared in 1852, "are not less than all other losses, the certain consequences of the impoverishment of their soil." In consequence, they had lost their "abundant legislative safeguards" against injuries from the "predatory States" to the north.[27] Governor Whitemarsh Seabrook, a prominent South Carolina sea island planter and friend of Ruffin's, wrote in the 1840s: "The period perhaps has arrived when not only the advancement of their pecuniary welfare, but it may be, the preservation of the domestic institutions of the South, depends on a radical change in the habits and practices of the tillers of its soil."[28] These men had a strong sense of Southeastern slavery being in a state of protracted and deepening land-based crisis. Accompanying anxieties led at best to intensified reformism, and at worst to bitter disunionism. Somewhere in between came emigration, but it was obvious to all that while this might serve as a partial solution for the emigrant it would tend only to add to the problems afflicting the seaboard communities.

The factor of land abundance unquestionably influenced a wide range of behavior and expectation. Emigration statistics alone show this very clearly. We largely ignore population movement here, not as a result of any unimportance, but because the majority of the Southeastern population failed to participate, and because the subsequent agricultural production of those who did move away strengthened, through competitive pressure, the case for improvement in the East.

Spare land also affected planter decisions through its widespread availability within the Old South itself. Farm sales by emigrants made it possible for extensive methods to continue in many areas, and local frontiers were still being approached in Georgia and in places where swamp drainage was being practiced. Land rotation, in John Solomon Otto's view, was widely resorted to by "plain folk" producers.[29]

Again, however, one has to guard against simplistic correlations. Land was rarely just lying there for the taking, virgin and instantly workable. Even formerly cultivated old-field could be a dense jungle of grasses, bushes, and trees, with major effort and expense necessary for its clearance. Draining swamps could also be an extended and costly affair. What is more, the new fields, whether from purchase or rotation, or from reclamation in swamps, forests, and abandoned land, tended to be of poor quality as a result of high acidity levels. They were usually very different from the comparatively calcareous tracts of the West, and soil amelioration was being proposed by Ruffin as a distinctively Eastern therapy.

Quality aside, fresh, uncultivated land was not widely available in the Old

South on the eve of the Civil War. Swamp drainage was mainly confined to tidewater, and almost all the internal frontiers of economic production had been reached.[30] Even where local factors of land abundance did encourage the survival of extensive methods of cultivation, these were not necessarily incompatible with improvement. Ruffin's basic exercises of marling and liming cannot properly be described as "intensive." They certainly might form one part of a generally intensive *program*, but they could yield major benefits even when they were not. Amelioration seems (by the details offered in chapters 8 and 9) to have been almost custom-made for a region of scarce capital, plentiful labor, and primitive methods of agricultural production.

Distinctions between extensive, traditional, new-land farming and intensive, reformed, old-land farming are often overstated. Many improvers applied their marl and lime to recently reclaimed land. James Hammond on the Savannah undertook the most extensive marling operations in the South, and much of the work was carried out on freshly drained swampland.[31] This accorded with Ruffin's advice that farmers should guard against marling old, overworked land, low in organic material, since an immediate effect was invariably a hastening of the decomposition and release of such constituents. Amelioration accelerated the depletion of nutrients, so—inconveniently—organic matter had to be added to weak soils at roughly the same time as the marl. Alternatively, or concomitantly, newly treated fields had to be cultivated in a careful, rotational manner.[32] In February 1843 Ruffin wrote to the Charleston *Mercury:* "If there be choice of lands for experiment, the best and earliest effects of marl may be expected on soils containing the most vegetable or other putrescent matter."[33]

There is, secondly, the issue of soil exhaustion. What was the point in trying to retrieve the irretrievable? Centuries of exploitative staple farming had surely ruined Southeastern soils—which had been thin and infertile to begin with. Pessimism, however, was not universal, as the growing population of the region shows, and it may well have been Ruffin's finest achievement to prove convincingly to those who would listen that "exhaustion" was a misleadingly static concept, especially for soils which had a manifestly curable defect. James Hammond informed Ruffin in 1844 of his "strong desire to beat the Western Planters on my *whole crop per acre.*"[34] The *American Farmer* suggested in 1859 that there was "no such thing as worn-out land: that expression conveys a falsehood; it is a very practical thing with . . . no very large means, to restore these lands to any degree of fertility they have ever possessed."[35]

This was not all fanciful. Many parts of eastern Britain, which were in the vanguard of agricultural advance in the eighteenth and nineteenth centuries, coming to include many of the country's most diversified and valuable farms, had formerly been characterized by poor, thin soils and low productive capacity.[36] Twentieth-century developments in the Southeastern United States have shown that once the necessary ameliorative and fertilizing work has been attended to, local soils can support a wide range of high-yielding forage and cash crops.[37] H. D. Foth and J. W. Shafer observe how the soils of the Southern Coastal Plain, once so problematical, now support some of the country's most successful agricultural enterprises.[38]

Soils are as barren or as acid as the farmer chooses to leave them. They are not fixed in perpetuity at a given level of fertility. The defects, of course, may be such that it makes good economic sense to let them lie unattended, but in the case of the sour lands of the Southeast the costs of retrieval (as shown in chapter 9) were comparatively low. Amelioration, on the whole, was resisted because it was bothersome.[39]

Climate has provided further deterministic ideas suggestive of limited regional capacity for adjustment and recuperation. In particular, there is the view that hot summers adversely affected grass and legume cultivation and stock rearing, thereby making it difficult to engage in the mixed farming that Ruffin viewed as the final phase of his reformed agriculture.

This again has to be queried. Climate certainly posed some major problems, but it also presented the Southeast with an extremely useful combination of mild winters and damp growing seasons. A number of official reports between the Civil War and the First World War were positively enthusiastic about the South's potential as a mixed-farming area. "It is not true," wrote C. W. Howard in 1874, "that artificial forage, plants, and grasses will not flourish at the South."[40] W. F. Ward in 1914 believed that the South was positively the best endowed part of the country for the production of animal foodstuffs.[41] More recently, J. F. Hart, while noting a lack of native forage plants guaranteeing all-year grazing in the Southeast, identifies an abundance of introduced grasses, clovers, and other legumes which have proved effective in the region.[42] Ladd Haystead and Gilbert Fite also mention a wide range of successful modern forage crops.[43] The ubiquitous Southeastern acid soils known as "ultisols" are seen by S. W. Buol, F. D. Hole, and F. J. McCracken to "represent a vast potential for agricultural production. They develop in climates that have long frost-free seasons and an abundance of rainfall." Any limitations can be countered by liming and fertilizing.[44]

Possibilities for mixed farming help counter the fourth brand of determinism, that concerning the commanding influence of European and Northern cotton markets. So, of course, does the fact that the crop simply could not be grown competitively in the north of the region (where much diversification had already occurred by the time of the Civil War).

Cotton, as noted, suffered from frequent price depression, and its general vulnerability, both as a farm crop and as a market product, rendered it a highly unreliable means towards wealth, comfort, and security. "The vicissitudes of cotton planters were almost proverbial," writes Flanders. "There was absolutely no way of foretelling the result of a planting."[45] In such circumstances many farmers must have understood the case for broadening the base of their operations. What is more, Ruffin's scheme promised them not only diversity but a larger and earlier maturing cotton crop itself. On improved land, he insisted, increased unit-yield could easily compensate for decreased area-sowing. "I would not offer, with any hope of its being adopted, such unpalatable advice (however good) as to lessen the general *production* of cotton on each plantation—but only the *space planted* and tilled in cotton."[46] Enlarged staple production and mixed farming were not necessarily alternatives. With amelioration and the insertion of a major fodder-livestock-manure sequence, they could be secured together. Simple ideas of "rational" cotton versus "idealist" reform are, therefore, inappropriate.

The issue in fact rested on the planter's ability to dispense with myths of impotence, measure the full range of realistic objectives, and estimate what means were available for their pursuit. Knowledge and learning were central to the exercise. Thereafter, it was a matter of determination, effort, and intelligent day-to-day empiricism. Whitemarsh Seabrook considered these virtues to be very thin on the ground in South Carolina. "The prejudices of a planter," he wrote in 1828, "are strong and difficult of removal. . . . His repugnance to test a new project is a truth of daily observation. You may convince him by argument . . . yet you cannot sway him from his olden course."[47]

Even the most favored cotton-producing areas of the Southeast were beginning to experience long-term difficulties and sense the need for change. Seabrook himself shows this in his numerous writings on cotton.[48] James Hammond told the State Agricultural Society of South Carolina in 1841 that, in relation to cotton, "the period is probably close at hand when we shall be compelled to abandon its culture, if not altogether, at least in a great measure. This is a matter of the deepest concern to us in every point of view." The problem was competition "from our own kith and kin."[49]

In 1842 the Committee of Agriculture of the South Carolina House of Representatives produced a report arguing for an agricultural survey of the state (later entrusted to Ruffin). It announced that South Carolina's "palmy days" as a cotton producer were past. "Every year opens new lands in the West, where congeniality of soil and climate to this commodity, increases the product per acre, far beyond what can be reared at home. . . . We cannot expect that accident is continually to supply new staples suited to our soil and climate, and place us beyond the reach of contingent circumstance. We must resort to science to improve Agriculture."[50]

The low prices of these years help account for this pessimism, but it cannot be claimed that market pressures were somehow unreal or superficial. Even if temporary, they had a habit of reappearing with a worrying frequency.

The dictatorial power of the cotton market was resistible. The continuation of monoculture in parts of the Carolinas and Georgia was now as much the consequence of inertia, habit, and blind faith as of unanswerable economic logic.

One must certainly take account of powerful frontier, soil, climate, and market influences in the Southeast. Equally, however, one must forcefully reject any rigid, associated determinisms. Within the broad limits set by physical and market circumstances, a great deal of optionality was in evidence, and the principal controlling variables at work were the planter-entrepreneur and, less directly, the entire institution of slavery.

Questions concerning reform and adaptation, then, are perfectly in order for the Old South. Indeed the long-settled, Eastern margin of the slave economy ought, generally, to have the first claim on our attention since that was the area of greatest crisis, where the need to find ways to meet the problems of low yields, low profits, low land values, emigration, and (Ruffin would have added) the loss of slaves to freedom in the towns and to plantations in the Deep South was most acute. Slavery's capacity for change, adjustment, and self-retrieval was being put to the test there as in no other part of the section. Had there been a sound future for the institution, this, arguably, is where it would have been taking shape in the early nineteenth century. A good many of the agricultural problems of the seaboard would, in time, have spread far to the west and the south of the mountains. Slavery could not survive forever by simple nomadism. The story of the Old South is that of the first large body of planters who had decided to become permanent settlers and to make the best (variously conceived) of the land they occupied.

III

Analysis of his writings (as in chapter 3) shows that Ruffin valued slavery in terms that were largely noneconomic and that bore little relation to the specifics (as distinct from the purpose) of his reform program. Reform had to serve slavery. If it could not, then other means of support and defense had to be considered. Failure became increasingly evident after the early 1840s, and by the 1850s most of his public energies were directed towards the cause of secessionism. Just before his death he noted that his instructions had been "mostly slighted" and that the material benefit that had flowed from them was a mere fraction of what it might have been.[51]

There was no Ruffin-induced "agricultural revolution" in the Old South, as some have claimed.[52] The problem lay partly with Ruffin's idiosyncracies as a reformer, and his reluctance to resolve contradictions in his own economic and political thinking. It also lay with slavery itself. Although some land improvements could be undertaken fairly easily with a slave labor force, progress was hard to secure within the wider context of a slave economy and society. Slavery, working in the main through poor entrepreneurship and a defective transport system, contributed to limited learning and high input costs. These combined to reduce Ruffin's disciples to a tiny minority of Southeastern planters—even in tidewater, where most of the land-ameliorating resources lay, and even in Virginia, where Ruffin was active for most of his life as a farmer and an author.[53]

Slavery, moreover, imposed insistent social priorities. It is a fact of the highest importance that, despite all the pressures for economic change, the best and most concerned minds in the South could by force of overwhelming race and class considerations transcend strictly material preoccupations and identify existing social institutions as something much more precious than any prospect of agricultural recovery. What we are dealing with, at root, is a very profound intellectual crisis, for the recovery was a crucial long-term prerequisite for the survival of the institution. Plans for salvationist adaptation and reform *arose from and were at odds with* the developing articulation of race fear. I. A. Newby writes of "the peculiarly southern relationship between the competing economic, social and racial fears that determined its direction. When these factors clashed, white elites invariably showed most concern about race, and in this sense the racial dimension of the plantation regime overshadowed the economic dimension."[54]

Ruffin provides us not only with the agenda for a study of agricultural reform and economic adaptation; he also exemplifies, with unusual power, this fatal contest of priorities. He was, it should be stressed, no back-woodsman, likely to follow the crudest passions and opinions of the moment. In some ways he was the very epitome of Southern modernity, having more to offer his section in the way of progress at its agricultural foundations than anyone else alive at the time. Yet 12 April 1861 did not find him writing in his study, or lecturing to some farming society, but standing at the Iron Battery of Cummings' Point in Charleston Harbor, delightedly accepting the honor of firing what he believed to be the first shell of the Civil War. That was the main source of his fame thereafter. In June 1865, old, unwell, and unable to accept the ruin of slave society, he shot himself.

A dozen years earlier Ruffin had told the Virginia State Agricultural Society in Richmond that, despite all his labors on behalf of agricultural advance and the great social importance he attached to the production and accumulation of wealth in the South, he would not hesitate a moment to prefer the *"conditions of these slaveholding States, with all the . . . exhausting tillage and declining fertility, to the entire conditions of any other country on the face of the globe."*[55]

Chapter Two

Edmund Ruffin and the Cause of

Agricultural Reform

I

*E*DMUND RUFFIN was born in 1794 into a family of socially
elevated planters resident in Prince George County, Virginia, on
the south bank of the James River. His line of American descent
ran back seven generations to William Ruffin of Isle of Wight
County, who appeared in local court records as a farmer of substance in the
middle of the seventeenth century.[1] It would seem probable that this first
Ruffin was the son of William Ruthven and nephew of the third Earl of
Gowrie, who had been murdered by the King's men in Scotland in 1600.[2]
Long before his ascent to the British throne in 1603, James I, as a Scottish
monarch with episcopal and absolutist tendencies, had encountered vigorous and menacing challenge from the Presbyterian Ruthvens. After dis-
posing of the third earl and his older brother he set out, in the words of one
historian, to bring the whole house of Gowrie "to ruin, disgrace and extinction, by wiping the brood from the face of Scotland."[3] The younger Ruthven brothers escaped to England, but were pursued there after James
moved south at the Union. The elder (and the claimant to the title) slipped
the net and finally settled in France. His son emigrated to Virginia. As

"Ruthven" was normally pronounced with the "th" silent, the new surname of "Ruffin" was a simple phoneticism.[4]

The lineage remained decisively seigneurial between the seventeenth and
the nineteenth centuries, the family amassing large estates along the James
and intermarrying with Cockes, Harrisons, and Skipworths. Edmund's pa-
ternal grandfather developed political interests, serving in the Virginia
House of Delegates in the 1770s and 1780s and participating in the convention called to consider the adoption of the Federal Constitution in 1788
(voting against it, along with Patrick Henry, James Monroe, and other states'
rights men). His father, George Ruffin, was elected to the Virginia State legislature between 1803 and 1806. A nineteenth-century Ruffin describes his
forebears as "almost universally high spirited, high tempered, quick to take
and resent offence, but placable, except when their personal dignity was
invaded or even threatened; when, though not relentless, they were unforgiving. They have not generally been obtrusive of their opinions though
tenacious of them, and have been too independent and outspoken to make
politicians. . . . They have all relished rural pursuits."[5] Except for the observation about nonobtrusiveness, these words are all remarkably similar to
those applied to the third Edmund Ruffin, both by his contemporaries and
by himself.

Little is known of Edmund's mother. Her name was Jane Lucas and she
came from Surry County, adjoining Prince George. She died when he was
still an infant and he was brought up by his father's second wife, Rebecca
Cocke, also of Surry County and a member of one of Virginia's oldest and
most ubiquitous families.[6] These propinquities, added to the south-bank
locations of the earlier Ruffins, suggest that Edmund's ancestral traditions
and influences came from a very restricted patch of Virginia on the James
River. As American patches went, however, it was a fairly cosmopolitan
one. The James was an arm of the sea and brought ocean traders virtually to
the doorstep of the Ruffin plantation; Richmond, the new capital of the
state, was only a couple of dozen miles upriver; Williamsburg, the former
seat of government and home of the country's second oldest college, was a
county-and-a-half distant on the other side of the James; and Virginia itself
carried disproportionate influence in the highest councils of the land along
the banks of the Potomac. The experience of the family may have been the
fairly narrow and stereotyped one of Virginia tidewater planters, but it cannot be designated parochial.

Avery Craven describes the Ruffin "Evergreen" plantation near Coggin's

Point as "in importance only below 'Shirley,' 'Westover,' the 'Brandons,' 'Curle's Neck,' and the other great plantations of the tidewater region."[7] Most of Edmund's time appears to have been spent either in idleness or with books, apparently read "rather for amusement than for instruction." He did, however, work his way through a number of agricultural texts. By the time he was ten he had read all the plays of Shakespeare. Privacy and isolation were breached in 1810 when he went off to William and Mary College, some thirty-odd miles downstream. In the same year his father died and the management of the plantation was taken over by his guardian, Thomas Cocke. The studies at Williamsburg were brief and unsuccessful. Much of his attention was focused instead on Susan Travis, a daughter of Colonel Champion Travis of Williamsburg, whose family had been in James City County for almost two centuries. They married in 1811. In the summer of 1812, after his dismissal from William and Mary for academic incompetence, Edmund joined a volunteer company and was stationed at Norfolk. He saw no action in the war against the British and served for only six months.[8] After this brief academic, romantic, and military trip around the shores of the James River he returned home to take over the running of his estate at Coggin's Point, assuming the role of planter almost a full year before his twentieth birthday and knowing himself to be "totally ignorant of practical agriculture." Marriage and children, however, quickly gave him a sense of patriarchal responsibility, thereby invigorating his labors.[9]

A few years later, in February 1818, Ruffin had his slaves haul marl from a shallow pit on his plantation to some acres selected for experimental treatment, thus commencing one of the most celebrated exercises in scientific agriculture ever undertaken in America.[10] Within twenty years he had established himself as the South's leading agricultural reformer. In the future he would be acclaimed as the "father of soil chemistry" in America.[11] What combination of ideas and impulses caused him to develop so quickly from untutored novice to perceptive experimenter, we cannot tell. Grand notions of protecting slave society were not in evidence that early. The desire for material gain, however, was almost certainly an important factor—or, more negatively, the desire to avoid the fate that had befallen so many careless and ignorant Virginia planters. He had considered moving West, but the transappalachian wilderness could not have held much appeal for a tidewater aristocrat.[12] Better if possible to stay put and enjoy local status and social leadership, perpetuating the aristocratic lineage for at least another generation or two. He was an instinctive accumulator, as his later life shows, taking pleasure in buying land cheaply, improving it, counting the advance in profits and land values, assessing his wealth, and then judiciously distributing portions of his assets among his children.[13]

There was also intellectual stimulation, and from two sources in particular: John Taylor's *Arator* and Sir Humphry Davy's *Elements of Agricultural Chemistry*. Taylor—"the first and highest name"—was influential because he was Virginian, contemporary, opinionated, and wrong. Davy commanded attention as one of the finest chemists of the day and conveyed ideas which, to Ruffin's sharp mind, seemed of likely relevance to the lamentable condition of tidewater soils.[14] And behind these two volumes lay other agricultural works which Ruffin had been reading over the years.

A further important factor, he later contended, was his ignorance of practical farming: a source not so much of timidity and confusion as of confidence and "conceit,"[15] enabling him to plunge straight away into an application of Taylor's ideas on fallows, rotations, manures, and other matters which had recently been put before an interested Virginia readership. When these failed to work for him he discovered in Davy's book the notion that sterility in soils might be the consequence of acidity and, therefore, that the fundamental, ameliorating exercise of restoring lost calcium to the land might be necessary before any other improvements (such as those advanced by Taylor) could be profitably undertaken. Taylor's scheme had begun at stage two. Ruffin, with the help of a few words from Davy, was beginning to sketch the outlines of stage one. Good fortune assisted him in that the requisite calcareous material lay in some abundance a few feet below ground at Coggin's Point. The marling proved an instant success, experimentation continued, mistaken procedures were slowly corrected, detailed records were kept, and by 1821 a paper ("On the Composition of Soils, and Their Improvement by Calcareous Manures") was ready for publication in John Skinner's *American Farmer* in Baltimore.[16] Over the succeeding dozen years or so Ruffin completed the primary scientific work which earned him his key place in the development of agricultural science.

It was to be a magnificent, original, and solitary achievement. Acidity, he conclusively demonstrated, could be cured by the application of calcareous material, and this was available over most of the tidewater South. Marling and liming had long been common practice in Europe but were still largely unknown in the United States, and not even European scientists had subjected their results and observations on calcareous amelioration to systematic explanation. "The annunciation of a single fact, the result of analysis," declared ex-President Tyler in Richmond in 1853, "viz. the absence of lime from the soil, rescued us and the State from comparative abandonment,"[17] Millar, Turk and Foth, writing in a modern volume on agricultural chemistry, acclaim Ruffin as "probably the first man in the United States to acknowledge the prevalence of acidity and the need for lime in soils of the eastern United States," and point out that amelioration of acid soils is frequently regarded as "the 'backbone' of permanent agriculture in humid regions." The application of marl or any other liming material was, ideally, a first step towards generally improved farming. After acidity had been corrected, nitrogen-fixing rotation crops could grow more abundantly; organic matter in the soil, including barnyard manure, could decompose more rapidly; and fertilizers could more easily release their nutrients in available, soluble form. Craven properly describes Ruffin as "the greatest agriculturist in a rural civilization." For Lewis Cecil Gray he appears as "the most influential leader of Southern agriculture and one of the greatest agricultural figures America has produced."[18]

It was around 1820 that Ruffin made his first definite move into Southern public life, thus embarking on an irregular and idiosyncratic political career which came to dramatic fruition in the secessionist cause of the 1850s and early 1860s. In 1821 he was secretary to the delegates of the United Agricultural Societies of Virginia when they petitioned Congress to reduce the import duties of 1816, arguing that agriculturists should not in effect subsidize industry and that "the only object of duties on importation . . . ought to be exclusively the increase of the public revenue."[19] In 1824, following the precedents of political participation set by his father and grandfather, he successfully sought election to the senate in Richmond. His constituency comprised Prince George, Surry, Isle of Wight, Sussex, Southampton, and Greenville counties—a slice of territory lying between the James and the North Carolina border. The experience, however, proved an unhappy one. Ruffin never acquired fluency or confidence as a public speaker and was too unbending for the huddles and deals of a democratic assembly. He was, as James Oakes indicates, out of touch and a failure, and, disliking that, resigned his seat and returned to Coggin's Point before his term had run full course.[20] If an ambitious man at the highest levels of Southern rural society was unable to strike a pose on the political stage, alternatives were normally found in the pursuit of domestic style, elegance, and extravagance. For Ruffin that would have meant far too closeted and parasitic an existence.[21] He despised waste and the ignorance that usually accompanied it. If life was to be lived out on the plantation it had to have a public dimension, contributing to the welfare of Southern society and appeasing personal vanity. There had to be respectable and observed function and, one might add, some fame and drama as well. In his adult years Ruffin was a dour and humorless man, but he did need excitement and stimulation. Easily bored and depressed, he feared inaction and obscurity.

His lifeline lay in his marling experiments and, built upon these, his "plan" for the recovery of Virginia agriculture. As more information accumulated, Virginia widened into the Southeastern states in general, and agriculture became Southern society, polity, and, finally, survival. By the mid-1820s he had sufficiently ample records of his own operations and a clear enough idea of the real defects of tidewater soils to embark on the preparation of a book for the instruction of his fellow planters. This was completed in 1826, around the time of his resignation from the assembly in Richmond. He let his former guardian, Thomas Cocke, read it, despite his being a poor farmer and "a slow convert to my doctrine."[22] Cocke pronounced against the very existence of the book. Since the young planter had no reputation, he might seem to be presumptuous, offering advice to his peers and betters. It was the advice of a recluse and a snob, and was sufficiently discouraging to make Ruffin stick the manuscript away in a drawer for nearly six years. No one else was consulted, as far as one can tell, such being the isolation of the Southern experimenter. When he recovered his nerve and had the book published in Petersburg in 1832 as *An Essay on Calcareous Manures*, he seemed pleased with his achievement. "The fears of my friend Cocke were removed upon reading the book in print." It was, happily, "very favourably received by the public"—and that seemed conclusive enough proof of its worth. Seven hundred and fifty copies came out in the first edition.[23]

Ruffin had betrayed self-doubt as a writer. It is odd to discover that he also had a low regard for his own basic abilities as a farmer. Whatever the merits of his theories, he "always, & truly, disclaimed all pretensions of being . . . a good manager of business, a good economist—& . . . a good practical farmer." Success was due to his "plan" being sound enough to compensate for numerous errors of detail. "In the general, & from my departure, I never have been a man of business. I am very deficient in order & method. As a farmer, especial deficiencies are that I have no genius for, and little knowledge of machinery & its proper working—even of ploughs. . . . I am no judge of horses, or other live stock, & take no pleasure in their care & management. I cannot exercise the uniform & inflexible demeanour which is necessary for the proper & easy government & discipline of subordinates, & especially of slaves."[24] Such weaknesses, and the implied measure of boredom, may partly explain his decision to try to abandon farming in the 1830s. David Allmendinger goes so far as to suggest that Ruffin "had come to hate farming" itself, recoiling in particular from the complicated procedures that his own new system had spawned.[25]

II

Ruffin was absent from practical agriculture from 1833 until 1844, initially switching his attention to the launching of a new journal, the *Farmers' Register*. Many farming papers in America had had brief and bankrupted lives, and the South had little reputation for active interest in matters of agrarian reform,[26] but if Virginians had bought *Calcareous Manures,* and *Arator* before that, why not a well-produced journal as well—especially one with a new and coherent message? Prospectuses were sent out, the response from contributors was encouraging, and early in 1833 the first number of the *Farmers' Register* was issued, thus setting Ruffin forth on his "new . . . engrossing & expensive" business as an editor-publisher. By the early months of 1834 he had assembled a total of 1,215 subscribers from sixteen different states and the District of Columbia. The *Register* was to appear monthly and cost $5 a year. Marling was the central topic of concern, and the decade of its publication coincides with an extension of marling activity in a number of counties in lower Virginia. The period, Ruffin wrote later, "perhaps made up that portion of my life which was of most benefit to public interest & also to my own reputation." He described the work as "delightful."[27]

The first volume was published in part by J. W. Campbell of Petersburg and in part by Ruffin at his recently acquired Shellbanks plantation a few miles inland from Coggin's, but all subsequent ones came from Ruffin's own press in Petersburg, to which town he moved himself, his printing equipment, and his wife and children in 1835. Not once between that year and 1842 did he spend as much as a full day on his James River lands, and so final seemed his departure to Petersburg that he attempted to sell both his slaves and his acres in the mid-1830s. As it happened, he was unable to find a buyer. Supervision was left in the hands of an overseer, and then in 1839 his son Edmund Jr. took charge with a half share in the ownership. Unfortunately, Ruffin was almost totally without experience in commercial affairs when he began the *Register,* and this weakness was to plague him in the years to come. Basic farming operations apart, all he had been required to do through nearly twenty years of control on his plantation was make occasional purchases of slaves and of items for use on the farm and for family consumption and load his surplus grain onto coastal and river vessels calling at his James River landing. The marl which formed the basis of his operations did not have to be bought: it was merely dug from his land and hauled onto the fields. All in all, as he put it, he had been "shielded" from the complex world of business.[28]

The Petersburg printing establishment was a small one, latterly with a chief printer and four apprentices. Ruffin found himself unable to achieve economies and reduce the price of the *Register* below the initial $5. In consequence, he ran into problems of competition with state-guaranteed papers like the popular Albany *Cultivator,* which sold for only 25 cents a year. Such publications, Ruffin acknowledged, also gained from lower-cost Northern printing and engineering. "I find that low price is essential to general circulation," he wrote in 1835, recognizing as well that the problem was a circular one, the sales level being itself one of the determinants of price. A large market was both objective and precondition. There were also difficulties in gauging the precise level of demand in any one year. He sold all 1,400 copies of volume 1, and when more were sought by late subscribers he bought back old issues for resale, then undertook a reprinting of 500 copies. Most of the new magazines lay cluttering his office. Ruffin then turned his mind to the devising of special offers in order to increase the circulation. If purchasers sent him the name of a new subscriber, two copies would be supplied for the price of one. He was certain that this simple scheme would succeed and increased the regular print run from 2,000 to 4,000 copies, persisting at that level for four years. "All," however, "worked wrong." Few extra subscribers were found, many old ones abandoned the *Register* (some alleging discrimination in sales policy), and the number of magazines printed was generally about three times larger than the number sold. In addition to a weak market, there were losses to defaulting subscribers and absconding debt collectors. All these problems, in Ruffin's view, were basically due to "my ignorance of the business I was carrying on."[29]

Apparently undaunted, he began to explore fresh journalistic territory. In 1837 he brought out the *Southern Magazine* and in so doing started to take up political issues of a proto-secessionist nature. The journal was intended to "maintain the original state-rights doctrine, & the principles of the old republican party." And it was, as he saw it sometime after, bound to fail, given its purpose to expose corruption and tilt at the Whigs and the new Democrats. A meager two hundred subscribers came forward and the magazine closed after only two issues, despite contributions from Abel Ushur, Nathaniel Beverley Tucker, and, of course, Ruffin himself. This was followed by the slightly more successful *Bank Reformer*, running to six monthly issues of about 3,000 copies each. Ruffin's concern—already pursued briefly in the *Farmers' Register*—was to expose the iniquities of the banking system, lately much expanded. He had been greatly offended by the suspension of specie payment in Virginia in 1837 and again in 1839 and 1841. It seemed an affront to trusting farmers and tradesmen to be given paper promising payment in good metal and then to be told that the promise could no longer be kept. He resorted to the weekly practice of taking legal action against Petersburg banks for the nonpayment of five-dollar bills. It was impossible, he thought, that any court could find against him. "Yet, on three . . . different days of trial every whig magistrate did so decide upon a different point each time, each of inconceivable absurdity." If, he claimed, a Democrat found in his favor, a Whig was sent for to neutralize the judgment on the instructions of the banks. It was all "a disagreeable & dirty business."[30]

When Ruffin became aroused by what he saw as an issue of principle, he pursued it with intense commitment, totally persuaded by the virtue of his own argument, totally persuaded of the vice and malice of his quarry. He also had a self-confessed love of notoriety and admitted in old age to the lifelong "habit of speaking freely, & with as much sarcasm or censure as the subject deserved, exercised without caution."[31] It was probably a recklessness that he enjoyed for the most part, supported by an *amour-propre* of both class and intellect, but it did put him at serious risk in a town like Petersburg with a white population of only a few thousand. There he was one of a very small number of notable men of trade and opinion. Ruffin was noisily slandering some of his closest neighbors. Some of the diatribe was offered in the pages of the *Register* in the spring and summer of 1841, the articles coming out as a pamphlet later in the year: *Abuses of the Banking System*. He brought into his assault an element of agrarian populism, deriving from ancient notions of the financier as usurious parasite feeding off the product of innocent toil. In the final page he addressed the "Farmers of Virginia—mechanics—all who live by honest labor," asking them to condemn "in a voice of thunder" those who "live and fatten by depradating upon the property and fruits of the labor of the community." The title page carried quotations from President Tyler and Daniel Webster imbued with the idea of rural virtue imperiled by insidious, extraneous forces. The James River planter in Ruffin was genuinely distressed and perplexed by the novel spectacle of urban financial squalor.

In the summer of 1841 the Association for Promoting Currency and Banking Reform was set up by Ruffin in Petersburg, declaring that irredeemable, depreciated paper money was a source of "great and still increasing evils to the property interests, habits and morals of the people." On 4 September the first number of the *Bank Reformer* was published, promising monthly 16-page issues at $5 for two hundred copies and offering itself as an accumulating record of "banking frauds, and the present struggle against banking power."[32] The campaign did not have to proceed for very long, however. The worst abuses were ended a year later when payments were resumed. By the mid-1840s the Virginia banks were operating a conservative and cautious specie-to-circulation ratio of 1 : 2.8.[33]

In 1932 Avery Craven suggested that the *Farmers' Register* collapsed because complaints "poured in" from upset planters about excessive editorial dabbling in issues of finance and politics. This relatively trivial reason has been repeated by all subsequent historians who have discussed the matter.[34] It is not, however, one which accords with the available evidence. Craven's point, in fact, was supported by very little documentation, and this has not been enlarged at all in the course of fifty years. Ruffin did not really change the character of his paper. There was only one index reference to banking and related topics for 1837 and for 1838, three for 1839, and one for 1840. (The percentages of column space represented are 0.7, 0.2, 0.1, and 0.3 respectively.) These figures cover the forty-three issues following the suspension of May 1837. In 1841 there were as many as forty-five pieces (8.5 percent of the volume), but in 1842 the number fell back to only six (2.0 percent).[35] Clearly there was only one year in which the intrusion was pronounced, though hardly overwhelming.

Ruffin felt that on banking matters he was defending agriculturists, and it is entirely possible that a great many confused farmers, saving and trading insecurely with their disavowed paper money, were not at all troubled by his occasional fulminations against the urban interests. These were early days for casual, sophisticated cynicism about the promises on bank notes. Nor was there any particular reason why the planter community as a whole should have been upset by an issue which had political overtones. Agriculture was already politically charged—on slavery, on the tariff, on emigration, and on the whole matter of Southern economic strength and Southern power within the Union.

The "political" charge, in fact, is based on a single letter which appeared in the *Register* in October 1841 referring to early promises in the journal to keep clear of politics, and observing inconsistency between these and the recent involvement with financial affairs, the country's "most fruitful source of political vituperation." No other outraged farmers were cited. Indeed the correspondent commented, "Some of my nearest friends are to the full as *abstract,* I was going to say *distracted,* about the banks, as you are." Ruffin had no difficulty in refuting the accusation. His original prospectus had declared the "fourth class of subjects" for the *Register* to be: "The discussion of such subjects of political economy as are connected with the preservation and support of the interests of agriculture." Recent banking troubles fitted the bill perfectly. A number of outspoken Democrats in Virginia were also complaining of the abuses of paper money, and to a considerable extent they represented farmer opinion. James Sharp has shown that whereas the towns of Petersburg and Richmond were decidedly soft-money and Whiggish in their affiliations in the late 1830s and early 1840s, the tidewater counties to the south of the James and to the west of Nansemond County were usually strongly Democratic and attached to the hard-money wing of the party. Even some of the tidewater Whig constituencies held reservations about paper money and suspensions. The main consequence of the banking furor for Ruffin was intense personal hostility from within financial circles and consequent social discomfort within Petersburg—of which town, he declared in 1841, he was "entirely disinclined to remain a resident."[36]

Ruffin was very self-critical when commenting on his own business skills and believed that he had been guilty of "injudicious conduct" in his management of the *Register.* He also viewed the influence of the banking fracas as "malignant." But the main problem, he insisted, was the condition of the planter market for such publications. "The great and unceasing and all-important obstacle to the proper maintenance and consequent full measure of utility of the Farmers' Register," he wrote in 1842, "is the general apathy and want of all public support, and *even of enlightened self-interest,* by the agricultural community of this state." The subscription list had experienced little growth over the years. One might guess at an average of around 1,300 in the 1830s, compared with 3,000 or so for all thirty-plus agricultural periodicals nationwide. As late as August 1841 Ruffin claimed that his list of subscribers was "larger than at any previous time," though in the fall of

1842, some months after he had announced the impending closure of the enterprise, the number had dropped to just under 1,000. It included a fair range of professional men as well as farmers, and by the early 1840s almost half the readership was non-Virginian. Many were subscribers in name only—an abuse which Ruffin initially tolerated. If a man did not cancel his subscription before the end of the year, he was automatically sent the volume for the next. The slack assumptions underlying such practice proved very damaging, especially in a market adversely affected by the financial troubles of 1837 and the price falls of subsequent years. It would not have taken many farmers long to discover that, despite initial good intentions, they were not really making much use of the paper. Equally, however, it did not take Ruffin long to run out of patience. In 1837 he began to enforce one of the resolutions of the recent Editorial Convention of Virginia. "The names of all subscribers whose ability to pay may be unknown to the publisher, and who remain indebted on open account at the end of two years, from the time when the advanced payment was due, shall be erased from the list of subscribers."[37]

In 1839 he claimed that the application of this rule had swept away between one hundred and three hundred defaulters a year: "It *shall* be done even if at the total loss of all such subscribers." The credit system of selling had, he thought, permitted "enormous abuse," and was pernicious enough to break even the most popular of journals.[38] When he received transferred subscribers from the *Carolina Planter* after its collapse in 1841, he declared that any of these who failed to pay up within six months of receiving the paper would likewise have their subscriptions canceled.[39]

Bills for arrears sent out in June and early July 1841 amounted to almost $5,000. On 25 August, Ruffin recorded that not one cent had been paid. By the end of 1842 the debt had risen to $8,000, the rise no doubt encouraged by the fact that Ruffin's sanctions lost all force when the decision to close down was announced early in the year. Of this, only $600 was ever retrieved. Other losses resulted from the 4,000-copy printings of the mid-1830s and from the habit many subscribers had of lending their *Registers* to nonsubscribers, failing to recover them, and claiming free duplicates from Petersburg. Despite difficulties, however, the paper made a decisive profit in its early years,[40] and it is doubtful if it (as distinct from the printing business as a whole) ever showed a loss over a full year. But the margins were clearly being squeezed. Complaining about defaults in 1841, Ruffin declared that the "publication has never been of so little profit as for this year." For some time, he observed in 1842, "there has not been enough of clear profit to pay for a capable clerk." Current arrears were in excess of all the net income the *Register* had ever secured.[41] There is, it should be stressed, no documented connection between defaulting and the financial disputes. Aggrieved farmers could have used that method of signaling their disapproval, but there is no clear suggestion from Ruffin that they did, and of course the banking problem had acquired serious dimensions long before 1841.

The mounting debt was both bothersome and dispiriting. Ruffin could, of course, have struggled on with his reliable customers, financing any deficits in common proprietor-editor fashion by digging into his own pocket. Money, however, had already been lost in the short-lived *Southern Magazine* and in the *Bank Reformer* (most copies of the latter having been given away). He had also suffered major setbacks in attempts to make money from investment—mainly in railway stock: $5,000 nominal in the Petersburg Railroad Company, $10,000 in the Greenville Railroad Company, and $12,000 in the Raleigh and Gaston Railroad. When prices fell in the 1837 crash and he consulted his investing friends in Petersburg about the best course of action, he discovered that they had all sold out sometime before. No one had tipped him off. He also invested money in water power and in cotton factories, but again there was personal letdown and loss. Further embarrassment came from property investments in Petersburg. Before the crash his estate had been valued at around $100,000. Losses—excluding those attending the disposal of the publishing works—amounted to about $30,000.[42] Ruffin was far from being ruined, but his financial experience had been a profoundly unhappy and disturbing one.

Little short of sustained farmer enthusiasm could have kept editor and business going. The agricultural community, however, was not only letting him down financially but failing to send in material which the journal could publish. This was a common problem, but it was one which seemed to be getting progressively worse on the *Register*. Ruffin had insisted as early as 1833 that without a generous supply of planter submissions "the *Register*'s usefulness will soon diminish, and its existence perhaps will not last much longer."[43] It was vital, he insisted in 1839, that it recruit "the pens of its readers." Tours by the editor and reprints from other journals were no substitutes for the clear, homely voice of local experience. The issues for the last two months of 1833, of 1837, and of 1841 have been examined for evidence of decrease in original contributions, these numbering 65 columns (25 percent of the total) in the first year, 25 (10 percent) in the second, and

24½ (13 percent) in the third. If Ruffin's own detectable pieces (signed as well as anonymous) are included, the figures become 104 (41 percent), 56 (24 percent), and 46 (24 percent). He too was contributing less. In the selected months for 1837 and 1841 three-quarters of the journal was composed of cuttings. The overall bulk was also diminishing: 768 pages and 610 index headings in volume 1; 524 pages and 204 headings in volume 10.

This failure grieved him until the end of his life. "I . . . retired," he wrote in 1851, "from that bond of connexion with the public in Virginia—disappointed & mortified—soured with the injustice & ingratitude of my countrymen & with a determination never to renew a connexion with the public in any form."[44]

He had to function in both the urban and rural spheres if his ideas were to have a major impact on agriculture. This proved to be too difficult and too wearing. From his town quarters he tried to stimulate planters in the rural fastness of the Old South, but they remained on the whole unresponsive. As a reformer he needed the urban world—for publishing, distribution, meetings, fairs, rail communication, markets, perhaps sometimes for finance as well. But it proved too threatening. Ruffin withdrew from it in 1842 and never returned. The dichotomy was later to take on larger and more ominous dimensions as conflict intensified between the urbanizing North and the slave South. Already in the 1840s he was championing the cause of beleaguered rural patriarchy, and he continued to do so up to the Civil War without any of the uncertainty and ambivalence shown by most of his fellow Virginians.

His overwhelming desire now was to return to plantation life and "perfect seclusion" in an attempt to recapture some of the old spirit of success in the field. Whatever his professed defects as a practical farmer, that was the one occupation in which he had excelled. His editorship of the *Register* had helped stock his mind with a host of new ideas on the specifics of improved agriculture. Rather surprisingly, given his declared anti-Virginia sentiments, he sought his way back not in some distant corner of the state or beyond but in his old county of Prince George—among the very farmers whom he had lately decided to abandon. He could not easily go back to Coggin's Point since his son Edmund Jr. was now part owner and full-time manager. Efforts to purchase land elsewhere in the county, however, proved abortive. Successful marling, ironically, had raised land values and reduced the numbers of plantations on the market.[45]

It would be futile to attempt to measure the agricultural impact of the

Register. It certainly coincided with a quite rapid extension of ameliorative practices in lower Virginia, but it may be that journal and improvement were both, for a while, products of optimistic and expansionist times. It was essentially a paper in which Ruffin could address the larger tidewater planters of the border states on the virtues of marling and diversifying, and through which a few of these planters could exchange results and ideas of their own (gaining a bit of publicity and prestige as they did so). It was a thoroughly patrician exercise. The circulation figures make it very clear that the great mass of Old South farmers were effectively unaware of its existence.

III

Late in 1842 Ruffin was presented with an unexpected and welcome opportunity to get out of Virginia for a time. James Hammond, the recently elected governor of South Carolina, wrote to him in November saying he hoped some arrangement could be made to get him south on a remunerated basis "to examine a few localities . . . & look over a few plantations."[46] Hammond had been a subscriber to the *Farmers' Register* and had lately embarked on very extensive marling operations by the Savannah River in Barnwell District.[47] He had already begun to publicize his findings. Fired by Southern nationalism, personal ambition, and enthusiasm for the possibilities of agricultural recovery through soil improvement and crop diversification, he came to be regarded by Ruffin as his best and most influential disciple.[48] By mid-December he was able, at the behest of the Agricultural Committee of the House of Representatives, to send Ruffin a formal invitation to undertake an agricultural survey of the state.[49]

   Ruffin had already enjoyed some direct contacts with the planters in and around Charleston. Communications had been sent to the *Farmers' Register* and it was clear from these, as well as from pieces lifted from other Southern journals, that there was some genuine curiosity in South Carolina about the virtues of marling. Former geological reports, moreover, had suggested that the state was peculiarly well endowed with calcareous resources. On 15 April 1840 Ruffin arrived in Wilmington, North Carolina, as a guest of the recently completed Wilmington Railroad, and on the afternoon of the sixteenth embarked on the company's steamship for an additional fifteen-hour journey to Charleston. He spent twelve hours in the city, experiencing some fine weather, and a good deal of frustration at having to leave so soon. He

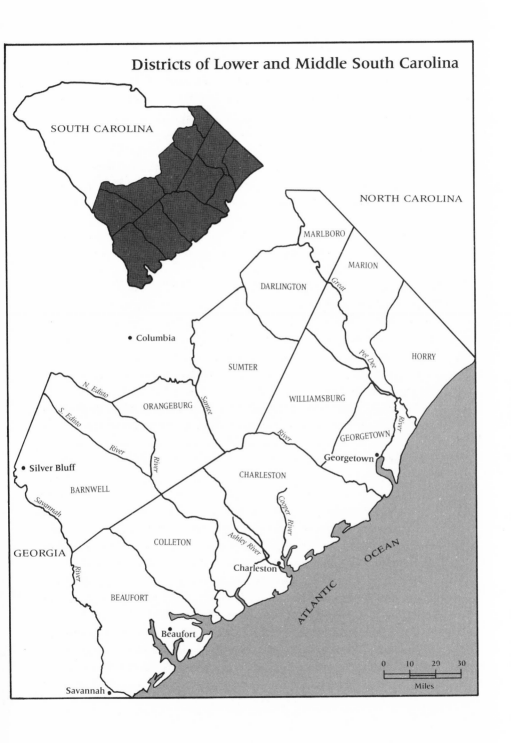

Districts of Lower and Middle South Carolina

SOUTH CAROLINA

NORTH CAROLINA

MARLBORO

MARION

DARLINGTON

• Columbia

SUMTER

HORRY

N. Edisto

S. Edisto

ORANGEBURG

Santee

WILLIAMSBURG

River

GEORGETOWN

River

• Silver Bluff

River

Georgetown •

BARNWELL

River

CHARLESTON

GEORGIA

Savannah

COLLETON

Cooper River

Ashley River

ATLANTIC OCEAN

River

Charleston •

BEAUFORT

Beaufort •

Savannah •

| 0 | 10 | 20 | 30 |

Miles

was "highly gratified with all that was seen and met with," enjoying the attentions of so many "warm-hearted southrons" and likening Charleston to "a gentleman born and bred." The Nullification crisis of 1832 had demonstrated that the state could nourish the heated sectionalism that Ruffin was already finding so inviting, and by 1842 it had a disunionist governor who pursued the patriotic cause of advanced farming as well as railing against the bankers.[50]

After some initial hestitation he decided to accept the appointment, being without either farm or "present employment." Hammond wanted him to take a two-year post with an annual salary of $2,000, but the duration seemed excessive to Ruffin and so the period was shortened to a single year. His task, as "Agricultural and Geological Surveyor," of searching for calcareous deposits and visiting and instructing planters, was bound to be an onerous one, taking him into "most uncertain & irregular" places. The terrain was unfamiliar, transport facilities were poor, and the climate enervating through much of the year. Hammond, moreover, had told him to expect an ambivalent welcome. He would find South Carolinians polite and hospitable but would also run up against "much indifference, much ignorance, much conceit, much obstinacy & some opposition."[51]

Ruffin began work in January 1843. He was forty-nine years old and some four hundred miles distant from his home and family in Petersburg. This was to be the most social and the most outdoor of his years as an agricultural observer and instructor. It also marked the end of a phase in his life, for his months in the state were the last of his career as a full-time reformer.

In the period covered by his own notes, from 28 January to 12 September, he describes extensive explorations of territory both above and below the fall line. An outline of his itinerary can serve as rough measure of the range and intensity of his work.[52] He spent most of his first month in the vicinity of Charleston. He examined promising ground along the banks of the Cooper and Ashley and around the Santee Canal, spent some time on James Island, and attended to office arrangements and specimen analysis in Charleston itself (using a room in Robert Mills's Fireproof Building). Distances of up to forty miles were recorded for individual days. At the end of February he set off for Beaufort by way of Edisto and Jehossa, and from Beaufort made trips to Lady, Distance, Port Royal, and St. Helena islands, his work in these less bountiful parts taking up about a couple of weeks. From there he moved around the headwaters of the Broad River and down to the

Savannah at Purysburg, then striking back east by a lonely and troublesome inland route running along the southern boundaries of Barnwell and Orangeburg districts. He arrived at the Santee River near Eutaw Ferry on 18 March. The journey from the Savannah had taken only four days and the surveying, inevitably, had been very cursory. He traveled on the Santee and around the relatively congenial Charleston hinterland until the end of the month, making some useful discoveries, and then headed east for Georgetown and the rice lands at the mouth of the Pee Dee River. A further two weeks were spent there in helpful company before he set off upriver to examine what turned out to be the finest marl exposures in the whole state. He got as far as Mar's Bluff near the Marlborough District boundary, after which he turned speedily back to Charleston across Black Mingo Creek and the Black and Cooper rivers. He arrived on 24 April and set sail the following day for Wilmington and a three-week break in Virginia. The one tidewater area he had ignored was Horry in the northeast. This was, by Ruffin's description, the "dark corner" of South Carolina. As he had no expectation of finding knowledgeable farmers there, he considered it pointless to make a visit.[53]

After his return on 10 May he retraced some former routes up the Cooper and Santee, pushing on into Orangeburg and arriving at Columbia on the twenty-first to meet planters assembling for a state agricultural convention. After a few days of surveying in the neighborhood of Orangeburg village he headed west again into Barnwell and spent a busy two weeks on the Savannah River and its eastern creeks. The main interest here was the Silver Bluff plantation of Governor Hammond, where large-scale marling had begun in 1841. "It was with much interest that I first saw the marled fields of which I had published the report," he wrote.[54] Ruffin stayed with Hammond between 9 and 16 June, rounding off this second visit to the Savannah with a short trip to Augusta. From there he moved north to Edgefield and then east to Columbia—his first brief journey on the piedmont. The hot season had begun and he wanted to stay well clear of the insalubrious coastlands. The capital replaced Charleston as his home base. During the last week of the month he examined a variety of exposures in the western parts of Sumter and Clarendon districts, keeping close to the Wateree and Upper Santee river system. At the beginning of July he stopped in Columbia for a few days' rest. On the fourth he rode upcountry to Monticello in Fairfield to participate in another agricultural convention. The tenth found him back in Charleston and packing for a second trip home. Ill health had begun to interfere with his work and he decided to seek relaxation and medical treatment in Virginia. This time he was away for six weeks.

He got back to Columbia by rail on the evening of 24 August. By the following afternoon he was in his buggy heading north again to Fairfield. There were no accumulations of marl to be found above tidewater, but there was a good deal of limestone which could form the basis for lime production. Unfortunately, Ruffin had made only a partial recovery in Petersburg. Headaches and biliousness afflicted him in acute form. His route passed through Monticello in a straight northwesterly direction to Unionville and Limestone Springs, with diversions to Spartanburg and the Nesbitt ironworks on the Broad River. By now he was in the most northerly part of the state, and after five days of sickness and confinement at Limestone Springs he passed over the North Carolina border on his way back to Flat Rock in the Blue Ridge Mountains "to seek a perfectly healthy climate" and a week or two's rest. He arrived on 13 September, and closed his diary. "These notes of late have been so little agricultural in their character . . . that I shall cease taking the trouble to continue them." He found his way home again to Virginia and returned to South Carolina for the last time as surveyor later in the fall. The diary was not revived, so it may be assumed that little was achieved. His physical condition deteriorated further. Most of his early enthusiasm for exploration and good company had left him. It was now a straightforward matter of discharging his remaining obligations—with some delegation if need be. Field labors planned for the late fall of 1843 were handed over to his son Julian.[55]

He was present in the state through most of the last weeks of the year, fulfilling his contractual twelve months and working on the completion of his lengthy and detailed official report. Clear notice of his intention to leave was submitted at the end of November. Hammond was disappointed, having hoped that Ruffin might still be persuaded to stay on for the two-year period originally suggested. He acknowledged the services received in a brief, tart note, pointing out how much more effective Ruffin's work would have been if substantially extended. Since Ruffin's personal interests and comforts were at stake, however, he acknowledged he had no alternative but to agree to his departure. Ruffin himself suggested a successor: "an obscure & unknown teacher of a school in Petersburg" by the name of Michael Tuomey.[56] The survey was continued to good effect and Tuomey won the close friendship of Hammond and much professional success in the lower South as a geologist and agricultural chemist.[57]

Ruffin's report was published at the end of 1843 and extracts appeared in the Charleston *Southern Agriculturist*. But despite his hard work and the associations which he had formed with some of the scientists and seigneurs of the state, he was unable to view his months in South Carolina as a particularly happy and productive period. His health, he felt, had been permanently damaged, and the planters, though amicable, had been generally unresponsive. In undertaking the survey, he wrote in 1851, he had hoped "to enrich the state & thereby to exalt my own reputation. But I have been greatly disappointed in the issue; I am compelled to believe that the results have not yet amounted in value to the state to one-thousandth part as much as I had expected."[58]

What strikes one as extraordinary, reading Ruffin's spare and evocative journal, is how personal and solitary the whole exercise was. A man was appointed to survey the geology and agriculture of a state the size of Scotland without the benefit of any staff. A couple of outriders would certainly have been useful for spotting the most promising calcareous formations, helping Ruffin select the rewarding routes, assisting in the evenings with specimen analysis, and getting on with the work when he was ill or back home in Virginia. On 11 May he recorded help from the chemist, Dr. John Lawrence Smith, while working on his marl collection in Charleston, but that is the only evidence of professional support. When he finally abandoned his travels in South Carolina he had to call in his twenty-two-year-old son, and then find a permanent replacement in a Petersburg school. He was a fortnight in the state before he met his employer, James Hammond, and then only by a brief social exchange at a Charleston hotel. He also had to make his own transport arrangements, hiring a keelboat in late February at 50 cents a day for the vessel and 50 cents each for the two oarsmen. This he considered expensive, and also inconvenient. The coastal rivers were awkward to navigate, there was much exposure to the elements, and the labor was not always available when required. Despite some excitements on windy days and on ebb tides, he decided before the end of the month to abandon regular water transport and buy himself a horse and four-wheeled buggy, costing $145. This strayed off uncertain tracks, labored through sandy state roads, and plowed seat-deep into swamps and creeks. In wet weather—even in summer—he had to don a greatcoat and raise his umbrella. But the vehicle rattled around the state quite nicely for the most part and could see him through a forty-mile day without too much discomfort.[59]

Ruffin had little choice but to rely heavily on the planter community for any advice he needed. He had no comprehensive geology map of South Carolina to guide him, so had to make-do with reported sightings. Once the presence of calcareous deposits had been certified in a particular area he could then start to look around more independently, examining river bluffs and boring with augers to determine the age, thickness, dip, quality, and accessibility of the strata. With a good number of findings, he could make deductions for a wide area with some precision. But the hospitable planter had usually to start him off—the process typically beginning with a letter telling Ruffin about the supposed marl and inviting him to come and stay. The host could then offer letters of introduction to other possibly helpful men in the neighborhood—or, better still, ride out with him for a day or two. His tendency to linger down on the coast in the later winter and spring and race through some of the humbler regions upcountry owed something no doubt to a partiality to comfort and good conversation, but it probably owed more to the availability of introductions and the number of helpful planters around who knew about the survey. It was another patrician exercise, and only very occasionally did Ruffin stray into the dwellings of the poor and the "houses of entertainment" where board and lodging had to be paid for.[60]

His reception by famous Carolinians must have pleased him enormously. Almost all were unknown to him personally, but most were familiar with his reputation. It was illness, rarely people, that demoralized him in the state. The conchologist Edmund Ravenel, he recorded, "received me with the hearty welcome which I have found from every stranger whom I have sought or made my host." Planters entertained without too much competitive display and conducted themselves with "temperate conviviality." Whitemarsh Seabrook, a future governor, devoted two weeks in late February and early March to conducting him around the Edisto Island and Beaufort areas. Ruffin also stayed, or conversed, with people of repute such as William Anderson, John Bachman, Robert Barnwell, William Elliot, Wade Hampton II, Thomas Heriot, Joseph Johnson, Mitchell King, David and Louisa McCord, John Richardson—and, of course, James Hammond. Information could be exchanged and wits sharpened in a social milieu that was much more intimate than Virginia's. Charleston made its contribution, and so too did the climate. Summer heat and "swamp miasma" forced tidewater planters and their families out of their low-lying estates and up onto the nearest dry elevations. Pine barrens were a favorite locale. "By such annual

meetings . . . ," wrote Ruffin, "the selfish feelings & prejudices which se-
cluded life is apt to induce are removed, & social feeling & social virtues are
cultivated. . . . Every planter's business & opinions become known to
all. . . . The careless & indolent were stimulated also by the good-natured
jeers of his neighbors. . . . A good miscellaneous literacy was established."[61]

There were also some lively agricultural societies. Despite a declared fear
of public occasions, Ruffin answered questions at a club on the lower
Cooper, at the Edisto Agricultural Society, in Beaufort Town House, at the
Black Oak Club House, and at the Georgetown Court House. He also delivered an address to an agricultural convention at Monticello, in Fairfield
County, to which six hundred people had turned up. Two other formal ses-
sions, with the Pee Dee and Edgefield societies, were cancelled, the latter
without any line of apology. This was about the only time in the state when
he felt rudely let down.[62]

Despite all the interest and farming intelligence on display, Ruffin was
frequently astonished to discover how ill-informed South Carolinians were
on matters which he considered to be of vital importance to sound agriculture. There were many people who did not know what marl looked like,
and he was in the state eight weeks before he saw anyone actually engaged
in a marling operation. "It is," he wrote after a meeting with planters in
Beaufort, "both astonishing & mortifying to me to find such general ignorance in regard to the use of calcareous manures, upon which I have so long
been writing & publishing & have sent so many copies of my publications to
the State." Even Governor Hammond had remained dismissive until as late
as 1840, and confessed to Ruffin that he had applied much influence and
energy in the late 1830s to opposing an agricultural survey of the state.
Audiences at meetings seemed interested, and often promised to begin experiments at once, but after Ruffin moved on the enthusiasm usually died
away.[63]

His claim in 1851 that he had expected a response a thousand times
greater than that actually realized must have been a little disingenuous. He
could not have anticipated a rapidly extending use of marl among such ill-
informed and conservative planters and where the solitary proselytizer had
been at work for less than a year. A middle-aged man riding around in an
open buggy, concerned about his luggage and his specimens, troubled by
bad weather, bad roads, and bad health and dependent on whatever judicious or injudicious private assistance presented itself, could hardly expect
to alter the entrenched traditions of remunerative staple farming. In 1843

he spoke of "the peculiar difficulties of a first investigation" and an aggravating "want of time" in characterizing his survey, and a decade or so later, in an address berating the planters of the state for their persisting, exhaustive monocultural ways, he declared how greatly disappointed he had been by his failure. It was a "subject of painful reflection" that he had been unable to stimulate marling and acquire "some just claim to be deemed a public benefactor." The number of marl experimenters was falling, not rising. Farmers insisted on pursuing "the greatest *immediate* production and profit" at the expense of "the greatest *continued* products and profits." Their capital losses were obscured by respectable incomes and by narrowness of accounting vision. Any talk of land-resting was met with the ignorant reply: "What! lose two crops in every five years? I cannot afford to lose even one." Many of the most notable farmers were "ready enough to accept and to apply to themselves . . . the name of 'land killers!' "64

At least, however, they now knew that if they wished to commence ameliorative operations, resources were at hand. Ruffin had shown that fine marl underlay most of the low country, and usually at no great depth. The Santee beds, running from Georgetown and Charleston west to the Savannah at Barnwell District, were the richest he had found anywhere, and the state as a whole seemed the best endowed in all of the Southeast.65

IV

By the end of 1843 Ruffin was back in Virginia. Shortly before leaving South Carolina he had received an invitation from the farmers of Prince George County to attend a presentation and dinner in his honor in Garysville, the town closest to Coggin's Point. The occasion materialized the day after he returned home, and he delivered a speech which, uncommonly, extolled the achievements of local farmers. Only one newspaper, however, carried any report of the proceedings. Both the Richmond *Whig* and the *Enquirer,* though invited to publish details, had chosen to ignore the event. Ruffin was, as he wrote later, "deeply mortified." Such lack of interest revived his sense of Virginia neglect and sharpened his resolve to withdraw once and for all from any form of public service.66 The kindness of the Garysville farmers themselves counted for little.

In October 1843 he had written from South Carolina to his eldest son, Edmund Jr., instructing him to purchase a plantation being sold in Hanover County to the northeast of Richmond. The land was bought at the seemingly inflated price of $17 an acre.[67] At the beginning of January, Ruffin began to move his personal effects out of Petersburg. The transfer to the farm which he named Marlbourne took more than two weeks to complete. There were 977 acres, most of them lying low along the Pamunkey River, but a substantial portion comprising rough upland grazing. At the age of fifty he had at last moved right away from the James, having sold his remaining share of the Coggin's Point lands to Edmund Jr. for $10,800. The retreat, however, was not intended as any sort of retirement. The farm was "wretchedly out of order." Old tested schemes had to be set in motion again and the plantation restored to a high level of production. Ruffin, indeed, was about to embark on his most successful phase as a practical farmer. It was to last for over a decade, after which he abandoned full-time farming for good. The main tasks were easily identified: soil amelioration over the entire extent of the property, and draining of the stiff wet land down by the stream. "I trust," he wrote in 1844, "that a few years of marling will put a new face on the fields."[68]

The job was more or less finished by the end of the 1840s. Drainage, however, involved the slow and laborious construction of large networks of covered ditches, and as late as 1851 these were still far from completion. Farm vehicles and a wide range of advanced equipment—McCormick reapers, harrows, and threshing machines—were purchased, and a good body of livestock built up for subsistence and manure. The entire labor force at the start came from Coggin's Point, Ruffin and Edmund Jr. dividing the total number between them. They apparently had no reservations about breaking up families in the process. Twenty-nine slaves moved north to Marlbourne: twenty-three hands, comprising twelve men under a foreman, three women, two boys, and five small children; and half a dozen house servants. Beyond these, Ruffin required a gardener and a carriage driver. At Whitsun or Christmas some slaves might be allowed to travel down to the old plantation to spend a day or two with their families, and on occasions people would be lent out to Edmund Jr., or to Julian, who farmed the small "Ruthven" plantation in Prince George County. Ruffin's sons were periodically short of hands, and were themselves prepared to lend out labor when the need arose at Marlbourne.[69]

Ruffin also brought in an overseer from Coggin's, an apparently hard-working young man by the name of Talley who was given a salary of $300 per year. By April 1846, however, he was in the employ of Julian Ruffin. In his exile from Virginia society Ruffin could be almost constantly on the property himself. Most supervisory functions could also be confidently left to his foreman-slave, Jem Sykes, who took charge of the whole plantation when Ruffin went away on occasional trips. Despite a reluctance to venture out-of-doors before breakfast, or in bad weather, Ruffin appears to have been a fairly active field farmer. All his indispositions, he claimed in 1851, were the consequence of his "habitual exposure to the heat of the sun, & often to other inclemencies of the weather or season." Labor during the day was followed by reading or writing in the evening.[70]

His "Farm Journal," kept between 1844 and 1851, ran to around a quarter of a million words, largely concerning day-to-day agricultural matters and conveying great energy of application and intensity of interest. Ruffin clearly felt himself to be back in the sphere of honest toil, uncontaminated by the corrupted world beyond. As a man with frustrated public ambitions, however, he could hardly be described as contented. The old patrician flame still burned. Authority, status, and fame could be only tenuously preserved in the private domain of master and slaves. The personal reflections in "Incidents of My Life," written for his family in the early 1850s, reveal a chronically unsettled and unhappy frame of mind, with Ruffin dwelling insistently on past failures and grievances and straining towards self-justification and self-acclaim. Self-criticism was usually muted and trivial. He also wrote a little on agricultural and, later, political affairs for newspapers and journals, thereby renewing some of the old "bond of connexion" with the Virginia public. In 1849, for example, he recorded his progress at Marlbourne for the pages of the Richmond *Southern Planter.*[71]

Marling was the foundation of improvement. Oddly, Ruffin had bought a plantation which lacked its own available supplies, but Carter Braxton on the adjoining property had substantial deposits and agreed to give him free access.[72] Ruffin was so eager, and had stocked the plantation with hands and equipment so quickly, that he succeeded in hauling the first loads onto his fields a week or two after arriving at Marlbourne. By 15 March 1844 he had moved 1,406 cartloads, and by the end of the year 67,875 bushels had been distributed over 252½ acres. Whatever disappointments he had encountered after his first experimental applications of 1818, his own successes as a planter, and those of the various farmers who documented their increased yields in the *Farmers' Register,* had served to consolidate his faith in marl as the one true and unfailing basis of profitable farming. In 1845 an additional 75,512 bushels were laid on the fields; in 1846, 35,545; in 1847, 42,575; in 1848, 55,106; and in 1848, 56,169—approaching a third of a million in just six years.[73]

The effort required the labor of a near-specialist force, supplemented whenever possible by slaves who could be spared from other tasks on the farm. This work was combined with carefully considered schemes of rotation. The particular one Ruffin was aiming for in 1847 was a six-year shift of corn sown with peas; peas for seed, fodder, and manuring; wheat sown with clover; clover for mowing and grazing; clover for grazing and manuring; and, finally, wheat again. In practice he had two or three variants of this in operation on different parts of the plantation. Hogs were fed on corn, peas, and clover, and large quantities of corn were retained for domestic consumption. Commercially, the main objective was wheat production, with roughly a third of the land under that grain in any one year. Cargoes were loaded onto vessels at his landing on the Pamunkey and carried off to Richmond and Baltimore. Smaller amounts were sold locally from his barn.[74] It was a fairly simple existence, involving substantial selling but an absolute minimum of physical contact with the outside world.

In June 1849 Ruffin made a major addition to the plantation by buying a nearby 323-acre tract of land, comprising poor fields and some forest. He paid $1,586.50, and in August joined this up to Marlbourne by purchasing three hundred intervening acres for $2,480, thereby reducing the length of his boundaries, saving on fencing, and gaining control over the outlets for his drainage ditches.[75] By the end of the 1840s Marlbourne had grown from 977 to 1,600 acres. The expansion of both production and area was achieved without any significant increase in the labor force.

The predictable and desired consequence of amelioration, drainage, and rotation was a rapid improvement in the profitability of the farm. Figures available for 1844 to 1848 show, sequentially, a loss of $74 and then net gains of $2,237, $3,545, $6,391, and $5,810. These sums amply retrieved the original cost of the plantation, and with most of the $10,800 in hand from the transfer of his old lands to Edmund Jr., Ruffin had no difficulty in assembling the funds needed for enlargement in 1849. By 1850 he valued his personal estate at $81,000. He ranked now among the half dozen wealthiest landowners in Hanover County.[76] He had presented annuities equal to the interest on $4,000 to each of his children either when they left school or came of age (although those who were still at home had deductions made as "a moderate charge for board etc."). In 1850 he was tempted to divide up his property in its entirety, but balked at the idea of selling his land and thereby putting an end to "all further accumulation." Additional settlements were arranged for all but his two youngest children, and in 1855 he finally decided that the time had come to pass over the mass of his estate. The value, by then, had risen to $150,000.[77]

Towards the end of 1854 Ruffin handed the running of Marlbourne to his second son, Julian, as the first step towards his retirement. Family fortunes had been radically improved and he was becoming weary of day-to-day farming, especially under the afflictions of what seemed premature senility. "In my 58th year," he wrote in 1851, "I am in body & mind as if 12 or 15 years older." Three of his children—Rebecca, Jane, and Ella—died in 1855, causing him the most acute desolation. The death of Jane in particular brought on something approaching derangement. Such blows rendered him "still less inclined to bear the labors & perplexities of conducting any regular business—for which indeed my interest had nearly ceased." Since Julian had been forced by family obligations to return to his own farm, and since Ruffin had no inclination to bring in an overseer, the time had now come to place Marlbourne in other hands. Keeping $25,000 for himself, he divided the bulk of his estate in roughly equal proportions among his five surviving children. Not wishing to compromise the authority of the new owners, he decided to leave Marlbourne as soon as all the business had been settled.[78] From then until his death in 1865 he moved around the various family properties, spending quite a lot of time in the cottage behind Edmund Jr.'s grand new Beechwood mansion, some way west of the old Coggin's house. He usually managed to keep well clear of farming work.[79]

V

A notable feature of this generally very private period was Ruffin's gradual reentry into the community of Virginia planters. No doubt he was energized by his own recent successes at Marlbourne. Virginia, largely unaware of its past sins, was glad to welcome him back. He always knew he had had "many warm & grateful admirers & approvers," and he was pleased to discover that old enemies could later become friends. Back in 1842 he had given up a briefly held secretaryship of the State Board of Agriculture, and in 1845 had spurned the presidency of the Virginia State Agricultural Society, later describing this and a subsequent body as "abortions."[80] In 1852, however, the formation of a new state society found him in a much more receptive frame of mind. Members apparently agreed now with his views on the malfunctioning of such societies, and elected him their president. This time he accepted. "It seemed as if . . . my former services to agriculture were now first brought to light and fully recognized." In October 1851 he became the subject of a short biographical account in *De Bow's Review,* and the accompanying portrait, though a poor likeness, gave him wider visual recognition in Virginia. Shortly after, his social confidence was further boosted by an invitation to attend the annual meeting of the South Central Agricultural Society in Macon, Georgia. There he received a kindly and gratifying welcome from planters and their wives and reciprocated with an extemporaneous address. In November 1852 he had a similarly encouraging reception in Charleston, despite his delivery of a long tirade against the practices of South Carolina farmers.[81]

He attended a number of Virginia State Agricultural Society meetings and prepared reports and addresses, but decided against serving as president for a second term. In 1853 he assumed the position of first vice-president. The year, however, saw a vigorous recruitment drive and it was decided that a grand fair should be held in Richmond in the fall. The occasion marked Ruffin's full restoration into the public life and esteem of Virginia. He was accorded the role of benefactor and patriarch. "Edmund Ruffin," wrote a newspaper correspondent of one of the meetings, "entered the Hall a little late, and his entrance was the signal for a warm applause. . . . Imagine a venerable man, with clear, quick, grey eyes, erect figure, firm confident step, fresh, healthy, rosy cheeks, and hair as white as silver hanging on his shoulders. Ruffin is a small man, retiring and quiet. . . . As he entered he was surrounded, shook by the hand, and every mark of reverence and affection given him."[82] Ruffin himself took note of the "outward & loud demonstrations" and the manifest fact that he was "the chief object of interest." The Richmond *Whig,* an old adversary from Petersburg days, placed him in "the order of great intellects"; ex-President Tyler lauded him as the man who had singlehandedly turned the tide of emigration from the state; and the author Nathaniel Cabell inserted him squarely in the pantheon of great Virginians: "He now belongs to us all, and him we hail as the field marshall of the army of farmers and planters of the Old Dominion."[83] Many other individuals and newspapers offered tributes in similar vein.

By the late 1850s he was still with the society, attending fairs, executive committee meetings, and discussions with other farming bodies. He also took on the presidency again between 1857 and 1859,[84] but much of the effort was political and organizational in nature and his diary notes contain few references to specifically agricultural issues. Ruffin recorded no particular pleasure or excitement in the work. "I am," he wrote in November 1858,

Edmund Ruffin, 1794–1865.
(Valentine Museum, Richmond, Virginia.)

"tired of the burdensome duties of my office, & will be glad when I can be honorably released from them." He had, he claimed, been vigorous in attacking peculation, extravagance, neglect, fraud, extortion, and plunder, gaining for his trouble "neither applause nor thanks from the public, nor even from the Society." Some unpopularity had also resulted from his role in shifting the annual fair from Richmond to Petersburg in 1858, thereby removing a good deal of profitable trade from well-connected individuals in the capital. Ill feeling and controversy helped bring about his withdrawal from the presidency in November 1859, some weeks before the expiration of his term of office.[85]

Ruffin also made fresh contributions to agricultural literature in the 1850s. He sent off some articles to journals; published a fine pamphlet, *On Opposite Results of Exhausting and Fertilizing Systems of Agriculture* (his 1852 Charleston address); brought together an assortment of short pieces in a volume entitled *Essays and Notes on Agriculture;* and wrote a prizewinning paper on the defects of agricultural education in the South.[86] A fifth and final edition of *Calcareous Manures* came out in 1852, and in 1861 he completed the geological and agricultural notes which he labeled *Sketches of Lower North Carolina.* But his principal literary effort was directed towards social and political matters, and arose from his intensifying concern with disunion and the defense of slavery. The most famous of these was *The Political Economy of Slavery,* and the most extended, his speculative *Anticipations of the Future.*

Financial returns from some of these offerings appear to have been meager. At the end of 1861 his publishers in Richmond informed him that only twenty copies of *Calcareous Manures* and thirty-one of *Essays and Notes* had been sold over the preceding three years, earning him a paltry $6.65.[87] Ruffin may well have lost the bulk of his agricultural readership after he closed down the *Farmers' Register* in 1842. He had been acclaimed in 1853 less as a present vital force than as a reforming planter of a past generation. Hundreds of farmers who applauded his movements around the fair had never tried marl and were never likely to. Many, no doubt, had never read a word he had written. No agricultural revolution in Ruffin's name had taken place over the state of Virginia as a whole.[88] Planters in Richmond in 1853 may well have been indulging in a little facile sentimentality, celebrating a remnant of Old Virginia and in the process celebrating themselves and their now threatened heritage.

If this is true, and if Ruffin was aware that the approbation may have been

to a degree valedictory and contrived, it may offer an explanation—along
with his retirement from farming, his growing disillusionment with the state
society, and the changing circumstances of the South—of his increasingly
passionate involvement with affairs of an almost exclusively political nature.
It was probably an easy transfer of emphasis. Ruffin was a Southerner and
planter first and foremost. Much of his commitment to agricultural reform
had been a function of sectional anxieties and of a wish to secure recognition
as leader of a salvationist cause. Secession, he declared, tragically, in 1860,
had been "literally . . . the one great idea of my life."[89]

VI

In the words of one of his granddaughters, Ruffin was "a hater of the
North." For him, "right was right . . . and wrong was wrong and there was
no compromise."[90] Throughout the 1850s and the war years his opinions
had not a breath of accommodation about them. It had to be all or nothing:
secession and survival or continuing union and gradual liquidation. Such
extremism—visionary as well as simplistic—placed him squarely among
the fire-eaters like Robert Barnwell Rhett and William Lowndes Yancey. It
also served to alienate him once again from the Virginia public.[91] Virginians
had a comparatively small slave population, they were aware of their close
and developing economic ties with the North, and they saw that they would
probably be the first to suffer from an invasion by Union troops and ships.
For Ruffin, however, their caution represented shortsighted cowardice: Virginia's interests as a slave state were Southern, and its duty was to build up
the defenses of mind and material so as to act as bulwark and morale-lifter
against Yankee presumption.

  Before the 1830s he had, like many in his state, been "opposed to slavery,
& a speculative abolitionist."[92] On the other hand, his affiliations had generally been with states' rights republicanism (in accordance with family tradition), and this had almost certainly been strengthened by Calhoun's stand
during the Nullification crisis in 1832 and, later, by his conversations with
some of the South Carolina planters visited during his extensive "Survey"
travels. Growth of abolitionism in the North represented the most serious
threat yet to such principles, and this, combined with Ruffin's almost total
unfamiliarity with the world beyond the Potomac, his class arrogance, and
his ready capacity for defensive animus, converted him quite quickly into a
rigid Yankeephobe. A full quarter-century before the Civil War he declared

that "the South, *and the Union,* have everything to fear, (and danger far greater than from servile insurrections) from the restless, mad, and *sustained* action of Northern abolitionists."[93] The intensity and hyperbole were already in place.

There is no need to enlarge much on Ruffin's views after the mid-1840s. They did not develop. They merely became particularized around individual affairs such as the Wilmot Proviso, the Nashville conventions, the Kansas-Nebraska Act, the Harpers Ferry raid, and the campaign and election of Abraham Lincoln. The basic rationale lay in the protection of slavery, and legitimacy came from the old Jeffersonian idea that the South had originally comprised "separate & sovereign states, which had voluntarily entered into the Union, & had reserved the right to withdraw from it!." If slavery disappeared, by *diktat,* by pressure, or by slow erosion, the South would face the degradation of Guadeloupe and the "bloody horrors" of St. Domingo, and in the end "the extinction of the white race, and the brutal barbarism of the black." It was essentially a question of race control and race survival. The defense of the protecting institution required the destruction of the Union. Secession could come peacefully, for the North would be unwilling to pour millions of dollars and thousands of lives into a war it could not win. An independent South would have no difficulty in surviving. Cotton and slaves would see to that.[94]

Now in his sixties, Ruffin began traveling around the section, secessionism now his "latest & greatest" cause. He attended the Southern convention in Montgomery in 1858, getting to know Barnwell Rhett and collaborating with William Yancey in the formation of what was to prove the ineffectual and short-lived League of United Southerners. Senators and representatives were cajoled in Washington, as were the large numbers of planters and politicians who took their ease at White Sulphur Springs in the Virginia mountains. North Carolina was accessible and frequently visited, and in September 1860 Ruffin traveled west to the Unionist state of Kentucky, where his daughter Mildred lived. He made several visits to South Carolina. In November 1860 he and Rhett took a trip to Milledgeville, then capital of Georgia, to talk to Joseph E. Brown, the secessionist governor, and a number of prominent legislators. He followed the news of the Democratic convention in Charleston in April and May 1860 and then went off a few weeks later to Baltimore and Richmond for the separate meetings of the two wings of the party. One of his most dramatic excursions took place within Virginia itself. In November 1859 he went to Harpers Ferry, hoping to see

John Brown's hanging and make whatever political capital he could from the raid of 16 October. Morbidly curious, he sought, and was granted, permission to join the cadets of the Virginia Military Institute. He was fitted out with cap, overcoat, and arms, and on the morning of 2 December found himself marching and wheeling around the place of execution with young men who could have been his grandchildren. The procedures, and Brown's "animal courage," he observed in minute detail. Ruffin secured Northern pikes intended for the slaves and distributed them, as symbolic evidence of vile Yankee intent, to all the state governors of the South. On 6 November 1860, the day of "the momentous election," he cast his vote in the Garysville Court House for Breckinridge and Lane and then made straight for Petersburg and the train to Columbia. On the way south he circulated secessionist literature among his fellow passengers and threw out small bundles at every station he passed through. When he arrived at his hotel, Barnwell Rhett and two of his sons were among the first callers. In Sumterville he was greeted by cannon fire and serenaded by a large band of Minute Men. There he also gave one of the very rare speeches of his campaign. Moving on to Charleston he found even noisier celebration. The outcome of the election was now clear.[95]

These were among the happiest days of Ruffin's life. "In addition to the exciting & important, & most gratifying political events, of the progress of secession, I have myself been made the subject of kind feeling & favor, & of general appreciation, such as I had never before experienced, & never expected to receive." Brief trips to Georgia and Virginia were followed by a return to South Carolina in December for the secession convention in Charleston. Ruffin was given a seat in the assembly as an honored visitor and on 20 December he witnessed the unanimous vote for withdrawal from the Union and the formal signing of the Ordinance of Secession. Amid scenes of jubilation South Carolina had declared itself to be an independent state. Others could now follow its lead. Around the end of the year he traveled south to witness similar momentous scenes in Florida, this time being permitted to address the convention during its deliberations. In March 1861 he gave a speech before a large disunionist meeting at Goldsborough, North Carolina, being "warmly welcomed & with enthusiasm."[96]

He was soon back in South Carolina, and on the fateful morning of 12 April stood as a private in the Palmetto Guards at the Iron Battery on Morris Island near Charleston. The decision had been taken to fire on the Union citadel of Fort Sumter at the mouth of Charleston harbor. For his services to the Southern cause Ruffin was given the distinction of pulling the lanyard for what he believed to be the first shot. "Of course I was highly gratified by the compliment," he recorded, "& delighted to perform the service—which I did. The shell struck the fort, at the north-east angle of the parapet."[97] It carried with it Ruffin's most intense sectional hopes. The man who had intended to save the South by agrarian reform had finally resorted to cannon fire. "My whole service, on this occasion," he wrote, "was indeed in evidence & in earnest (as I had designed it should be,) of my readily embarking in the 'rebellion' which I had so long advocated in words, & of my readiness to encounter all the consequent risks to life & property."[98]

Ruffin, it is clear, was no average Southern nationalist. There was, within defensive, sectional thinking, considerable room for the formation of compromise solutions. He could have no truck with these. The fact of his extremism has to be firmly established, for it reveals a heady fusion of simplistic logic with nationalist emotion, and a quite blinding attachment to the institution of slavery. It is clearly of interest to the historian that the Southerner with the greatest intellectual stake in economic reform was also one of the Southerners who set his heart and mind most passionately against any sort of interference with his section's historic institutional base. Ruffin himself recognized that his were "*extreme* opinions." Their unpopularity is revealed by his revived isolation in Virginia, where notions of possible accommodation prevailed right up until the spring of 1861. In August 1860, in the company of 1,600 people at White Sulphur Springs, he noted that there were many present "from the more southern states—most of them contingent or conditional disunionists. . . . I find myself alone, as an avowed disunionist *per se*, & I avow that opinion upon every occasion."[99] Ruffin sought the militant South identified by John Hope Franklin more than a century later but did not believe he had found it.

He welcomed drama and sectional misfortune as a means of simplifying issues for the wavering millions. John Brown and Abraham Lincoln became his secret heroes. They could do more for the cause than any amount of speechifying from Rhett or Yancey. On the day he heard of the Harpers Ferry raid he wrote: "Such a practical exercise of abolition principles is needed to stir the sluggish blood of the south."[100] On 7 November, traveling through North Carolina, he heard from the telegraph that Lincoln would probably carry New York, the key state in the election. "It is good news for me," he declared in his diary.[101]

It is also clear from Ruffin's pen that he took pleasure in the expression of strong opinions and in the animosity they could arouse. He lapsed quickly into impatience, frustration, and hatred, much of it self-regarding. His approach to problems tended to be hasty and instinctive. The tigers of wrath, as in Blake's Proverbs of Hell, were wiser than the horses of instruction. The world had to be simplified into Manichean categories, and the evil wrenched out at its roots. Behavior in public was also affected by the admitted flippancies of "vanity & love of notoriety."[102] It would have been difficult to have been a notorious conditional secessionist.

VII

The Civil War that began with Ruffin's cannon fire brought with it, in the manner almost of simple theatrical tragedy, his years of most terrible suffering. It presented acute private grief and led to the total inversion of his most cherished public causes: the perpetuation of slavery, the revival of agriculture, and the independence of the South. His pride, conceits, and intensity of conviction in the past had provoked much enmity and conflict, but the contexts had been provincial and he had usually been able to withdraw into some rural fastness. Now, however, he had pitted his passions against much more powerful and violent furies, and this time there was to be no earthly retreat.

The early excitements of Fort Sumter and the state secession conventions were followed by sobering observations of the realities of armed conflict. In the summer of 1861 Ruffin participated marginally in the victorious encounter at Bull Run near Manassas Junction, being much affected afterwards by the scale of the mortality and the agonies of the wounded. In 1862 he was involved in action around Richmond and Coggin's Point, and in 1863 in Charleston. For the most part, however, his role in the hostilities settled quickly into that of a helpless observer, confined to the outer periphery of public affairs. Old secessionists, he noted, were given little part to play in the running of the war. Their day was over.[103]

Pressures resulting from war damage, food shortage, and the conscription of his sons forced him back into occasional plantation work. At Coggin's he regarded himself "as *consulting agriculturist*" to Edmund Jr. Further responsibilities were assumed for a time at Julian's Ruthven. In June 1861 he was showing the Coggin's labor force how to cure clover in cocks and furnishing the overseer with his *Essays and Notes on Agriculture,* which contained the necessary directions. Two years later he recorded a Saturday of prolonged ditching work at Marlbourne in which he had performed his supervisory functions "with unwearied interest."[104] These, however, were rare moments of satisfaction. He no longer had the proprietorial enthusiasm or physical strength for sustained practical farming.

He spent most of his time at Coggin's Point, with odd periods in Richmond and at other family plantations. Reading and private writing had to be his main pursuits. It was 1862 before he visited Marlbourne, having stayed away since his daughter Elizabeth Sayre died there in 1860. From the very first weeks of the war lower Virginia had become an important theater for the operations of the contending forces. It lay close to Washington, it was the location of the Confederate capital, and its great tidal rivers offered powerful blockading temptations to the Union navy. Coggin's and Marlbourne lay horribly exposed on the James and the Pamunkey, and both were occupied and looted, with some consequent slave desertion. Acts of war and destruction, and the manner of their commission, served to intensify Ruffin's already extreme detestation of the North: "the vilest and most malignant people . . . in Christendom." The Yankees now stood before him in his own state, guilty of numberless vices and outrages, and directed from the White House by a "clown & mountebank," a "low & vulgar blackguard." With the fall of New Orleans, only a year into the war, he first admitted the awful "possibility of subjugation to the North." By April 1863 the Confederacy seemed "in great peril of defeat—& not from the enemy's arms, but from the scarcity & high prices of provisions, & the impossibility of the government feeding the horses of the army." Hopes for British and French support—even for Southern reabsorption in the British empire— proved forlorn, and by the late months of 1864, with Sherman's capture of Atlanta, Thomas's destruction of the western forces at Nashville, and the bloody advance of Grant's Army of the Potomac towards Richmond, Ruffin knew it was all but over.[105] Richmond was evacuated on 3 April 1865 after a prolonged siege. Less than a week later the Confederate army surrendered at Appomattox.

Accompanying this disastrous course of public events, spelling for Ruffin the final, dreadful materialization of Northern rule and the end of slavery, was a series of tragedies within his family. A grandson, Julian, was killed at Seven Pines in 1862. In January 1863 he received news that his daughter Mildred had died in Kentucky from some form of paralysis. On 16 May 1864 his son Julian was killed in battle at Drewry's Bluff. His youngest son, Charles, in 1862 went off on six months' irregular leave from the Palmetto

Guard. "His honorable death," Ruffin wrote with unforgiving fury, "would be to me a blessing, compared to his continuing to live & act as he has done." Sometime later Charles deserted completely.[106]

Ruffin was denied philosophical serenity in old age. It would not have been in character and the calamities that had befallen him were much too bitter. In 1863 he spent some hours on 20 January cataloguing all his grievances against his native state. "It seems to me, that, but for the accident of Fort Sumter, my patriotic labors & efforts would [have] been unknown—& my name almost forgotten in my own country, & by the generation which I have zealously & effectively labored to serve." He would be happy, however, to accept the opinion common among his "ignorant neighbors" that he alone had been responsible for the Civil War. Encroaching disaster was certainly not tempering his spirit of defiance. To be seen, however falsely, as chief cause of a separation of North and South, "even at all the general expense of blood & property, & ruin to individuals, which it will cost," would constitute all the "glory and fame" he required.[107]

Renown as a farming reformer now seemed inconsequential. The fighting became in itself a reason for living, as so many other supports crumbled around him. "Except for the deep interest I feel in the present war . . . ," he declared in January 1863, "I have no inducement to desire the extension of my life." It was no idle, melodramatic aside. There was a serious logic implied in the statement and it was one he was prepared to see through. When Richmond fell to Union forces two years later, Ruffin decided that the time had come to end his life. The destruction of the Confederacy's defense and independence was "now consummated."[108] He had not tutored himself to be able to accept this. His violent secessionist impulses were still at work. If his country could not escape from the Union, then he would have to do it on his own account.

He sat down for three days in mid-June in Edmund Jr.'s house, Redmoor, in Amelia County west of Petersburg, and wrote out an extended suicide note of much nobility and simplicity.[109] Gone at last were the recriminations and the self-pity. The very coolness and steadiness of the lines carry their own drama. Virginia, for once, was spared vilification. Only the Yankees brought out the old defamatory excesses. He offered a remarkably detached explanation of his coming death, listing and organizing the considerations as though engaged in some elegant exercise in scholarly persuasion. The disinterest, however, may well have been that of a spiritually dead man, standing beyond common fear and passion. This ossification, we may presume, carried its own horror. He had, he thought, performed good works for the farmers of the South, and especially lower Virginia. Much extra wealth had accrued, although it could have been ten times more had his instructions not been "mostly slighted & neglected wastefully." As for his other great cause, secession, that was now "trampled in the dust." This was the ultimate failure, and the Almighty himself seemed to have had a hand in it. "I do not think that any particular prayer of mine, even for the most laudable & unobjectionable objectives, (so far as I could judge,)," Ruffin wrote, "has ever been answered."

He asked to be buried within a few hours of his death, wrapped in an old sheet or blanket, like "our brave soldiers who were slain in battle," or placed in a coffin of roughest workmanship. "Have no company assembled, other than the few nearest friends or neighbors. . . . Do not have or attempt to have any religious or clerical services—which would now be improper." His last words were reserved for the people who had stimulated much of his interest in Southern economic reform and who had provoked his later efforts to pull the slave states out of the Union: "With what will be near to my latest breath, I here repeat, and would willingly proclaim, my unmitigated hatred to Yankee rule—to all political, social, & business connection with Yankees, & to the perfidious, malignant, & vile Yankee race." There followed the pathetic postscript: "Kept waiting by successive visitors to my son, until their departure at 12.15 p.m."[110] It was 18 June 1865: ten weeks on from Appomattox. The postbellum period was already too far advanced. A few minutes after closing his diary in a barely legible hand, Ruffin positioned his gun against a trunk on the floor, placed the muzzle in his mouth, and, pressing down with a forked twig, shot himself through the head at the second attempt.[111]

Chapter Three

Edmund Ruffin and the

Defense of Slavery

I

RUFFIN'S passionate attachment to the slave society is clear from the actions documented. It also manifests itself powerfully in his pamphleteering and his diary writing, and increasingly so over the last decade or two of his life. Of particular interest in his literary work, however, is his failure to formulate any coherent *economic* case for the institution of slavery. This says much for his honesty, but it leaves him open to charges of inconsistency and incompleteness as a reformer. His arguments for slavery were not those of an economist but of a conservative patriarch and racist. He was pursuing economic revival to save an institution, was employing that institution in the process, and had good reason to believe that the institution was itself blocking reform. The confusion of means and ends was never resolved, and no one in the South at the time was much interested in drawing attention to it. It was, for the most part, irresolvable, and in the end helped drive Ruffin into the crudities of secessionism.

Slave-owning planters were as much a part of slavery as were the unfree laborers themselves. As Ruffin viewed them, with his *Register* and South

Carolina experiences in mind, they were badly educated, complacent, careless, and spendthrift. Subscriptions to farming papers were limited and grudging, and did not guarantee regular reading, understanding, or ability to put new schemes of improvement into effective operation. What was more, high profits from monoculture on some of the less depleted lands blinded people to the possibilities of yet better returns from diversified farming. Planters, he declared in Charleston, though generally honorable and public-spirited, did not object to being called "land killers." As for Virginia, the great evils at work could be "summed up in the single word, *ignorance.*" There was also the debilitating and impoverishing "hospitality of Old Virginia" which the mass of good-hearted planters insisted on perpetuating.[1] Ruffin's criticisms were incessant and wide-ranging, but he drew back from general, institutional analysis.

He also questioned the capacities of the slaves themselves. Since the institution had developed under a primitive agricultural regime, laborers had been extremely ill instructed and, with no improvement in practical education, would "always remain unfit agents for operations which . . . would be greatly superior in effect and in profit."[2] Whatever the task, the planter had to contend with the slaves' God-given "feebleness of mind and indolence of body."[3] Ruffin believed it was possible to fit them into improved systems of farming, as the experience of parts of tidewater Virginia had shown, but this was difficult, not only because of physical awkwardness but because of management difficulties concerning redeployment and supervision.[4]

There could also be limits to the level of skill and understanding attainable. "I have been much amused to hear, from Mr. Sayre, of some of the remarks of Jem. Sykes, the foreman, (my former overseer,) about the crops and the land," Ruffin wrote in his diary in July 1857, some time after he had given up active farming at Marlbourne. He was gratified to learn that Sykes gave him most of the credit for the present productiveness of the plantation, but was at the same time surprised that the slave had the wit to do so. "I did not expect a negro, even of superior intelligence as he is, to look back to causes so remote, & of such slow & gradual action."[5] It was a curious observation, considering that Sykes had helped supervise huge marling operations, extensive drainage improvements, and experiments with crop rotations as recently as the late 1840s and early 1850s, and had occasionally been required to run the business on his own for short periods. Clearly Ruffin's instruction of his slaves, including his black overseer, had been of a largely mechanical sort. Explanatory conversation must have been kept to a minimum. Slavery, and its accompanying racist skepticism, caused widespread underutilization of slave ability. "Since blacks were inferior," writes Eugene Genovese, "they had to be enslaved and taught to work; but, being inferior, they could hardly be expected to work up to Anglo-Saxon expectations."[6]

Ruffin made no great effort to rest his proslavery arguments on economic considerations. Here he was in rough accord with the two other most celebrated propagandists of slavery, his fellow Virginians Thomas Dew and George Fitzhugh. He read Dew's *Essay on Slavery* twice in the 1830s and once in the 1850s, describing it in 1858 as "the earliest modern work that justified & defended the institution of slavery," as well as the best argument available in print.[7] Fitzhugh's *Sociology for the South* and *Cannibals All!* were both read at least a couple of times. Ruffin declared the author to be profound and original, but guilty of careless and sometimes misleading writing. Fairly or unfairly, he did not regard Fitzhugh as any sort of influence. "Many of the positions which he has assumed, I have also entertained & presented, in regard to slavery."[8] Ruffin did not believe that slavery possessed economic strength generally superior to that of a free-labor system. It was, however, better than any other system available to the South. The question, as Thomas Dew wrote in 1832, was not one of the general, comparative merits of free and slave labor but of "the relative amounts of labor which may be obtained from *slaves before and after their emancipation.*"[9] The unfree black was the basic and peculiar datum of Southern society, and all comparative thinking about the institution had to be based on Southern reality. Ruffin's relativism is always clear: "It would," he wrote in 1859, "be extremely disadvantageous, if not ruinous, for either Massachusetts or Virginia to exchange its own established labor system entirely for that of the other."[10]

Slavery did, however, have some intrinsic economic virtues. It obliterated idleness and secured continuity of work; it suited areas of sparse population, unattractive to Europeans; and it conformed with the socialist ideal of associated labor being more productive than that of individuals or families, adding the essential ingredient of the single directing mind.[11] Moreover, the unit of black slave labor in the South was generally cheaper, more reliable, more industrious, and less intractable than the unit of black hireling labor. Free workers also involved substantial costs for the community at large— "in pauper support, legal judicial and penal expenses, and police and a standing army."[12]

The benefit of coercion and continuity in slave labor, however. stemmed in large part from the alleged laziness of the slave. Slavery was necessary to make *blacks* work.[13] And even when forced to labor, their only incentive was the avoidance of punishment. It was, Ruffin declared, "an unquestionable general truth, that the labor of a free man, for any stated time, is more than the labor of a slave": probably around 50 percent more. Awkward implications here were resolved with the contention that slaves performed a sufficient margin of extra work in aggregate over the months and years to compensate for their relative slowness and inefficiency per diem. If wage laborers worked as hard, then they usually were not free by any normal meaning of the term.[14]

Ruffin believed that the most productive worker of all was the proprietor-farmer. This was a view held by the British philosopher and economist John Stuart Mill—a man whom Ruffin, unlike Fitzhugh, was prepared to describe as "distinguished (and generally correct)."[15] Adam Smith thought much the same and, despite his distaste for slavery, was another favorite of Ruffin's. Such farmers would be "the most diligent, hard-working careful and frugal of laborers—because every member of the family is not only under more perfect direction and control of the proprietors, but also has every additional stimulus to exertion and care that self-interest, family affection, and the pride of proprietorship can offer." The grander ways of Southern planters, by comparison, interfered with agricultural improvement and damaged the section's propensity to save: "In proportion to their respective amounts of capital and labor, the small northern farmer would make and save double as much profit and accumulation as would a large southern slaveholder."[16] These Yankee virtues must have appealed to Ruffin, for he had a very strong provident and accumulative instinct himself.

The salability of labor was another feature of the system which troubled him. Transfers from Virginia to the lower South helped raise slave prices and, in a strict accounting sense, depressed returns on capital. They also made it increasingly difficult for border planters to purchase extra labor themselves. "At the present high prices of slaves," Ruffin wrote in 1859, "no undertakers can afford to make new and complete agricultural investments."[17]

In economic terms, then, slavery, with its "peculiar and incidental evils,"[18] was seriously flawed. The pessimism must have been disturbing for a man whose reform program was both motivated by and dependent upon the institution. He envisaged no other system of labor and entrepreneurship

which might be suitable for farming in the South. (The small slaveless farmers in the upcountry regions of the South Atlantic states were viewed as
being largely beyond any movement of agricultural advance. He certainly
did not address them in his writings.) Free blacks were an abomination and
there was no attraction in any "substitution of a laboring class of foreigners
and Yankees."[19] The agricultural revolution which he proposed was not one
which *needed* slavery, or one which could, on balance, be *helped* by slavery,
but one which had *inherited* slavery and which derived much of its rationale
from the *defense* of slavery. Ruffin could not stand above the highly charged
ideological conditions of his section, and had no wish to. He was quite
prepared to remain intellectually amphibious: scientist and reformer on the
one hand, secessionist and slavery propagandist on the other. He was alert
to the possibility that the two prime objectives of his public life, though
intimately related, might stand in conflict with each other. The realization of
this devastating contradiction is best brought out in the address he gave in
the State Capitol in Richmond in 1853:

> No one appreciates more highly than myself the advantages to a nation
> of producing and accumulating wealth by the individual members of
> the great community, and especially, as the greatest public gain, the
> increase of agricultural production and riches. To advocate and urge the
> forwarding of the latter results is the especial object of my present ser-
> vice and employment, as it has been one of the most important objects
> of all my public efforts and labors. Still, God forbid that we should
> deem the accumulation of wealth—even if from its most beneficial and
> best possible source, the fertilization and culture of the soil—as com-
> pensation for the loss or deterioration of the mental and moral qualities
> of southern men, and more especially of southern women! *And if
> brought to the hard necessity of choosing between the two conditions, with
> their opposite disadvantages, I would not hesitate a moment to prefer the
> entire existing social, domestic and industrial conditions of these slaveholding
> states, with all the now existing evils of indolence and waste, and generally
> exhausting tillage and declining fertility, to the entire conditions of any other
> country on the face of the globe.*[20]

That was his resoundingly clear choice and it serves as a paradigm both
for his own failure and for that of the late antebellum South as a whole to
achieve any productive intellectual coherence. Material advance was
needed to retain population and resist the Yankee. On the other hand, such

advance, if it came, might erode the very foundations of planter civilization and power. The basic dilemma was an ancient one, although a number of societies had attempted to resolve it by conservative programs of controlled reform. Not even this could be attempted in the South, now that the fundamental social institution had come to be regarded as inviolable. It was the rock against which abstract and partial formulations for economic improvement were doomed to founder. Men might dream of agricultural sophistication and industrial strength but, as the greatest reformer of them all insisted, these would have to remain imaginary if their realization meant any alterations to slavery or the culture and patriarchy which had grown up around it. Southern civilization, in such intellectual circumstances, had to survive on increasingly ethereal and phantasmagoric foundations. A man of Ruffin's intellectual ability was able in his Richmond address to see the South's much-vaunted "mental and moral qualities" as somehow capable of survival and vitality in a society of "indolence and waste . . . and declining fertility." It was a collapse of the reasoning mind under destructive pressures emanating from class defensiveness and racist insecurity.

II

Ruffin's cultural case for slavery was more substantial than his economic one, but it was weak and fabricated nonetheless. The benefits he adduced for the slaves—plantation welfare, protection against economic vagaries, and Christianization—can be ignored.[21] These were inevitably part of any comprehensive defense of slavery, serving to display humanitarian virtue and underscore contrasts with the viciousness of alternative social and economic systems. The hypocrisy of abolitionists had to be exposed, and Ruffin did it largely in the manner of Fitzhugh.[22] But such considerations, however sincerely cited, could not possibly have been central ones. Ruffin agreed with his friend James Hammond that slaves were the essential "mud-sill" of society. One of the institution's greatest strengths, he suggested in 1853, was that it confined "the drudgery and brutalizing effects of continued toil to the inferior race."[23] The terminology speaks for itself.

Slavery, as Ruffin saw it, served to civilize *whites* rather than blacks, and only the wealthy whites at that. The argument had strong antidemocratic overtones. Slavery gave a more secure underpinning to the perpetuation of upper-class power, privilege, and refinement. A stable and civilized society should provide high income, abundant free time, and a monopoly of political control for a small aristocracy. If slavery were to be pronounced "unjust and wrongful," he wrote, "it is in the same manner as property, wealth, and political rank and power, in almost every civilized and even free country, are possessed by a small number of the people, while the far greater number are without land or other property" and confined to an existence of "unceasing toil and privation."[24]

Ruffin asserted that in the slave states there had developed a large and informed elite of unusual "mental improvement" and breadth of vision, their social virtues squarely based on the leisure and material means deriving from slavery. This was where the South gained over the small owner-occupier farmers in other parts of the advanced world, pursuing their narrow Millian lives of all-absorbing industry and thrift, and afflicted in consequence by a "brutal rudeness of manners, and ignorance" and an accompanying "moral degradation."[25] It was, of course, a woefully slender argument, not only because it was so crassly dismissive of other rural societies about which Ruffin chose to know very little, but also because of his overall ambiguity on the qualities of planter culture. There was, of course, a small minority of *grands seigneurs* of great refinement and learning, and Ruffin's familiarity or friendship with many of these around the James River and in tidewater South Carolina must have colored his outlook. There was also the developing, self-absorbing myth of the gentle, hospitable, idiosyncratic South: the web, as Newby calls it, "as enticing as gossamer."[26]

But the wider realities, as Ruffin himself documented, were harsher, plainer, and less flattering to the section. An intellectually vigorous body of planters would have been more attentive to his own agricultural prescriptions than in fact it was, and he had attacked them frequently and viciously for their paralyzing ignorance. These were the people whom he abandoned in the mid-1840s when he retreated to Marlbourne; who, according to his suicide note, had "slighted & neglected" his reform plans.[27] He knew too that leisure, and the opportunities it gave for moral and mental improvement, could be misused: "The facility for obtaining the comforts and pleasures of life also invite to [*sic*] self-indulgence, indolence, and negligent and expensive habits."[28] Built into slave-farming, moreover, was a pronounced separation of individual production units, inhibiting the social intercourse which he perceived was vital to cultural advance.[29] Ruffin accepted that "the necessary dispersed residences of the superior class of population" was a consequence of slavery, but the problem was not one which he chose to discuss.[30] Neither did he examine the similar difficulties created by the low degree of urbanization and the stunted development of transport in the South. Education was another area where the facts were depressing—a number of them heatedly publicized by Ruffin himself.[31]

Ruffin's sociocultural argument was slipshod and cavalier: a propagandist mixture of bald assertion and blanket denunciation. In the end, it distills down into little more than hardfaced planter conservatism.

III

The principal determinant of Ruffin's intense attachment to slavery was racist fear. The introduction of this issue implies no harsh criticism of him. Attacking a Southern planter for being a white supremacist is about as useful as berating the ocean for being wet. The vice was also rife in the North and in Europe, and in the South it fed off troubling local conditions. Africans had been held in bondage for centuries; their history, dimly understood or thoroughly misunderstood, seemed to invite contempt; their submissive role had generated simplisitic doubt over their natural ability; their forced enslavement fed fears of retaliatory violence; and the idea of their translation into free men and women, assuming normal rights and responsibilities and initiatives within Southern society, was one that beggared the white imagination. For Ruffin (as for Dew) the option of African colonization was an unreal one.[32] Labor would be lost, high costs would afflict the taxpayer, and no colony could hope to survive on its own. Liberia was demonstrating the futility of the exercise.[33]

The blacks had to stay where they were and slavery, in consequence, had to be rigidly maintained. The likely results of emancipation were all too evident if one glanced at the behavior of the quarter million free Negroes in the Southern states. They were, Ruffin insisted, a horrid blight on society, and their numbers could not be allowed to increase. They had a universal reputation for "ignorance, indolence, improvidence, and poverty—and very generally, also, for vicious habits, and numerous violations of the criminal laws."[34] Those guilty of criminal acts who could give no evidence of participation in honest toil should be pulled back into slavery. Others with habits of idleness or drunkenness should be hired out to the highest bidder. Somehow or other all these "vicious, unmanageable and shameless" people had to be socially repositioned, with minimal regard for legal niceties.[35] These views were published by Ruffin in pamphlet form and distributed throughout the Southern states under the title *The Free Negro Nuisance and*

How to Abate It.[36] Grim warnings were on display overseas, most notably in Haiti, Jamaica, and Liberia.[37] Turmoil, barbarity, and impoverishment awaited any society that permitted freedom for its black population.

The whole world, in fact, could be viewed in simple supremacist terms. Latin America, said Ruffin, was largely occupied by "mongrel races" who were "everywhere spreading and maintaining desolation."[38] In India, the British *raj* was cruel and unjust, and the repression of the Mutineers in 1857 and 1858 had been particularly barbaric, but there were higher considerations to be taken into account, it being essential for "the well-being of the world, that the European & superior race shall be dominant in Hindostan, as well as elsewhere—& therefore that the British rule shall be re-established & maintained."[39] In the Arrow War between Britain and China in 1857 he considered it appropriate for the supposedly half-civilized Chinese that they be subject to "extensive conquest" by their attackers. That also remained the best hope for the Japanese. Africa too needed more "white masters" to attend to agricultural production and Christianization.[40]

All nonwhites, for Ruffin, were intellectually and morally flawed, and blacks were in a specially degraded class of their own. Jem Sykes, the foreman at Marlbourne, was reliable enough to be trusted with the keys of the plantation, but he was not expected to have any understanding of the processes of agricultural improvement. The Negro race had been designed "inferior in intellect to the white." Blacks could not abide working on their own. They were prone to "inertness & cowardice."[41] In 1862 Ruffin visited the prodigious black pianist Thomas Green Bethune. Despite blindness and extreme youth, Bethune possessed what Ruffin acknowledged was a remarkable talent. The source of this, however, was something freakish, since Bethune was manifestly "an idiot, of unusually low order of intellect" who paced around like a monkey. He had "true & even exaggerated features of the negro type—& his profile is almost as much like pictures I have seen of the Ourang Otang [sic]."[42]

Hearing that a black man had graduated from the University of Cambridge, Ruffin recorded his view of "the possibility of one negro in a hundred thousand cases being capable of receiving a college education."[43] This conceivably was written in a spirit of some geniality. Ruffin did not in fact regard himself as peculiarly stern on racial matters. He avoided sitting with blacks in a Washington church in 1858, not because of any objections to rubbing shoulders, but for fear of being mistaken by others "for a rabid abolitionist." He came close to gallantry in a train in North Carolina when he gave up his seat for white women and found it taken by two black maidservants. "Theirs was not the color of the ladies to whom my invitation had been given, but I said nothing." Later on he sat down next to one of them: something which, he was sure, would have shocked a Northerner.[44] After the Nat Turner rebellion in the early 1830s he incurred considerable odium for trying to secure the pardon of a falsely convicted slave, and thirty years later could still deplore the "general community-insanity" of the white population which had led to the execution of large numbers of innocent blacks.[45] He had no evident fear of the slaves on his own plantations. Shortly before the Civil War began in 1861 he recorded his habit of never locking doors or securing windows at night.[46] These slight blurrings on the very edges of Ruffin's prejudice, however, reveal no notable liberalism or sentimentality. If anything, they underline the patrician obstinacy of the man.

The generally harsh and derogatory phraseology displays a simple, primitive racism in which there is virtually no room for intellectual maneuver. This cannot, however, be attributed to sheer bigotry. Open-mindedness, curiosity, and intellectual receptivity are hardly characteristic of a zealot's cast of mind and are much in evidence in Ruffin's scientific writings. His diaries, moreover, reveal catholicity of taste in reading: philosophy, religion, economics, political science, chemistry, geology, history, biography, and a very large quantity of romantic fiction as well. In religious matters he was broadly Jeffersonian: a liberal, deistic Episcopalian who attended church in a spirit of noblesse oblige. He rejected what he saw as the absurd dogmas of the Trinity, treated much of the Bible with a skeptic's contempt, and could find no profound meaning in the Crucifixion.[47] He detested Calvinism as tyrannical and satanic. The Pilgrim Fathers had been "hard, & ferocious bigots."[48]

Apart from a few loose references to divine ordainment, he sought no religious justification for slavery. It assisted the process of Christianization, but its moral rationale was not to be found in scripture. The old and persistent notion that slavery was the fulfillment of Noah's curse on Ham, and slaves the degraded descendants, was one that he rejected unequivocally. A merciful God would not have approved a curse based on commonplace sin to be visited on perhaps a third of all humanity.[49] On the history of races, he got the instruction he wanted in the work of his distinguished Lutheran friend Dr. John Bachman of Charleston. He found his *The Unity of the Human Race* fascinating and powerfully argued on the common origin of ethnic groups.[50] Scientific conclusions of this sort did not trouble him. They were of no practical relevance to the racial circumstances of the antebellum South.

Ruffin, then, took no bigotry or inanity from religion to apply to his thinking on race and slavery. It is impossible to explain his attachment to the institution with reference to any special peculiarity of mind. He was assuming his ideological position very much within the concrete circumstances of Southern society. The most powerful of these were the numerical strength, economic importance, and cultural deprivation of the black population, these serving, in the context of growing emancipationism, to arouse deep-seated racist and class fears in the minds of the planter community.[51] Ruffin's central position on slavery was that slaves could not possibly be freed. Confined, they propped up white society; liberated, they would obliterate it. Other considerations were secondary.

His cultural argument was something fabricated around a hard core of class conservatism, and his economic argument was pursued with uncertainty and ambivalence. *The attachment was to slavery as an instrument of survival rather than of progress.* Its defense was a far more compelling consideration than the pursuit of agricultural advance. If the latter had to be sacrificed in the maw of slavery, then that was a grim necessity, but a necessity nonetheless. Racist anxiety meant that the program for agricultural reform had to be one-dimensional. It had to be formulated in exclusively abstract, scientific terms. If progress ran up against fundamental institutional barriers, then it could run no farther. Institutional change was never on the agenda.

Part Two

The Possibilities for Land Amelioration in

the Old South

Chapter Four

Land Acidity and Its Treatment

T HE first chapter has identified some of the major issues attending any analysis of reform in Southeastern slave agriculture. The second and third have examined the agricultural activities and social preoccupations of the principal reformer of the day, Edmund Ruffin of Virginia. Now it is time to look at the reforms themselves and their precise relevance to the physical and economic circumstances of the Old South.

The principal function of marl and lime—terms which can at this stage be used interchangeably—was the correction of soil acidity.[1] Such correction meant reducing acidity to a tolerable level, or removing it altogether. This was no mere chemical tinkering: something which might make the land incrementally more productive but which could be easily dispensed with if other improvements could be readily implemented. Soil acidity has always been one of the most powerful and most fundamental negative forces at work in agriculture, depressing yields to levels at which farming could cease to be economically viable. The alleviation of acidity was, and remains, one of the most crucial exercises that can be undertaken by a farmer.

Ruffin's broad conclusions on the importance of the question and the urgent need for marling on the sour soils of the Old South have been amply borne out by the work of modern scientists. C. E. Millar, L. M. Turk, and H. D. Foth acclaim his contribution and refer to the amelioration of acid soils as "a fundamental and essential practice." A former president of the American

Society of Agronomy declares that there is probably no other exercise that "affects soils as a plant medium as much as liming acid soils." F. E. Bear writes that as "lime has been shown to have a profound influence on many soil productivity factors, its application is considered the first step in a sound fertility program on acid soils." Lime, in N. C. Brady's view, is "vital to successful agriculture in most humid regions."[2]

Southeastern soils, as we shall see later, reveal a very pronounced tendency towards acidity. They are, in fact, among the worst afflicted in North America. Any simple statement about damaging levels of acidity over a wide extent of country would, however, obscure the considerable complexity of the question. The degree of acidity can vary a good deal within quite a small area and its effects can differ markedly between one crop and another. It is rarely uniform even in a single field or through whatever portion of a soil profile a plant's roots are spreading. It may also change quite noticeably on one little patch over the course of a year, with a probability of increase in the damp summer months. A given measure of acidity, moreover, might be more harmful to a particular crop on one sort of soil than it is on another. Climate adds a further complication. Plants, writes Sir John Russell, "can tolerate more acidity . . . in cool wet conditions than in those warmer and drier."[3] It is clear from an examination of the scientific literature that although the importance of acidity is unchallenged, the general relationships between different degrees of acidity and the responses of different crops in different climatic and pedological environments are still only imperfectly understood, much of the research establishing correlations but only surmising as to precise causes. This has obvious practical implications. Whatever form the correction of acidity takes, it is never a simple practice with guaranteed, standardized results. "The action of lime . . . is so complex," wrote Justus von Liebig in 1863, "that from its favourable influence upon one field, it is scarcely ever possible to form an opinion of its probable action upon another field."[4] An antebellum cotton planter in the Deep South might learn very little of service from reading about a Virginia farmer's experiments with marl on wheat. Indeed, if he copied the Virginian down to the finest practical detail he risked damaging his crop and losing his investment.

As soil acidity is a central reference point in this study, it is essential that the meaning of the term be clarified and its associated problems described. This must, of course, be abbreviated in a historical work, but a fair degree of chemical and other scientific detail does nonetheless have to be presented here to provide a basic minimum of elucidation.

The standard measure of acidity is the pH scale, which indicates the hydrogen (H) ion concentration in a soil. Since the scale is reciprocal, it advances in inverse relation to the degree of acidity; and since it is logarithmic, a difference of 1 (working from neutrality) corresponds to multiplication or division by 10 and a difference of 2 to multiplication or division by 100, and so on. As commonly presented, the effective pH range runs from 3 to 10, with 7 or thereabouts representing neutrality and anything below that, acidity. The ideal range for most crops appears to be 6.5 to 7.

The causes of acidity lie mainly with rain and its movement through the soil. Hydrogen ions are produced by the dissociation of acid molecules, usually when dissolved in water. Water also leaches away base ions, thereby permitting their replacement by the hydrogen, and if leaching continues and is not compensated for by any artificial replenishment of bases in the form of lime, the imbalance increases and the acidity intensifies. "For the formation of acid soils," writes V. A. Chernov, ". . . the soil must undergo lixiviation, percolation through it of atmospheric precipitation. Under such conditions, there would be washed out from the soil first the readily soluble salts and then the difficultly soluble salts. After removal of the salts, *among them calcium carbonate*, there are created the necessary conditions for the replacement of absorbed cations of the soils by hydrogen ions of the soil solution."[5] Crudely, if water washes through a soil it removes the alkalinity and leaves behind the acidity. Soils have enormous reserves of hydrogen (and aluminum) ions, ready to become active when the bases disappear. According to Millar, Turk, and Foth, a medium-textured soil may

Table 1. *pH and Acidity and Alkalinity Intensity*

soil pH	soil reaction
3.0–4.5	acidity: extreme
4.5–5.0	acidity: very strong
5.0–5.5	acidity: strong
5.5–6.0	acidity: medium
6.0–6.5	acidity: slight
6.5–7.0	acidity: very slight
7.0	neutrality
7.0–8.0	alkalinity: slight
8.0–8.5	alkalinity: moderate
8.5–9.5	alkalinity: strong
9.5–10.0	alkalinity: very strong

Source: Based mainly on Truog, "Lime in Relation to Availability of Plant Nutrients," p. 2.

have up to 50,000 times more latent than active acidity.[6] The basic point to be stressed is that relatively free-draining soils in damp climates (especially in areas where open cultivation has removed much of the old natural protection against the impact of rain) have a natural tendency towards acidity.

It is the view of virtually all soil scientists that the principal consequences of acidity are indirect. High hydrogen-ion concentrations per se do not bring about depressed plant growth, as water culture experiments (isolating hydrogen as a possible determinant) have clearly shown. What acidity does— and this is the crucial point—is influence the availability to plants of a variety of important chemical compounds. In particular it lowers the supply of accessible nutrients and enlarges that of toxins. Some scientists stress the former, some the latter, although there seems to be unanimity that acidity attacks the plants on both fronts.

The two principal nutrients affected are nitrogen and phosphorous, which, along with potash, constitute the main sources of plant sustenance. The presence of available nitrogen in the soil is controlled by microbial activity. Under ideal conditions the nitrogen present in different combinations in organic matter in the soil is converted into ammonium compounds, then into nitrous acid, then into nitrites, and finally into nitrates, the soluble form in which nitrogen is most easily taken up by the plants. The most important bacteria assisting this process, *Nitrosomonas* and *Nitrobacter*, are, however, highly sensitive to acid conditions. The acidity, it seems, does not need to be all that pronounced before their activity is reduced and nitrification slowed down. This can happen up to pH levels of 6. The problem not only applies to organic matter present in the ground: it also affects the efficiency of farm manure and nitrogenous fertilizers. Nitrogen fixing—the conversion of free nitrogen into nitrates—is another important contribution that bacteria can make to fertility, either operating in nodules attached to the roots of leguminous plants such as clover and alfalfa, or, like the organism *Azobacter*, functioning nonsymbiotically. Most symbiotic bacteria are adversely affected by moderate to strong acidity. *Azobacters* also have low tolerance and function poorly if the soil reaction is less than 6. All of these nitrate-generating organisms therefore, although able to operate in conditions of slight acidity, do seem to suffer markedly when pH falls below 6, thereby progressively depriving the crop of its vital nitrogenous nutrients. "Nitrification and nitrogen fixing," writes Brady, "take place vigorously in mineral soils only at pH values well above 5.5."[7]

The problem with phosphorous can also be very serious, and again it is not merely a question of the availability of food already present in the soil but of the utility of fertilizers which may have been added to it. In Emil Truog's view, "If lime produced no other benefit than its favourable influence on phosphate availability, it would usually pay to use it." If the soil reaction is less than 6.5, he writes, "the influence on availability rapidly becomes less favourable."[8] Other authors suggest that at 5 it becomes almost totally unavailable. Acid soils tend to have a good deal of iron and aluminum in solution, and what happens is that these minerals combine with phosphorous to produce complex phosphates of iron and aluminum which have low solubility. Plants, accordingly, can absorb them only very slowly, or not at all. Phosphorous, in short, is trapped in an acid soil. If, on the other hand, there is very weak acidity and other elements like calcium are in abundance, phosphorous will tend to form quite different liaisons, producing compounds which are highly soluble and, therefore, available to the plants. The best range on the pH scale for phosphorous is 6.5 to 7.5—around neutrality. On such a soil, with other conditions right, one would expect optimum returns from applications of phosphatic fertilizers such as bones, superphosphate of lime, and most guanos. Conversely, on even a moderately acid soil, the use of such manures may be a waste of time and money.

The calcium deficiency of leached acid soils may also have a direct, damaging effect on plant nutrition. There is a common view that calcium is relatively inconsequential in itself as a plant food, but this has been selectively questioned by some authors. Frank Moser, for example, has stressed its importance for cotton, and C. B. Harston and W. A. Albrecht have suggested that it is a crucial food for leguminous crops such as clover and peas.[9]

The toxic effects of acid soils have much to do with the strong correlation between acidity and amounts of soluble aluminum and manganese. Aluminum accumulates in plant roots and interferes with nutrition, while manganese gets right into the tissues and has an adverse effect on metabolism. The problem of aluminum toxicity has been given special emphasis by some soil chemists attempting to explain low crop yields on sour soils.[10] It does seem, however, that this is only serious on land of very pronounced acidity. Aluminum is harmful in solution, and solubility begins at a pH level of 6, or a little lower, increasing quite rapidly between 5 and 4.5, and then very rapidly below 4.5. In other words, a plant growing in a soil with a reaction of 5.8 would tend to be affected more by nitrogen and phosphorous defi-

ciencies than by aluminum poisoning. In a strongly acid soil, however, toxicity and nutrient unavailability would be doing their damage in tandem. "It
is quite generally believed," write Millar, Turk, and Foth, "that toxic concentrations of aluminum and manganese are a major factor in contributing
to the poor growth in strongly acid soils."[11]

Other acid-soil constituents, harmful to many plants, are soluble ferrous
compounds. Annie Hurd-Karrer has also observed correlations between
acidity and the presence of toxic sodium thiocyanite, sodium chlorate, sodium borate, sodium arsenite, ammonium thiocyanate, and ammonium
sulfamate.[12] It ought to be noted as well that many fungi can operate in acid
soils and cause a variety of plant diseases, some of them highly damaging.

All these problems can find alleviation through the addition of appropriate quantities of calcium carbonate. The end result is that crops have improved supplies of crop nutrients and, on the worst soils, are spared the
damage wrought by aluminum, manganese, and fungi. Nutrition and de-
toxication, rather than acidity as such, are the main issues. There can be no
short-circuiting by simply boosting the nutrient supply (in the manner of
John Taylor of Caroline) through applications of manures which might not
be able to work properly in acid conditions. The Southern planter working
sour land could not make a simple choice between, say, marl and guano.
Usually he needed both. In 1942 W. G. Ogg took Scottish farmers to task for
forgetting that "the use of artificials [fertilizers] does not obviate the need
for liming but increases it." Any enlargement of crops from such applications might well prove temporary, since it meant "that more lime is being
removed from the soil, and in some cases the fertilizer itself causes lime to
be washed out in the drainage water."[13] Liming was the top priority, and
indeed could be at least a partial substitute for manuring. Lime, writes A. R.
Midgely, "by increasing availability of plant nutrients, reduces the need for
added fertilizers."[14]

Treatment with calcium carbonate is the only well known way of reducing
soil acidity, and its effects have been well documented and much acclaimed
over the centuries. "It is," wrote James Hammond with reference to marl,
"the grand agent that prepares for the crop nearly all the food which the earth
furnishes."[15] Liming permits or accelerates the decomposition of organic
matter in the soil; it releases trapped phosphorous; it causes the removal of
soluble toxic substances (and indeed can convert some of them into nutrients); and it helps make soluble some useful salts which hitherto were
unavailable to plants—for example, silicate of potash, which strengthens the

stems of cereals and grasses. Most of these functions are very obviously of the greatest importance. Without easy decomposition, organic matter in the ground—weeds, leaves, woody fibers, dead roots—yields little to the crop. "Poor and acid soils," wrote Ruffin, "cannot be improved durably, or profitably, by putrescent manures, without previously making them calcareous, and thereby correcting the defect in their constitution."[16] Amelioration, moreover, is frequently a prerequisite for the growth of nitrogen-fixing leguminous crops such as clover, cowpeas, and alfalfa—often vital crops in advanced systems of rotation farming. Lime can help too by combining with sulphuric acid in the soil to produce sulphate of lime, more commonly known as gypsum or plaster and a salt of much value to clovers. The judicious application of calcium carbonate clearly is not only important in a variety of immediate ways; it can be crucial in permitting other forms of soil improvement involving fertilizers and rotations to go ahead successfully.

It may also produce a physical improvement in the soil. Shelly or sandy marls and lime help loosen up heavy soils; clay marls can add weight and absorbency to light ones. Ebenezer Emmons neatly summed up the combination of functions in 1852. Calcium carbonate, he wrote, acted *"vitally, chemically* and *physically. Vital,* in being a constituent element of plants; *chemical,* in its action upon silicates and organic matter; *physical,* in imparting friability to argillaceous soils, and compactness to sandy ones."[17]

There remains one final, and somewhat semantic, matter to be considered. Marling and liming may be roughly interchangeable terms in relatively abstract discussion. Over centuries of European usage, however, marling in particular has acquired much definitional ambiguity and, certainly on farms, has never been a simple synonym for liming. This has owed something to marl's variety of forms and appearances as an "earth": to the range of its physical as well as its chemical properties. Ruffin did much to tidy up the conceptual problem. He expressed irritation with the terminological slackness that prevailed in Britain, even among elevated commentators such as Arthur Young. For Ruffin, the purpose of marling was unequivocally that of *"making a soil calcareous."*[18] For British farmers, however, marling was also commonly associated—to a much greater degree than in America—with the mechanical function of altering the structure of a soil. Earths locally known as marls sometimes contained little or no carbonate of lime. Much of the emphasis in fact *was* placed on calcareous treatment. William Marshall wrote of marl in this way in the late eighteenth century. Many of his contemporaries did likewise, and in the 1850s *Morton's*

Cyclopedia of Agriculture described it as an "unctuous, clayey, chalky, or sandy earth, of calcareous nature."[19] But there remained enough variety of usage to cause Ruffin legitimate concern. Numerous British farming books, after all, were in circulation in the United States. He exaggerated somewhat when he wrote that "no two operations called by the same name, can well differ more," although almost a century later Sir William Ashley, in a study of British agriculture, had to confess that he had "no knowledge . . . just what that mysterious thing marling really meant."[20]

Insofar as the confusion has been resolved, this has sometimes been effected by undue narrowing. In their recent history of British farming, J. D. Chambers and G. E. Mingay discuss marl without any reference to calcareous content. Lime and chalk, they suggest, broke down heavy clays. "Marl had the contrary effect of binding thin and sandy soils."[21] The same emphasis appears in R. E. Prothero's classic study of English agriculture.[22] Such citations are offered simply to establish that British usage, ancient and modern, is best disregarded. In Ruffin's opinion, an American farmer trying to learn about marling from English sources would be "more apt to be deceived and misled, than enlightened."[23]

Ruffin wrote that he applied the term *marl* "to any compound or mixture of earths of which *carbonate of lime* in any form constitutes either the sole or chief value as manure, and is in such large proportion as to be an important value—and of which compound the mass is soft enough to be excavated and broken down by ordinary digging utensils. This definition is sufficiently plain and precise."[24] Happily, Ruffin was a sufficiently powerful propagandist to ensure that the definition was widely adopted by both practical farmers and scientific writers. Marl, in short, was a calcareous earth, and we might add some extra precision by suggesting, in accordance with other contemporary definitions, that it was one containing at least 20 percent carbonate of lime.[25] Ruffin's notion of marl as a calcareous manure derived from prior usage in Virginia,[26] and the only exception, it seems, to the almost immediate and universal acceptance of his terminological precision in America was the habit of applying the word to greensand. This, like marl proper, was found abundantly along the Eastern seaboard, but in its pure form it contained no lime whatever, its fertilizing powers being ascribed to its often substantial potassic (and sometimes phosphatic) content. There were, however, earths that Ruffin and others beyond New Jersey were quite happy to call "greensand marls," in which greensand happened to be mixed with a sufficient quantity of calcareous material.[27]

The carbonate of lime in marl was normally derived from shell fragments which had accumulated in Tertiary marine and freshwater deposits, the dominant geological formations of the tidewater South. As one might expect, the nature of the matrix varied a great deal. There was, in consequence, a large array of different marls: clay marls, loam marls, sandy marls, peat marls, ferruginous marls, stony marls, and the greensand marls. Then, depending on the color of the accompanying material, there were blue, red, white, yellow, and brown marls.[28] "No mineral," wrote a U.S. superintendent of agriculture, Thomas Clemson, "varies more in its physical character than marl."[29] The lime content also changed a good deal from one deposit to another and in some places could be as high as 95 percent.[30] Such physical and chemical variety meant, of course, that marl had no uniform effect. Land receiving greensand marl, for example, stood to gain from both carbonate of lime and potash. This was fine in the sense that benefits could come in more than one form, but it also caused difficulties given that no simple set of rules could be devised for universal application.

As a calcareous manure, marl belonged to the same category of soil improver as lime. It differed from lime, however, in a number of important respects. Being earthy, it was much less pure as a source of calcium, and also heavier and more slow-acting.[31] Impurity, though, had some nutritional advantages, as suggested, and the bulkier marls could also add substance to light soils, in the British fashion. Marl, moreover, could be applied to the soil without any prior physical or chemical processing. Unlike chalk or limestone in their natural states, it usually had the property of crumbling into powder when exposed to the atmosphere.[32] The principal chemical effects on the soil were, however, the same. The most important of these without question was the alleviation of soil acidity.

Chapter Five

The Soils, Crops, and Calcareous Resources

of the Southeast

I

*T*HE principal cause of acidity, as observed, is the leaching action of rainwater, percolating through the soil and dissolving out soluble bases like calcium or moving them to depths beyond the reach of crop roots. "Soils," writes A. R. Midgely, "are influenced by climate . . . to such an extent that they can be regarded as a product of it." Identical rock bases produce quite different soils in different climatic regions. Acidity will almost invariably be most pronounced in areas of high rainfall and where the soils are light and open, with a low water-holding capacity. An annual precipitation of 25 inches is usually enough to set the process in motion. Most of the Southeast has an average ranging between 40 and 50 inches: relatively high by American standards.[1] Moreover, the ground is often very exposed as a result of clean-row cultivation of crops such as cotton and tobacco.[2] Indeed, any cultivation will tend to encourage acidity, not only because it destroys the natural mat of protective vegetation but because the whole object of the exercise is to produce plants which can be removed for consumption or sale. When these are taken off the land, bases which they have absorbed are removed with them. The point need not be labored that much of the Old South, especially the northern parts, had been under heavy cultivation for a century or more.

The soils of the South, in particular those on the great sweep of uncon-solidated alluvium which forms the Coastal Plain, tend additionally to be light and free-draining. Rainwater passes easily through most of them. Some have a degree of dusty fineness which, to a Midwestern or European eye, seems startling for cultivable land.

Almost all Southern soils are classified as podzols of one sort or another—a category partly defined by acidity.[3] "Well developed podzol soils," writes Midgely, "are very acidic." Podzolization is described by Millar, Turk, and Foth as a process "by which soils are depleted of bases." Robert Pearson and Fred Adams write that "most of the acid soils of the Southern U.S.A. fall within the Red-Yellow Podzololic group. . . . The soils are highly leached, acid in reaction, and low in organic matter."[4]

One of the best of this category, in the view of J. W. Batten and J. S. Gibson, is the ubiquitous Norfolk series, but it needs generous and careful attention: "a minimum of drainage, heavy liming and fertilizing, and also crop rotation." These soils run from Virginia to Texas and normally have a markedly acidic reaction of 5 to 5.5. Other coastal-plain subcategories, they suggest, lie in the same range and most of them require substantial applica-tions of calcareous material. Averaging out maxima and minima (un-weighted) for the piedmont, one arrives at a range of 5.1 to 5.8. In the mountains every major soil type has reactions lying between 5 and 5.5. Red-Yellow podzols are described by Batten and Gibson as "rather strongly acidic" and "rather poor for agriculture" in their natural state.[5] B. T. Bunt-ing notes how they occur on a variety of parent materials and have prob-lematically high aluminum and iron contents: they are normally "well drained and are acid, devoid of free lime." In the Grey-Brown podzols com-mon in Delaware, Maryland, and much of Virginia he observes that calcium carbonate has generally been leached down to an inaccessible depth of over fifteen feet.[6] As for the Ground-Water and Half-Bog podzols of the Carolina and Georgia coasts, these are designated "acid" and "strongly acid" by J. R. Henderson.[7] The Southeast, according to J. F. Hart, has "soils which are poor even by Southern standards, and much of the land simply is not worth cultivating."[8] Frank Moser points out that there are soils in the region with reactions as low as 4, and that general acidity means that "calcium must be supplied to assure maximum production."[9]

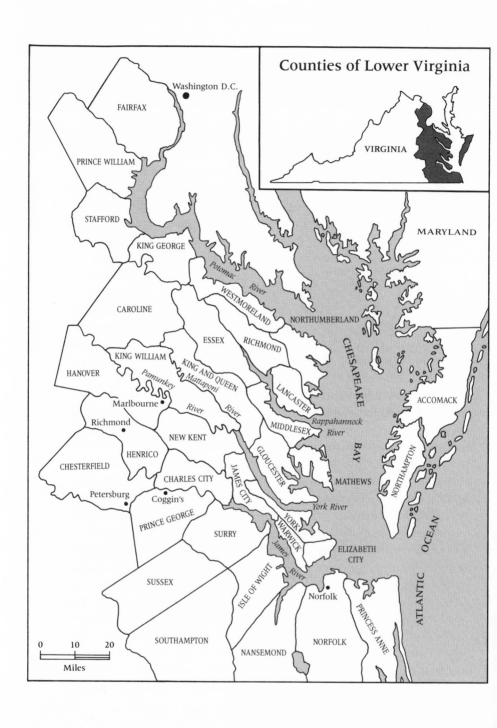

Counties of Lower Virginia

FAIRFAX

Washington D.C.

PRINCE WILLIAM

STAFFORD

KING GEORGE

Potomac River

CAROLINE

WESTMORELAND

NORTHUMBERLAND

ESSEX

RICHMOND

KING WILLIAM

KING AND QUEEN

HANOVER

Pamunkey

Mattaponi

River

River

LANCASTER

Marlbourne

Richmond

NEW KENT

MIDDLESEX

Rappahannock River

CHESAPEAKE

BAY

ACCOMACK

NORTHAMPTON

HENRICO

CHESTERFIELD

CHARLES CITY

GLOUCESTER

JAMES CITY

MATHEWS

Petersburg

Coggin's

York River

PRINCE GEORGE

YORK

WARWICK

SURRY

James

ELIZABETH CITY

SUSSEX

ISLE OF WIGHT

River

Norfolk

PRINCESS ANNE

0   10   20

Miles

SOUTHAMPTON

NANSEMOND

NORFOLK

ATLANTIC OCEAN

MARYLAND

VIRGINIA

Ten samples of Maryland soils, selected by L. B. Golden, N. Gammon, and R. P. Thomas to represent the variety in the state, showed three with a slightly alkaline reaction and all the rest as acidic, four of them with the relatively extreme pHs of 5.0, 4.8, 4.7, and 4.3.[10] Readings on sandy soils in the vicinity of Williamsburg, Virginia, in 1981—an important marling area, according to Ruffin—gave results of 4.9 and 4.7.[11] Ralph Cummings observed in 1945 that although the use of lime in North Carolina had shown a tenfold increase over the previous decade, even that "phenomenal" expansion was insufficient to deal comprehensively with acidity. Annual consumption still needed to be trebled, he suggested. The state is dominated by so-called ultisols: "very acid, highly leached, and weathered."[12] James Clay, Douglas Orr, and Alfred Stuart have shown just how extensive the problem remains. All the mountain soils (save "stony land") are acidic. Thirteen of the fifteen piedmont categories and fifteen of the eighteen coastal-plain groups are similarly designated. They point out that because of leaching and resultant calcium loss almost "all North Carolina soils require application of lime and fertilizer before they are suitable for the more commonly grown row crops and pastures."[13]

A survey of Beaufort and Jasper counties in tidewater South Carolina draws attention to problems of low natural fertility: "Nearly all of the soils . . . have an acid surface layer unless they have been limed recently. Most of the soils are acid throughout. . . . Many upland soils are naturally extremely acid to strongly acid."[14] Elmer Fippin of Cornell University told the South Carolina Agricultural Society in 1915 that the South had not yet gotten down to any extensive study of the acidity problem. Almost all soils of the section were "deficient in lime for successful production of humus forming crops." The judicious use of lime of one sort or another had been "demonstrated to be essential to best results throughout large areas of the Southern coast states."[15] M. E. Walker and A. W. White stress the high calcium requirement of Georgia soils. Despite a great increase in liming up to the early 1960s, it still fell "far short of the estimated needs," particularly in the lower parts of the state where a quarter of the soils tested had reactions of less than 5.5.[16] In 1968 it was suggested that the application of calcareous material in the six states from Georgia up to Delaware was conducted on a highly inadequate scale. Actual consumption was little more than a third of the optimum, with Virginia and South Carolina the most negligent areas.[17]

II

There is ample evidence here to establish beyond reasonable doubt that the Old South was, and is, a region of pronounced soil acidity. The seriousness of the problem, however, is not a simple function of the pH readings. Plants vary a good deal in acid sensitivity.

It would seem that all the main crops generally stood to gain from a reduction in acidity levels, some of them very substantially. Roy Donahue, John Shickluna, and Lynn Robertson identify cotton, barley, sugar beet, alfalfa, beans, soy beans, peas, red clover, and sweet clover as plants with high calcareous requirements and corn, wheat, tobacco, trefoil, and peanuts as ones with moderate needs. Buckwheat, oats, rye, potatoes, rice, and vetch gain very little from lime, and blueberries and cranberries can get by with hardly any at all.[18] Experiments carried out in Ohio in the 1930s showed that corn, wheat, timothy, alfalfa, and alsike and mammoth clover gave their highest yields at the near-neutral reaction of pH 6.8 and that oats, barley, red and sweet clover (and alfalfa again) all peaked at the slightly alkaline reaction of pH 7.5. At the very acidic level of 4.7, however, oats achieved only 77 percent of their maximum, wheat 68 percent, corn 34 percent, timothy 31 percent, mammoth clover 16 percent, alsike clover 13 percent, red clover 12 percent, alfalfa 2 percent, and both sweet clover and barley a dramatic zero.[19]

Neither tobacco nor cotton was included in the Ohio experiments. Tobacco is the one major Southeastern staple which generally does better on sour soils than on neutral ones. Although classified by Pearson and Adams as "relatively sensitive" to acidity, tobacco is a crop for which flavor rather than yield is the central consideration. On infertile, sandy soils the plant produces the mild, thin, light-colored leaf which is best suited to the tastes of North American and West European markets: the so-called "Virginia" as distinct from "Turkish" tobacco.[20] Ruffin himself acknowledged that Virginia's past success with tobacco may have owed much to the *lack* of calcareous matter in the soil.[21] According to B. C. Akehurst, American producers only need concern themselves about liming when the pH is below 5.2—that is, when acidity is becoming very pronounced.[22]

With cotton, the picture is somewhat more complex. Some authors, such as Louis Thompson and I. de V. Malherbe, suggest that it is fairly tolerant of acidity and that liming may not always produce substantial rewards.[23] Pearson and Adams, bringing together figures from different experiments which compare yields before and after amelioration on soils of marked acidity, indicate increases ranging from as low as 1 percent to as high as 446 percent.[24] Walker and White, referring to trials in Georgia, come to the conclusion that cotton is, on the whole, "lime responsive."[25] W. R. Paden and W. H. Garman, working in South Carolina in 1947, found that soil of pH 5 gave an 18 percent increment when corrected to pH 6, and of 20 percent when raised to pH 6.5. In addition (and this was something widely recognized in the antebellum period),[26] crops matured earlier when the acidity was lowered, with an increase of 41 percent in the first picking after an adjustment from pH 5 to pH 6 (and of 51 percent to pH 6.5). Accordingly, they advised farmers of "the importance of liming acid soils in order to have the maximum amount of cotton ready for harvest at the earliest possible date."[27] Cotton can survive quite a substantial degree of acidity, but stands to gain considerably from corrections towards neutrality. The desirability of amelioration in strictly economic terms will, as with most plants, be a function of cost, of the requirements of accompanying crops in a rotation, and of the degree of acidity encountered.

The point to be stressed above all others is that many of the crops central to diversified, rotation farming are *highly* dependent on amelioration—in particular a wide range of legumes such as clover, alfalfa, and peas. These raise the nitrogenous content of a soil and provide fodder for manure-producing and consumable livestock, very vital productivity- and profit-raising functions on a plantation. The correction of acidity, in short, does not have to work directly on a crop; it can yield indirect benefits through what might be termed leguminous nutrition. Acid-tolerant crops, writes N. C. Brady, will still be responsive to amelioration through "the stimulating influence of lime upon the legume which preceded them in a rotation."[28] E. N. Fergus, Carsie Hammonds, and Hayden Rogers observed in 1949 that cotton can thrive on fairly acid soils, but that if "grown in a rotation with legumes, the soils should have a pH of about 6.5. This means that most of the soils on which cotton is grown should receive lime."[29]

Calcareous manures, it seems, are an irrelevance for only a small minority of Southeastern crops which can tolerate high acidity *and* which are produced within essentially nonrotational (or primitive-rotational) systems of farming—and, of course, for plants grown on the odd pockets of naturally limey soil in the region. In Ruffin's view these latter were the exceptions which proved the rule. In Virginia, he contended, there was "no doubt but that every acre of our shelly land has been as much tilled, and as little manured, as any in the country—and that it is still the richest and most valuable of all our old cleared land." Of the calcareous canebrake soils of Alabama, he observed how some planters were securing crops of red clover "more productive, valuable, and far more enduring" than anything ever grown on improved land in Virginia—without the benefit of marling.[30]

In consequence of Ruffin's perceptions and labors, the antebellum South had quite a widespread awareness of the problem of soil acidity. "It was nearly forty years ago," he wrote in 1860, "that I first came to believe, and then asserted, and soon after published, the then entirely novel fact of the general (and almost universal) and entire absence of *carbonate* of lime as a natural constituent of the soils of our Atlantic slope. . . . No scientific inquirer had before even suspected this remarkable fact. But every scientific observation, made in later times, has served to confirm my then unsupported position."[31] Professor William Gilham declared in a paper to the Virginia State Agricultural Society in 1853 that it was well known that "the much greater number of soils of Tide Water Virginia are not productive without the aid of lime . . . and in considerable quantities."[32] John R. Edmunds, addressing the same body later in the year, observed that one of the "distinctive features in the soils of this State is absence of carbonate of lime in nearly all." This deficiency, he went on, was "abundant cause for sterility."[33] The North Carolina *Farmer's Journal* noted in 1852 that "most of the worn out lands of our State" were "greatly deficient" in lime.[34] Governor Whitemarsh Seabrook of South Carolina observed in 1854 that calcareous manure was "indispensable to the fruition and development of plants, and that nearly all of the soils of our State require its application."[35]

In an official report of 1859, Thomas Clemson noted how the majority of soils to the east of the Appalachians derived from old, often crystalline rocks which "contain less lime than soils of a different origin" and insisted that all, "without exception, would be benefited by the application of lime" in whatever form it could be found.[36]

III

Marl was not some narrowly localized resource, its application easy to advocate in the abstract but impossible to effect, practically and economically, on any noteworthy scale. Many thousands of farmers could make profitable use of it if they had a mind to. It was found very extensively in the Tertiary formations which ran from southern New Jersey to the Gulf of Mexico,[37] and its presence was being increasingly publicized in the antebellum period through books, farming journals, government reports, and geological surveys. The planter could, moreover, prove that he had it on his farm by the simplest of tests. All he had to do was put a piece in a glass of water, wait for the initial air bubbles to escape, and then add a few drops of acid or strong vinegar: any resultant effervesence was fairly certain evidence that carbonate of lime was present.[38]

Of all the states in the region, only Delaware was scantily provided. There was some greensand, but not all of it was mixed with calcareous material and the accessible beds were confined to Newcastle County in the north. There appear to have been no shell marls whatever in the state.[39] In neighboring Maryland, however, these were found in considerable abundance. Professor J. T. Ducatel, in his 1830s geological survey, referred to a very extensive underlying deposit of shell marl, although the southwesterly dip of the beds meant that they generally lay too far beneath the surface to be of service to Eastern Shore farmers south of Talbot and Caroline counties. Marl was also absent above the fall line, but in the remaining counties around the Potomac and the Chesapeake it was widely available, and there was a lot of calciferous greensand around as well.[40] Joseph Kennedy of the U.S. Census Office observed in 1852 that marl could be found in abundance in St. Marys, Queen Anne, and Caroline. A great deal of this was easy to get at.[41] Ducatel wrote that there were beds accessible to the great majority of Calvert planters and that in some estates it appeared in every field, exposed by springs and streams or lying at only a small depth from the surface.

Virginia was even more generously provided. Once again, however, there was little or none to be had above the falls.[42] This in fact was the case throughout the Old South: the geological formations of the piedmont, being of a much greater age than those to the east, were virtually devoid of loose, shelly material. In the extreme east of Virginia, too—as in the southeastern counties of Maryland—there was little available, either because it had been washed away during recent encroachments of the sea or because it lay at too great a depth. In Norfolk it was discovered seventy feet down.[43] Away from the shoreline of the Piankatank there were few deposits in Mathews, and it was effectively absent on the Eastern Shore.[44]

However, one only had to move a little way inland—from Mathews to Gloucester, or from Norfolk to Nansemond—to discover generous supplies. "It is found," wrote one observer, "in the sides and bottoms of ravines, with which the land near the rivers, creeks, and branches is much broken. . . . In some places, it is found almost at the surface, and in others at a depth of several feet." In the tidewater counties south of the James, according to a government report of 1870, there were "inexhaustible beds of shell-marl lying . . . but a few feet below the surface." It was also "found abundantly" and "readily accessible" in many localities between the James and Potomac. Of Nansemond, south of the James, it was written in 1842: "Nearly every water course and ravine has a bountiful supply, and that of the very best quality." In Surry, suggested Ruffin, marl could be had more easily and more cheaply than in any other part of Virginia. Calcareous earth, he believed, also underlay the whole county of Sussex.[45]

Between the James and the York a great deal of highly calcareous white marl was available.[46] In Charles City marl was "found very abundant" in the middle range of the county.[47] New Kent was also well supplied, and in James City it was "accessible to almost all."[48] In the neighborhood of the Pamunkey River, the principal headwater of the York, there were extensive deposits of rich greensand marl. The tidewater region of Hanover County had substantial quantities that were of great service to Ruffin at Marlbourne in the 1840s.[49] In King William the marl was "supplied most bountifully so that numerous landowners own beds, and none are far removed from some of good quality."[50] Further extensive deposits were found in the counties between the York and the Rappahannock, especially in Gloucester and Middlesex.[51]

The principal marl region of Virginia, then, extended from the Rappahannock on the north to some way inland from the James River on the south, and from the fall line on the west to the lowest of the tidewater counties on the east. The deposits therein seem to have been widespread, close to the surface or exposed, and of moderately high calcareous content.

North Carolina's resources, according to Ebenezer Emmons in the 1850s, were less impressive. The Tertiary marls, he wrote, were "always isolated, or confined comparatively within narrow limits." They generally had an excess of silicious material and a relatively low lime content. They vanished above the fall line, and the deposits in some of the lowest tidewater counties were often too deep for profitable digging.[52]

Most of the accessible beds lay along the banks of the principal rivers—the Roanoke, the Tar, the Neuse, and the Cape Fear. Supplies on the Roanoke were quite substantial, in Emmons' view. In Halifax, however, the marl lay at considerable depth and, accordingly, was exposed only in large ravines.[53] On the Tar, it was available from Nash down through Edgecombe and Pitt to the sea at Beaufort, though good dry exposures became less common the nearer one came to the sea.[54] The Neuse had marl from Wake down to Carteret. Beds also lay exposed along its main tributary, the Trent, in Jones County. Thomas Antisell reported a "marly limestone" in the north of Wake County, and near Raleigh Professor McLenahan found what he described as a "silicious shelly limestone." Downstream, in Wayne, the same sort of deposits reappeared alongside the more orthodox shell marls.[55]

The best-endowed counties appear to have been Lenoir and Craven.[56] To the south the only remaining areas of significance were the lower flood plains of the Cape Fear and Northeast Cape Fear rivers. In 1840 Ruffin, on a brief visit to North Carolina, found some marl by the Northeast Cape Fear near Rocky Point and pronounced it "the richest and most valuable . . . I have ever known," some of it having a lime content of as much as 95 percent. He also saw strata in the vicinities of Ashemoore and Wilmington in New Hanover. More of his discoveries in the same region were recorded in 1844.[57] Emmons, some years later, concentrated his attention on the Cape Fear, declaring its basin to be rich in marl and greensand, and advising local planters to take advantage of the bounty available to them.[58]

In South Carolina, Ruffin undertook his agricultural and geological survey in 1843, with Michael Tuomey replacing him the following year. Their findings confirmed what a number of people had supposed since the mid-1830s—that South Carolina was very richly supplied. Marl had been reported on all the major rivers from the Pee Dee down to the Savannah.[59] In 1838 Lardner Vanuxem, the Pennsylvania geologist, took note of the already documented deposit at Shell Bluff on the Savannah twenty-five miles downstream from Augusta,[60] and in 1841 James Hammond, who had a plantation twelve miles away in Barnwell District, made use of this to commence what eventually became the largest marling operations in the South.[61]

According to the *Southern Agriculturist*, Ruffin's 1843 report showed that the state possessed "immense supplies of the richest marl ever found in any part of the world—the most easily found—the most easily obtained—the most easily conveyed from its bed."[62] He identified two main beds: the Pee Dee, a Cretaceous rather than Tertiary formation, exposed principally along the Great Pee Dee and its tributaries in Marion, Williamsburg, and Georgetown districts in the northeast, and the Great Carolinian, extending from the same area southwest to the Savannah River and into Georgia, with the inland limit running across the state some twenty-five to thirty-five

miles downstream from the fall line.[63] Both beds appeared together in the
northeast. Over much of tidewater, especially between the Santee and
Edisto, exposures were generally abundant and highly calcareous. On the
Santee, beds were particularly rich in St. John's Parish in Charleston District,
near Black Oak—"a section of the State abounding more with marl than
any other."[64] On the right bank of the Santee along the dozen miles from
Echaw Creek to Lenud's Ferry, it appeared on every plantation. The beds all
the way to above Eutaw Spring in St. John's Parish he described as "the
richest known." Supplies were available as far up as Orangeburg District,
with other deposits appearing as far inland as Potato Creek in Sumter.[65]

In the great swamps in Charleston District, between the Santee and the
Ashley rivers, there was, Ruffin wrote in 1853, a lot more "of the richest
quality" to be had if planters would dig just a few feet below the surface.
This had already been demonstrated by the extensive exposures opened
during the digging of the Santee canal, linking the Cooper and Santee
rivers.[66] On the Ashley, in the words of an 1838 report, it was "so abundant, that it is brought to Charleston, and is used for filling up the streets."[67]
The city itself stood above a deeply set stratum of marl. Ruffin noted that
much of the Ashley marl was hidden by tidal marsh, but that from nine
miles above Charleston, wherever there were good-sized banks, exposures
ran along the whole course of the river.[68] He also made some discoveries on
the Edisto River and its tributaries. On the Savannah at Shell Bluff, most of
the marl, by James Hammond's account, was "hard and compact, of a grey
color, containing 50 to 60 per cent. of lime," and crumbling "on exposure to
the seasons and in handling."[69]

Little exploration was undertaken in Georgia. Discussions of marl beds
there were usually pitched at a level of high generality. It was Ruffin's opinion in 1844 that Georgia was "much more bounteously bestowed" than
North Carolina. The younger Southern states generally, he observed a few
years later, had "a ten-fold better supply of far richer and cheaper marl than
is found in Virginia."[70] In the late 1840s the distinguished Scottish geologist
Sir Charles Lyell observed large areas of shelly deposits in parts of the lower
counties of the state, but his remarks did not constitute any sort of systematic evaluation.[71] A report by a subcommittee of the South Central Agricultural Society to the Georgia Senate and House of Representatives around
the same time noted that "marls appear to increase in richness as they extend southward. They enter Georgia in a broad belt extending, from some
20 miles below Augusta, to the sea, and running parallel to, and a short

distance below, the last falls in our rivers, and pass out westward near Columbus, extending south into Florida, and occupying near two-thirds of our States."[72] Detailed information on marl reserves, however, was not provided, and the whole point of the committee's communication with the legislature was to plead for a $10,000 appropriation to finance a comprehensive survey of Georgia by "a competent Geologist" who would be able to "seek out her hidden treasures of mineral manures, learn their value by his chemical knowledge, and teach their application to the condition of our varied soils."[73] A brief report, by Dr. Joseph Jones, was sponsored by the Cotton Planters' Convention in the state, but this did not appear until 1860.[74]

It is clear, even from these impressionistic observations, that marl was in widespread supply in the newer geological formations of the Coastal Plain, and was generally of a high calcareous content. It did not appear above the falls and it frequently lay too deep in areas close to the sea, but there was nevertheless a good, solid belt up to a hundred miles or more wide running south through tidewater counties from the Chesapeake to the Gulf states. The most conspicuous and accessible exposures were by rivers, but marl was also available in gullies and along road and rail tracks, or could be got at by digging sometimes through only a foot or two of covering earth.

IV

As for lime, the physical basis for production in the Southeast was, by contrast, somewhat restricted and sometimes remote. Large accumulations of oyster shells lay here and there along the coast, but many were manifestly exhaustible.[75] Limestone was patchily available in the interior. "The older calcareous formations of the Atlantic States," it was written in 1868, "constitute a belt of considerable breadth, coinciding nearly with the great eastern mountain chain of the continent, and having numerous offshoots and local outcrops, at greater or less distances from the main range."[76] However, the belt tended to run a little too far to the north and west.

Delaware had a patch of limestone on the state line with Pennsylvania, and Maryland's beds were confined to its northern counties. In Virginia—embracing a great deal of highland country before the separation of West Virginia in 1863—calcareous strata were much more in evidence, with good stone available throughout the length and breadth of the Great Valley and in many upland counties to both east and west. To the south, however, the formation swung away largely out of reach, leaving "localities of older limestones" in North Carolina "few and widely separated."[77] There was some stone-marl in a few locations near the coast, in Bladen and Craven, and an outlying band of older calcareous rock running south from Stokes to Catawba, but overall the resources were meager. "The deficiency of lime-stone in this State is notorious," wrote Ebenezer Emmons in 1860.[78]

The same could have been said about South Carolina, which the Ap-palachians missed altogether, and where notable beds were found only in the upper counties of York, Spartanburg, and Laurens. Some of the harder marls close to the coast, however, could be used for burning.[79] Georgia was more liberally supplied. There was an extensive patch of cretaceous lime-stone in one or two middle counties close to the Alabama border, and the belt of old mountain stone passed through the northwestern corner of the state.[80] In 1853 a quarrier from Kingston to the north of Atlanta secured freight reductions from two railway companies and offered limestone to farmers at rates ranging from $16 per car of eight tons in Atlanta to $31.25 in Augusta. He advised: "Make a log heap of large logs of about 14 feet long each. Let it be in the field, if possible, on which the lime is to be used. The heap should be at least 5 feet high, and long in proportion to the quantity of rock to be burned. The rock should be broken in pieces not larger than a man's fist, and then piled in the shape of a cone."[81]

The combination of such primitive technology and effectively scarce re-sources made the South an inconsequential producer of lime. There is no evidence of any vigorous entrepreneurship at work, rectifying the situation. Planters who did want lime commonly chose to buy it from the producers of the Schuylkill, the Hudson, and the coast of Maine.

Part Three

The Ruffin Reforms in Practice

Chapter Six

The Effects of Marling and Liming

———————◦◦◦◦◦◦———————

I

I have marled, Mr. Editor, God be praised, I have marled . . . ," declared a correspondent of the *Farmers' Register* in 1835. "And now my good sir, when my spirits are depressed, I generally take a walk to look at the corn on the marled land. When the cashier informs me that on such a day my note falls due, I walk to the marled land. If anything crosses me there I go, morning, noon, or night. Upon my word I begin to think marl will cure half the ills of my life."[1] The enthusiasm was shared by many farmers who witnessed dramatic improvements in crop yields and, with them, increased profits and enhanced land values.

It is virtually impossible to establish precise correlations between marling and the widely documented increases in the productiveness of the soil. Planters who marled did not always confine their improvements to that single practice. The use of farmyard manure and the wider resort to draining and ditching were all common features of general programs of land betterment which included marl, and these could, of course, make their own contributions to enlarged crop yields. The initial degree of soil acidity would also be a major determinant of the impact of marling, as would the efficiency with which the planter set about the operation. Weather, too, could have significant short-term effects, obscuring or exaggerating the benefits resulting from amelioration. James Hammond frequently felt unable to make an exact estimate of marl's worth because of the intrusion of climatic and other natural forces.[2] "Every disaster fastens on me and I never escape any flood, frost, drought, insect, or epidemic which afflicts the planting interest," he told Edmund Ruffin in a letter written in 1851.[3] And, of course, if we go beyond crop yields and also look at profits, land values, and population changes, the number of variables greatly increases and with them the difficulty of evaluation.

Circumspection must be introduced at the outset. Analysis, however, can still proceed. There is, for one thing, much evidence to suggest that many improvements accompanying marling ought to be viewed to a large degree as dependent variables. Rotational leguminous crops, as already noted, often could not be grown unless marl had been previously applied to the soil; and the benefits of manuring could be severely limited if the soil was allowed to remain acidic. The greater interest in draining and ditching (hardly very widespread in the South) was, in part at least, the consequence of a desire to maximize the gains expected from marling, or indeed to create or re-create cultivable land so that marl could be applied to it. Marl, in short, was, in the words of an 1842 report to the Virginia Board of Agriculture, "the main-spring of all our improvements": in some instances the *sine qua non,* in others the *encouraging* factor.[4]

"The increase of the first crop on worn acid soil," wrote Ruffin in 1832, "I have never known under fifty per cent., and often as much as one hundred—and the improvement continues to increase slowly under mild tillage. In this, and other general statements of effects, I suppose the land to bear not more than two crops in four years. and not to be subjected to grazing."[5] In the Williamsburg area of James City County he noted twofold to fourfold increases in yields up to 1840.[6] The highest figures generally were recorded for ridgelands between the river courses, formerly "universally acid in a high degree."[7] The other great Southern marler, Governor James Hammond, was getting less spectacular but nonetheless satisfactory results with his cotton in South Carolina. "My expectations for the first year have been fully justified," he wrote in 1842. "I did not calculate on any of these magical results which agricultural experimenters so often look for and so seldom realize to the full extent. I regard an increase of 20 per cent as a very handsome return."[8]

The crop which seems to have gained more than any other was corn. The results of various trials, as tabulated here, suggest that percentage yield

Table 2. *Marling and Corn Yields*

Farmer	County, State	Period†	Unmarled Yield per Acre‡ (Bushels)	Marled Yield per Acre‡ (Bushels)	Percentage§ Improvement‡
William Carmichael	Queen Anne, Md.	1824 to 1837	—	—	50.0
Richard Hill	King William, Va.	1811 to 1822	5.5	15.0	172.7
John Dickinson	King William, Va.	18? to 1835	—	—	200.0
Corbin Braxton	King William, Va.	1834 to late 1830s	17.5	40.0	128.6
Thomas Carter	King William, Va.	1827 to 1840	16.3	32.5	100.0
Thomas Robinson	King William, Va.	1834 to 1840	5.0	20.0	300.0
William Fontaine	King William, Va.	1835 to 1840	8.0	20.0	150.0
R. W. Tomlin	King William, Va.	1838 to 1850	20.0	55.0	175.0
H. B. Tomlin	King William, Va.	1838 to 1851/52	15.0	35.0	133.3
Mrs. Coulton	King William, Va.	1838 to 1852	17.5	40.0	128.6
W. F. Wickham	Hanover, Va.	1820 to 1840	17.5	35.0	100.0
Edmund Wickham	Hanover, Va.	1824 to 1840	16.3	32.5	100.0
Edmund Ruffin	Hanover, Va.	1844 to 1848	18.1	28.1	55.2
Carter Braxton	Hanover, Va.	1837 to 1840	15.0	30.0	100.0
Thomas Stubblefield	Gloucester, Va.	1830 to 1835	2.5	30.0	1,100.0
C. H. Minge	Charles City, Va.	1820/33 to 1836	5.0	25.0	400.0
C. H. Minge	Charles City, Va.	1837	—	—	200.0*
H. C. Richardson	James City, Va.	1829 to 1840	10.0	25.0	150.0

continued

Table 2. Continued

Farmer	County, State	Period†	Unmarled Yield per Acre‡ (Bushels)	Marled Yield per Acre‡ (Bushels)	Percentage§ Improvement‡
Edmund Ruffin	Prince George, Va.	1818	—	—	40.0*
Edmund Ruffin	Prince George, Va.	1821	22.5	33.5	48.9*
Edmund Ruffin	Prince George, Va.	1820	7.4	13.7	85.1*
Edmund Ruffin	Prince George, Va.	1813/15 to 1825/27	13.5	16.8	24.4
Edmund Ruffin	Prince George, Va.	1828	7.3	13.8	89.0*
Edmund Ruffin	Prince George, Va.	1831	5.0	11.0	120.0*
Edmund Harrison	Prince George, Va.	1833	5.0	20.5	302.0
Edmund Ruffin	Prince George, Va.	1818 to 1839	11.0	26.0	136.4
James Cocke	Prince George, Va.	1820 to 1839	7.0	27.0	285.7
Edward Marks	Prince George, Va.	1820 to 1839	10.0	22.5	125.0
John Marks	Prince George, Va.	1820 to 1839	10.0	25.0	150.0
John Bland	Prince George, Va.	1826 to 1839	10.0	30.0	200.0
Elgin Russell	Prince George, Va.	1827 to 1839	10.0	20.0	100.0
Theoderick Bland	Prince George, Va.	1830 to 1839	13.5	35.0	159.3
William Wilkins	Prince George, Va.	1833 to 1839	6.3	25.0	296.8
Richard Harrison	Prince George, Va.	1834 to 1839	10.0	20.0	100.0
Edmund Ruffin	Prince George, Va.	pre-1818 to 1840/42	14.2	24.0	69.0

David Tatum	Prince George, Va.	1850 to 1850/51	10.0	30.0	200.0
Peter Spratley	Surry, Va.	1834 to 1840	7.0	20.0	185.7
Bolling Jones	Surry, Va.	1834 to 1840	9.0	19.5	116.7
Mr. Cunningham	? N.C.	1841	—	—	100.0*
Mr. May	? N.C.	18? to 1851	—	—	300.0
Samuel Black	New Hanover, N.C.	1837 to 1838	—	—	75.0
C. Rumph	? S.C.	1838	6.0	30.0	400.0*
Francis Holmes	Colleton, S.C.	1844	17.0	22.5	32.4*
James Hammond	Barnwell, S.C.	1842	17.0	20.2	18.8*
James Hammond	Barnwell, S.C.	1843	—	—	−7.0*
James Hammond	Barnwell, S.C.	1845	—	—	12.6*
UNWEIGHTED AVERAGE			11.2	26.3	134.0

Note: Entries arranged in year-of-completion sequence, by county.

†Period over which comparisons are made; does not necessarily mean period during which marling was continuous. Starting dates sometimes a little uncertain.

‡Where a range is given in the sources, the two figures have been averaged out.

§Comparing sums of all cases where unmarled and marled yields are available.

*Signifies comparison of separate plots in same year.

Sources: Ruffin, *Calcareous Manures* (Sitterson, ed.), pp. 84–89; Ruffin, *Survey of South-Carolina*, "Tabular Statement of Marling Operations"; Tuomey, *Survey of South Carolina*, p. 50; *Farmers' Register* 3 (December 1835): 477–78, (January 1836): 555; *FR* 5 (December 1837): 511; *FR* 6 (June 1838): 144; *FR* 7 (February 1839): 115; *FR* 8 (August 1840): 491–97, 500, (November 1840): 683–89; *FR* 9 (January 1841): 20–21, 24–28, (May 1841): 264–66; *FR* 10 (April 1842): 190–91; *Southern Cultivator* 1 (March 1843):1, 4 (July 1846): 99; *Southern Planter* 13 (May 1853): 140–41; *SP* 14 (April 1854): 100–104.

Table 3. *Marling and Wheat Yields*

Farmer	County, State	Period†	Unmarled Yield per Acre‡ (Bushels)	Marled Yield per Acre‡ (Bushels)	Percentage§ Improvement‡
Richard Hill	King William, Va.	1812 to 1816/22	—	—	300.0
William Fontaine	King William, Va.	1834 to 1835	2.0	13.3	565.0
R. W. Tomlin	King William, Va.	1838 to 1851/52	3.5	22.6	545.7
H. B. Tomlin	King William, Va.	1838 to 1851/52	2.5	24.5	925.0
Mrs. Coulton	King William, Va.	1839 to 1851/52	3.0	24.0	700.0
W. F. Wickham	Hanover, Va.	1820 to 1840	—	—	75.0
Edmund Wickham	Hanover, Va.	1824 to 1840	—	—	100.0
Corbin Braxton	Hanover, Va.	1834 to 1840	—	—	110.0
Edmund Ruffin	Hanover, Va.	1845 to 1848	14.8	20.0	36.0
Anonymous	Gloucester, Va.	18? to 1839	—	12.5	—
Mr. Wynne	James City, Va.	1834 to 1844	1.0	10.0	900.0
Edmund Ruffin	Prince George, Va.	1819 to 1831	—	22.5	—
John Bland	Prince George, Va.	1826 to 1840	4.0	9.0	125.0

Edmund Wilkins	Prince George, Va.	1834 to 1840	5.0	15.0	200.0
Edmund Ruffin & Edmund Ruffin Jr.	Prince George, Va.	1813/19 to 1840/42	7.0	11.7	67.1
David Tatum	Prince George, Va.	1840 to 1850/51	—	20.0	—
Edward Marks	Prince George, Va.	1827 to 1851	—	13.7	—
John Marks	Prince George, Va.	1827 to 1851	—	9.8	—
Elgin Russell	Prince George, Va.	1827 to 1851	—	10.0	—
Richard Harrison	Prince George, Va.	1834 to 1851	—	13.0	—
H. W. Harrison	Prince George, Va.	18? to 1851	—	12.7	—
Edmund Ruffin Jr.	Prince George, Va.	18? to 1851	—	16.8	—
UNWEIGHTED AVERAGES			4.8	15.6	250.7

Note: Entries arranged in year-of-completion sequence, by county.

†Period over which comparisons are made: does not necessarily mean period during which marling was continuous. Starting dates sometimes a little uncertain.

‡Where a range is given in the sources, the two figures have been averaged out.

§Comparing sums of all cases where unmarled and marled yields are available.

Sources: Ruffin, *Calcareous Manures* (Sitterson, ed.), p. 96; ibid., (3d ed.), p. 254; *Survey of South Carolina.* "Tabular Statement of Marling Operations"; *Farmers' Register* 3 (January 1836): 552; *FR* 7 (September 1839): 575; *FR* 8 (November 1840): 684; *FR* 9 (January 1841): 25; *American Agriculturist* 4 (April 1845): 118; *Southern Planter* 9 (August 1849): 227–28; (May 1853): 140–41; *SP* 14 (April 1854): 100–103.

improvement was lower than for wheat, but the much greater frequency of references to marling for corn indicates that substantially larger acreages were involved. This is not surprising. Virginia, where so much of the marling took place, ranked as the third corn-growing state in the country in 1840, after Tennessee and Kentucky. The crop for that year was estimated at 34,577,591 bushels, compared with just over 25,371,829 for all the other main grains combined (wheat, rye, oats, barley, and buckwheat).[9] Significantly, Ruffin's first application of marl in 1818 was on land intended for corn. "I now constantly apply it to the ground cultivated in corn," one of his marling precursors, the Rev. John Singleton of Maryland, wrote in 1817, adding that it never failed on that crop.[10]

Increased production of corn was a matter of the greatest importance for farmers. It served as the principal food for slaves, it provided fodder for livestock, and its yields had lately been sinking to abysmally low levels. The 11.2-bushel average for unmarled land in Table 2 (crudely calculated from figures unweightable for acreage) is probably a fairly accurate indication of the sort of crop returns that could be expected. Ruffin wrote of a maximum of ten for his own neighborhood in Prince George County, "and more generally of five."[11] Lower Virginia as a whole, he estimated in 1841, frequently had yields of seven to eight, with the average standing somewhere between ten and twelve bushels.[12] The tabulated increase, after marl, of around fifteen bushels also seems to be in line with contemporary observation. Judicious marling, according to Ruffin in 1842, could add a good sixteen bushels to the crop, and the following year he suggested a post-improvement average of about twenty-four bushels in Virginia.[13]

Planters, needless to say, were delighted with such results and provided the farming journals with a stream of information about their good fortune (most of it, however, nonstatistical). "I had no idea the marl would have produced so great an effect," wrote Hill Carter of Shirley in August 1837, optimistically anticipating a massive sixty bushels from his thinnest and once most acidic soils.[14] Another planter, watching his rapidly advancing crop in 1835, was expecting thirty to forty bushels: "Mortal man," he commented, "would scarcely believe it."[15] James Hammond expressed similar surprise in 1847. "Such a crop," he wrote, "was never seen in these parts *nor anywhere* on pine land. It now looks like 30 bushels per acre."[16]

There is virtually no record of disappointment in the journals. These, of course, had a bias towards success, with propagandist editors such as Ruffin at work, and subscribers probably preferring not to publicize their failures.

The figures and comments available are, nonetheless, impressive, and Ruffin was a serious man of scientific disposition and unlikely to distort the facts, even by default. He was certainly prepared to question what he considered to be extravagant claims for marl's effects,[17] and his advice to farmers was that marling had always to be conducted with caution and intelligence, and its consequences seen in proper perspective. People who now got twenty-five bushels of corn, he pointed out in 1840, should bear in mind that many farmers farther west would regard such a yield with contempt, and indicative of approaching soil exhaustion.[18]

Figures for wheat giving yields to the acre are much more difficult to come by. In the nine cases in Table 3 where pre- and post-marling figures can be compared, unweighted averages suggest an improvement of 251 percent. This is almost double the increase for corn, but the size of the sample and the scale of the standard deviation invite extreme caution. The 11-bushel increment contrasts with Ruffin's suggested average of between four and eight for tidewater Virginia in the early 1840s.[19] Nevertheless he did write in 1832 that he was convinced from observation "that the increase of wheat from marling, is at least equal to that of corn, during the first few years—and is certainly greater afterwards, in comparison to its product before using marl," and in the 1850s he noted that yields could go up to twenty-five bushels or more if amelioration was combined with improving rotations involving legumes like clover and peas.[20]

The editor of the Richmond *Southern Planter* was impressed by the fact, in 1852, that the wheat crop of Virginia had doubled in the course of only nine years: "Whilst it is known that some farmers there have increased their wheat several hundred per cent. it is believed that nearly all who use calcareous manures have doubled their crops within the last seven years."[21] On six Prince George County farms alone, as a result of marling and possibly also of expanded acreages, wheat production rose from 1,358 bushels before any marling began (variously between 1818 and 1834) to 10,638 in 1851: roughly an eightfold increase.[22] It ought also to be stressed—to explain the scale of the improvement and to specify the sort of crisis that it was helping to relieve—that, as with corn, wheat yields in unmarled parts of the Eastern seaboard could be extremely low by national standards. The figure of 4.8 roughly suggested by Table 3 contrasts with state averages of, for example, 16 for Massachusetts, 15 for Pennsylvania, and 14 for Iowa and Wisconsin in 1850. In the same year Virginia, North Carolina, South Carolina, and Georgia had figures of 7, 7, 8, and 5 respectively, suggesting not only the obvious fact that the Old South was performing relatively badly in wheat but that the areas where marling was being pursued had been especially unproductive, even by the low standards of their own states.[23] For many farmers amelioration was an emergency measure.

Few figures are available for the effects of marl on cotton. As we only have information for a handful of producers, there is little point in tabulation. It does not appear that cotton responded quite so well as corn and wheat, and indeed a number of James Hammond's experiments registered substantial falls in yield. It was, nonetheless, generally held that marl could do good work on cotton. "Marl," wrote Ebenezer Emmons in 1860, "seems well adapted to all those crops where the product sought is made up of cellular tissue, as the lint of cotton . . . because lime is the basis of cellular tissue."[24] Ruffin insisted that it was just as effective on cotton as on corn.[25] "In many parts of South Carolina, where marl has been applied," observed James Hamilton in 1844, "the cotton crops have nearly, if not entirely duplicated."[26] James Hammond, however, thought it would be sufficient if he could increase his product by a fifth. "My expectation," he wrote in his diary in 1841, "is to make all my marled land bring 225 to 250 lb. (cleaned) average—*permanently*. If I succeed in this I shall be satisfied though the books promise a great deal more. . . . Ten years will fully test the experiment and if it fails I have no hope left but emigration."[27] Single-year experiments (seed measurement) between 1842 and 1845 show Hammond registering a low of minus 52 percent, a high of 98 percent, and an average of 18 percent.[28] In May 1850 he observed the splendid appearance of his crop, and told Ruffin, "I think marl will immortalize itself here this season."[29] Four other South Carolina planters in the late 1830s and mid-1840s enjoyed yield increases of between 13 and 103 percent.[30]

In addition to enlarging crops, marl could also speed them up. "Accompanied by two other friends, examined the crop and found the marled cotton far in advance of the unmarled," recorded Francis Holmes of South Carolina in his plantation book for 4 July 1844.[31] Ruffin considered the hastening of maturity to be especially important for the more northerly cotton growers, as it reduced the danger of frost damage in, or prior to, the picking season.[32] "The crop of this year," wrote James Hammond in 1843, "has satisfied me perfectly that cotton will mature at least a fortnight earlier on marled than on unmarled land."[33] Other planters noticed the same thing. Even if frost was not a major worry, the possibility that cotton could be sold sooner than usual was an attraction, offering the chance of relatively good returns before the massive quantities of unmarled cotton flooded the market.

For tobacco, oats, rye, potatoes, grasses, legumes, and other Southern crops there is an almost complete dearth of statistical data. Tobacco seems to have been largely ignored by the marlers. Calcareous earth might have damaged the product, so Ruffin never recommended its use.[34] Oats, on the other hand, seem to have reacted well. Peter Sprately of Surry County, Virginia, Thomas Robinson of King William in the same state, and Samuel Black of New Hanover, North Carolina, all recorded a doubling of their crops in the late 1830s (Robinson also reporting the same for his rye).[35] A year or two later Ruffin suggested that yield increases of eight to sixteen bushels an acre were being secured in lower Virginia.[36] As for roots, James Hammond noted that Irish potatoes "consume more lime than any other crop," and in an experiment in 1844 Francis Holmes found that marling more than doubled his potato crop and that a combination of marl and manure raised it by 400 percent.[37] Marl was recommended for grass in Virginia in 1857, and as early as 1824 the Maryland Academy of Science and Literature pronounced that it was not only good for small grains but "even more advantageous upon meadows, pasture grounds, and gardens."[38]

Of all the crops additional to corn, wheat, and cotton, however, the ones which seem to have gained most widely from the application of marl were legumes in general and clover in particular. Clover's intolerance of soil acidity was well attested in the nineteenth century and its luxuriant, if narrowly extended, growth on the calcareous canebrake soils of Alabama gave good indication of what could be expected when acid land received appropriate treatment.[39] Ruffin made his own discovery in the early 1820s, having earlier, after "years of disappointed efforts," given up clover as "utterly hopeless." In 1823, after marling, he got the first crop of red clover he had known "from any acid soil, without high improvement from putrescent manures." Further good yields of red as well as white clover followed: in 1831 a field of 18-inch high growth was the best he had ever seen on sandy soil.[40] A Prince Edward, Virginia, planter found his yield doubled in 1833 after marling, and another in King William described his 1835 crop as "knee high."[41] A few others reported satisfactory results from Spotsylvania, Surry, Nansemond, and stretches of land along the James River.[42]

A report to the Virginia State Board of Agriculture in 1842 on farming in Prince George County noted that on improved farms clover "is sown as soon as the land will bear it, generally with the first small grain crop after the marling. The culture of clover and application of putrescent manures are the chief means relied on to perfect the improvement begun by the marling. Until marl . . . is applied, clover will not grow, and manure yields no profit."[43] A Northern visitor, surveying eastern Virginia generally in 1847, noted that clover, which formerly could hardly be produced at all "without a heavy dressing of putrescent manures, grew luxuriantly upon the application of marl; and one or two crops of clover fallowed in, not only produced fine crops of wheat [through nitrogen fixing] but . . . also made a permanent change and improvement in the soil, which could be made by no other means."[44]

Ruffin's hope was that the development of rotations with clover would extend well to the south of tidewater Virginia. Observing the large crops that could be grown on the lime-rich soils of Rocky Point on the Cape Fear River in North Carolina, he asserted that "if the soil be but made calcareous, the warmth of climate of North Carolina, or even farther south, is no bar to profitable clover culture."[45] Another important leguminous crop was peas. James Hammond reported an "extraordinary" yield of 16½ bushels to the acre on marled land in 1846, and in 1849 he told Ruffin his peas were "outgrowing all precedent—all calculation—all decent limits. I must enlarge all my ideas and plans to be able to control them to a good purpose."[46]

Marl, therefore, could not only substantially boost the yields of three very important Southern cash and subsistence crops—cotton, corn, and wheat; it could also permit the growth on acid soils of legumes vital to rotation farming, providing fodder for livestock and nitrogen and extra animal manure for succeeding crops. Some portion of the increased yields of wheat and corn cited above must have been due to such indirect assistance.

It was not uncommon for farmers to marl a piece of land more than once to secure these various benefits. Generally, however, it seems that one good dose (especially if followed by the other improvements now possible) was enough to give substantially higher yields for decades: "for a period which may be called indefinite, from its remoteness," in Hammond's judgment.[47] Increased productiveness, moreover, was not the only benefit. As indicated earlier, marl had the capacity to improve soil texture, and this was well recognized at the time. Before marling, wrote Robert Tomlin of King William, sandy soils were "liable to be drifted by high winds in very dry weather."[48] Marl served to deepen such soils, in Ruffin's view, and made them "much less apt to wash." It could also help "old gullies . . . to produce vegetation," thereby reversing the process of soil depletion.[49] "My people," commented Hammond, "all say the marl has very much improved the land for working. The stiff parts are mellowed, and the light made more consistent."[50] It also got rid of vigorous acid-loving weeds such as sorrel, which were so difficult to kill off by physical means and which could effectively destroy a grain crop.[51] Lucas Benners of Craven County, North Carolina, wrote in 1835 that some of his land used to be knee-deep in red sorrel; now, after marling, it was not to be seen anywhere.[52]

More fancifully perhaps, but with some conviction, a number of people suggested that marl improved the health of both men and beasts on the plantations. It had, observed Ruffin, the capacity "of restraining or preventing the production of malaria, or the gaseous products of putrefaction of vegetable matter, injurious to health." This had not been believed at first, but the experience of a dozen years or so had been "enough to remove almost every doubt on this subject."[53] Hammond put marl in his stables in 1842 to improve the manure and noted with interest that few of his mules got sick and none died, whereas normally he had been losing an average of four a year. He attributed this "unexpected effect" to "the absorbtion of noxious gases by the marl."[54] "My wife says it has prevented the chickens having the gapes," wrote another puzzled planter. "She declares that never had she so little trouble with the young turkeys: and in fact she verily believes the health of the children is greatly improved."[55]

II

The principal result sought by the marling farmer, of course, was increased income. Through marl, Ruffin believed, the formerly indigent tidewater farmer was now guaranteed "a full and sure reward for his labors."[56] Planters in lower Virginia, observed *De Bow's Review* in the early 1850s, "who before had made only a few hundred dollars from their annual crops, were now found counting up their thousands."[57]

We have already seen how greatly Ruffin's income expanded at Marlbourne in Hanover County. Nine Prince George farmers calculated around 1840 that the increased annual value (gross) of their marketable commodities stood at $426, $466, $736, $1,020, $1,100, $1,800, $2,000, $3,000, and $3,200 respectively. Ruffin suggested that about a quarter of the total ought to be deducted for costs, so the average net individual increase stands at well over $1,000 a year.[58] In Hanover at about the same time Carter Braxton set a figure of $2,000 gross per annum on the increased value of his corn crop alone, while Corbin Braxton, William Fontaine, and Thomas

Robinson of King William suggested totals of $2,600, $750, and $700 a year respectively for all their market produce.[59] Using figures collected by George Powell, who had conducted the 1840 census in King William, and supplemented by others provided by William Fontaine (showing that eighty-nine farmers had marled 9,370 acres in the county), Ruffin calculated that the men in question were, in aggregate, producing $520,000 more grain than they had been before marling began. With an allowance of $4 an acre for costs, he estimated the net increase of "newly created capital" since pre-marling days at $483,020, giving the very high per capita figure of $5,427.[60] This is close to the sum of $5,000 which James Hammond considered to be his net gain from marling over the seven years between 1842 and 1849. "I have no fault to find with marl," he wrote. "I think on the whole it has improved my land 50 per cent."[61] The Georgian *Southern Cultivator* noted with great interest in 1844 that James Belin, a planter on the Pee Dee River in South Carolina, "thinks that the land he has marled, on which he has planted both cotton and corn, will yield him a profit, at the very lowest calculation, of *one hundred and fifty per cent. the present year!*"[62]

Higher profits, in turn, were translated into enhanced land values. Values could, of course, be calculated simply in terms of the amount of money yielded (or saved) by the product. Individual farmers supplied the journals with figures like 3.0, 3.5, 6.7, 7.0, 8.0, 8.5, 8.6, and 9.5 dollars for the product-value increment per acre.[63] The market value of the land, however, was something different, and it was a constant complaint of Ruffin's that this never quite matched the "intrinsic value."[64] Official assessment showed that Virginia tidewater lands (marled and unmarled together) had increased in value by 28 percent between 1838 and 1850, but in the view of the *Southern Planter* this was "not a fair index of their improvement, because lands there are generally rated below their productive value."[65] Values, of course, had been low to begin with as a result of soil weakness and economic depression. The late 1830s in particular were bad years for planters, standing in very sharp contrast to the generally prosperous 1850s. One must, therefore, guard against simplistic correlations with marling.

Around Williamsburg, land prices had sunk in some instances to a mere 75 cents an acre. By 1833 marled farms there were fetching up to $5 an acre, and by 1840 up to $10 or $12.[66] In Surry County, unmarled acres could fetch as little as $1 in the mid-1830s,[67] and similar depressed levels seem to have been quite common elsewhere in Virginia on the poorest, most acidic soils. By 1850, however, the *American Agriculturist* was referring

to prices of $10 to $30 for the most highly improved tidewater land.[68] A
Virginia planter in 1847 drew attention to typical leaps of from $2 to $30
after amelioration.[69] The 1850 census figures for the thirteen Virginia counties where marling was most widely practiced suggest, by contrast, an overall average of no more than $7.9 an acre, and a range of $4.8 (Prince
George) to $12.2 (Gloucester).[70] Even if due allowance is made for the
unmarled land that comes into these figures, it would seem very doubtful
that a price of $30 was at all widely achieved. The average for the marling
counties rose quite rapidly in the 1850s but was still only just over $12 on
the eve of the Civil War, and a few cents higher than the average for the state
as a whole.[71]

High individual figures are recorded in other states, but again must be
seen as exceptions. In the late 1830s a farm in Lenoir County, North Carolina, was sold at $125 an acre, thanks to its rich marl beds.[72] "We have
heard," wrote the *Southern Cultivator* in 1844, "of one gentleman who, a
year or two ago, bought a tract of land, having marl on it, for $1500, and
would not now take $6,000 for his purchase."[73] A planter in Edgecombe
County, North Carolina, where marling was widely practiced, observed in
1850 that such improvement had had the effect of "advancing the value of
land throughout the county, particularly in the vicinity of this village
[unnamed] where lands cannot be bought for less than $50 an acre."[74]
Edgecombe farmland, however, was valued at $5.5 an acre overall in 1850.
It was not until the 1860 census that figures appeared which were more
suggestive of agricultural progress: the average stood at $16.1, and the total
value of farmland was greater than in any other county in the state.[75]

Marl, therefore, helped raise land values. In some cases the increase was
probably quite dramatic, in particular where original levels were very depressed, where marling was followed by other improvements, where the
crops produced could fetch high prices, and where the farm was well situ-
ated in relation to transport facilities and the market. Generally, however,
the advances were probably only modest ones, often failing to reflect the full
extent of changes in productive value. Socially, this may have been no bad
thing. It prevented the exercise from becoming an essentially speculative
one whereby cheap acid land could be quickly improved at moderate cost
and then sold off after a few years at a greatly enhanced price. Even if land
had not been bought initially as a form of short-term investment, rapid
increases in market value might have tempted long-established planters into
selling up and taking their money West or into the lower South. Certainly

the reverse applied: investment and improvement *un*accompanied by a commensurate increase in land value impeded sales. If a farm became highly productive and profitable, but could not command an attractive price on the market, then it made sense to stay put and pocket whatever profits were going from *commodity* sales; and obviously the negative pressures for quitting the land and emigrating were substantially eased by high yields and enlarged incomes. "Where marl is introduced," it was observed of Prince George in 1842, "we hear no more of turning out land or of emigration to the west."[76] The former state of things, Ruffin told the farmers of the same county at the dinner in his honor in 1844, could "hardly be realized by those who were then children, or unborn. Twenty-five years ago, there was scarcely a proprietor in my neighborhood, and deriving his income from his cultivation, who did not desire to sell his land; and who was prevented only by the impossibility of finding a purchaser. . . . All wished to sell—none to buy. . . . Now mark the contrast since presented. In all of this my old neighborhood, and, so far as I know, throughout the whole county, not one individual, after beginning to marl, has emigrated or desired to emigrate."[77]

Around 1820, in the area of Williamsburg, all was decay and ruin. With a diminishing population in the region, William and Mary College, lately prosperous, had fallen on lean times. Recovery, however, at once set in with marling, and it was to that practice, Ruffin asserted, that "the College of William and Mary owes much of its progressive increase within seven years, of from only 17 students in 1834 to 140 at the present session [1840]."[78] Much of Virginia, according to a Nottoway County planter, was now "exchanging the dreary aspect of desertion and decay for one of greenness and prosperity."[79] An exile from the James River returned to his old territory in 1834 and pronounced himself amazed both by the changed appearance of the land and by the new mood of optimism which prevailed among the farmers: "The spirit of industry and improvement have sprung again into life, and the physical energies of the people seem to be endued with a new impulse."[80] Marling, wrote a North Carolina planter, had "had the effect of stopping emigration" throughout Edgecombe County.[81] Farther south, James Hammond's gloomy anticipations of a move West had been dispelled by the success of his improvements.

Again, however, there is a danger of overgeneralizing from the experience of a few planters and a few restricted areas and accepting too literally the enthusiastic claims of propagandists and of unknown men of uncertain reliability. If we look at population changes on a county-by-county basis between 1840 and 1850 we certainly find that Prince George and James City, two of the Virginia counties where Ruffin had observed substantial recovery, had increases of 5.9 and 6.4 percent respectively. Nansemond's population went up by 13.8 percent and Charles City's by 8.9 percent. For the eight remaining Virginia counties where marling was widely practiced, however, the figures are much less impressive: a 1.2 percent increase in Hanover, no increase at all in Middlesex, and falls in all the others—a 5.2 percent decrease, for example, in King William and a 12.4 percent decrease in Surry. The twelve counties as a whole show a fall of 0.3 percent. In Edgecombe, where marling was undertaken more extensively than in any other North Carolina county, there was a healthy increase of 9.4 percent, but in Charleston District—probably the main area of amelioration in South Carolina—it was a mere 1.4 percent.[82] Given the range of possible factors involved in any of these demographic changes, it would be foolish to talk in terms of simple correlations between marling and population increase or decrease. It does seem, however, that marling contributed only very locally to any demographic recovery in the Old South in the 1840s—a decade which ended nearly twenty years after the publication of *Calcareous Manures*. Without it, the decline of the tidewater population would probably have been somewhat greater, but the practice was clearly not widespread enough to have acted as a general check to emigration.

Avery Craven's remarks about marling representing "one of the great agricultural revolutions in American history" and Ruffin lifting tidewater Virginia from the depths of depression to abundant prosperity do, in the light of land value and population statistics, seem highly exaggerated.[83] Even with a longer time-span, census data suggest population stagnation—which, of course, taking natural increase into account, indicates net loss through emigration. Numbers in the dozen marling counties in Virginia grew from 111,366 in 1830 to 111,854 in 1860: an increase of only 0.4 percent. James City County certainly enjoyed an impressive 51 percent advance, but in Prince George the increase was only 0.5 percent and in King William there was a fall of 13.1 percent.[84]

Such statistics suggest that, despite its manifest benefits, marling was confined to a very small minority of planters, and that the calcareous earths of the Old South were grossly underutilized. We shall now see if this was really so, and look too at the extent of liming—a practice, as noted, very similar to marling in purpose and result, though more difficult to conduct because of greater risk and comparative scarcity.

Chapter Seven

The Extent of Amelioration and

Diversification

I

*T*HE extent of marling cannot be measured with much precision. In the case of a fertilizer like guano, which was almost exclusively an import, trade statistics permit fairly exact quantification. With marl, there are no such possibilities. Material came from within the South and, indeed, commonly from the very farms on which it was used. Census data are also thoroughly uninformative. Figures for the numbers of marlers are available for only a single county in a single year: King William, Virginia, 1840. The best one can do, with the assistance of localized contemporary comment, is sketch the broad areas within which marl came to be used and offer some judicious guesses as to the intensity of application in them. Close examination of manuscripts and the main farming journals enables one to pronounce on the matter with a fair degree of confidence.[1]

For Delaware, there is virtually no information at hand. In 1838 the *Delaware Journal* noted that farmers were finding marl daily in one or two of the lower parts of the state, but we hear little about experiments, yield improvements, or enhanced land values.[2] This may have had something to do with the availability there of the other main calcareous material, lime. Maryland is another state where marling seems to have been conducted on only a very limited scale. Some of the earliest experimentation had been undertaken there by the Reverend John Singleton of Talbot County in 1805 and succeeding years. He had discovered marl accidentally during the construction of a causeway, and thought that its shelly constitution might help in breaking down stiff clay.[3] By the 1820s the practice had spread to a number of other counties east of the Chesapeake, but it is unlikely that large numbers of planters were involved. Reports on Maryland geology and agricultural practice by Professor J. T. Ducatel in the 1830s make it clear that marl beds were not being widely utilized; the practice was occurring on a notable scale only in Talbot and Queen Annes counties. Ruffin complained of "neglect and ignorance." The 1850 survey of the state by Joseph Kennedy cited its use in five counties to the east of the Chesapeake (Talbot, Queen Annes, Caroline, Kent, and Cecil) and in three to the west (Anne Arundel, Calvert, and St. Marys). It was the only application specified for Queen Annes, Caroline, Cecil, Calvert, and St. Marys, and in two of them, Caroline and Cecil, it was identified as "the principal fertilizer." In the dozen remaining counties it was not mentioned.[4] The picture, then, is one of marling confined to the shores of the Chesapeake: on the east, above the Choptank; on the west, below Baltimore.

Virginia was the state in which the practice became most firmly and most extensively established. Ruffin's publications obviously had much to do with this. He was by no means, however, the first Virginian to try marl. Sometime before the Ruffins established themselves in Virginia, Captain John Smith observed: "*To manure the land* no place hath more white and blue *marle* than here."[5] George Washington made use of marl as far back as 1760, though without much success. Major William Short of Surry discovered it while digging a ditch and made an unproductive experiment around 1775. Thomas Cocke worked on three small patches of ground in Prince George in 1803, but did not take it up regularly until Ruffin persuasively elucidated its powers almost two decades later. Richard Hill and William Westmore of King William started marling on neighboring fields around 1814, and Hill persisted with it until he sold his estate in 1822.[6] According to Ruffin, however, "Henley Taylor and Archer Hankins, two plain and illiterate farmers, and near neighbours in James City county, were the earliest *successful* and continuing appliers of marl in Virginia," beginning sometime before 1816. They were glad to acknowledge its benefits but unable to understand how it worked. Ruffin later recalled that he had been in the habit of visiting the area at least once a year when Hankins and Taylor were busy at their farming, but had never heard of them or their experiments.[7]

His own trials began at Coggin's Point in 1818 and these proved crucial for the spread of the practice. Local planters were initially slow to follow his lead, and a number of those who did applied their marl carelessly and without accompanying improvements. Indeed it was partly through his fear that its reputation could be damaged as a result of misuse that he decided to write *Calcareous Manures*. One can name about a dozen Prince George planters who began marling in the 1820s, and continued to use it thereafter. Almost certainly there were many more, and Ruffin suggested that around 1830 "there was scarcely a land-holder" in the county "having marl and knowing it, who had not commenced its use, to greater or less extent."[8]

James City and York counties on the northern bank of the James, farther downstream, comprised another area of early advance. Marl was coming into general use on the poor, high land between the James and York rivers: "Almost every person who has marl," wrote Ruffin in 1833, "uses it to some extent—and it is accessible to almost all." James City, he commented some years later, was the county with the longest record of marling "as a regular business," and the broad area around Williamsburg he described as "the most interesting marling region of Virginia."[9] In King William, on the north bank of the Pamunkey, John Dickinson of Moor's Mount reported in 1835 that many of his acquaintances were applying it, and by 1840 at least 9,370 acres had been marled, by just under ninety individual farmers. Marl was abundant in the middle of Charles City County, and according to one planter's account in 1837, "the inhabitants are freely using it." In Hanover, "most decided benefit" had resulted from the employment of marl, in the view of an 1834 observer.[10]

Ruffin judged in 1842 that the practice was most extensive in his own county of Prince George, with James City in second place. The other counties in which it was "extensively applied" included the other four cited above—Hanover, King William, Charles City, and York—and also Surry, Isle of Wight, and Nansemond, along the southern shore of the James; King and Queen, Middlesex, and Gloucester, between the York and the Rappahannock; and New Kent, to the south of the York and the Pamunkey. It was also used to lesser degree in some of the adjoining counties. One reads of its application in Elizabeth City and Mathews, but the lowest of the tidewater counties, including those to the east of Chesapeake Bay, were generally unimportant marling areas. Others mentioned include Sussex, Essex, Caroline, Spotsylvania, and Stafford, but it would seem that only limited application was made in these more inland tidewater counties.[11] Also largely excluded from the marling region was the Northern Neck, between the Rappahannock and the Potomac.

The principal area, apparently, was a rough square embracing around 3,000 square miles with the southern line running from Portsmouth to Petersburg, the western line from Petersburg to about twenty miles north of Richmond, the northern line cutting across the tops of King William and King and Queen counties to the Rappahannock River, and the eastern line from the south bank of the Rappahannock down to Portsmouth (probably with a substantial curve to the west). Inland from tidewater, in the piedmont and mountain areas, the practice was virtually unknown. Articles in the journals on tobacco farming, soil exhaustion, and land improvements in central Virginia usually do not mention marl. If they do, it is usually to underline the fact that it was not in use.[12]

Marling, therefore, was largely confined to the central tidewater counties, representing about 5 percent of the area of the state. Some impression of the intensity of the practice might be gained from the King William County figures: eighty-nine farmers working 9,370 acres around 1840. The 1850 census gives a total farmland acreage of 151,442 and a total "improved" ("cleared land used for grazing, grass or tillage, or which is now fallow") acreage of 84,639.[13] Assuming similar figures for 1840, we can calculate that around 11 percent of the cleared land (and 6 percent of the total farmland) in King William was marled. In Prince George and James City counties the percentages were almost certainly higher, and in most of the other marling counties probably lower. It is, therefore, likely that over the central tidewater region as a whole the proportion of "improved" land which had been marled was well under 10 percent in 1840, and the proportion of all farmland less than 5 percent. As the journals provide very little evidence of any significant spread of marling after that year, 10 percent would serve as a realistic maximum for cleared land for the period up to 1860. This is low enough to explain why marling could run parallel with population loss in many of these counties. If nine out of ten farmers did not marl, then there was a large majority just as likely to join the ranks of the migrators as there would have been had no marling at all been practiced in their neighborhoods. "Marling," Ruffin observed of Virginia in 1842, "has not yet been extended over the hundredth part of the surface to which it may be profitably applied."[14] Advances in land values in lower Virginia, he pointed out a decade later, were the result of improving probably "not more than one-twentieth of the cultivated land" in tidewater. Underutilization persisted up to the Civil War and beyond. "There are . . . in many places," Samuel Jancey wrote of Virginia in 1864, "considerable tracts of land . . . that might be improved or renovated by the application of marl, which is found in abundance."[15] In 1868 Thomas Antisell viewed farmers in Virginia, like those in Maryland, as men who in general had not awakened "to the values of these sources of wealth . . . profusely scattered in the very positions where they can be made so highly beneficial."[16]

The people who publicized the details of their marling operations to the journals, or whose farming was observed and reported by Ruffin, tended to be planters with fairly large holdings—often literate men with an experimental cast of mind. Their names, therefore, are perhaps disproportionately prominent in the journals. But such is the degree of prominence that it can be safely assumed that the most effective marling was conducted by the Virginia gentry—operating individually on an extensive scale, and sometimes knowledgeable enough to attempt maximization of returns by spreading out into the various forms of diversified, rotation farming with increased livestock numbers and proportionately enlarged supplies of animal manure. The names scattered around this study are almost entirely those of tidewater grandees, many of them bound together by old ties of marriage: the Blands, the Braxtons, the Wickhams, Bolling Jones of Walnut Valley, John Selden of Westover, President John Tyler of Sherwood Forest, the Carters of Shirley, the Harrisons of Berkeley and the Brandons, the Cockes of Tarbay and Aberdeen, and the Minges of Sandy Point and Walnut Hill.

In North Carolina, marling was also confined mainly to the central tidewater counties, the practice, however, being even less extensive than in Virginia. The first application was apparently made by Lucas Benners, on the Neuse sixteen miles below New Bern in Craven County, in 1818, the same year Ruffin began his experiments. He met with failure initially, "and was of course laughed at and ridiculed," but he quickly corrected his mistakes and found good returns for his labors over the years that followed. His example, however, was "lost on the community," a fact which Ruffin later found "strange and lamentable" in an area so richly supplied with marl beds.[17] Colonel Isaac Croom, who had a plantation higher up the Neuse in Lenoir County and who had been in correspondence with Benners, started marling in the mid-1830s, and in 1838 Samuel Black commenced operations on a small scale in New Hanover County after reading Ruffin's book. By 1840 another five planters were reportedly using marl along the Neuse and the Trent, and small quantities were being applied to gardens in Wilmington. Between then and 1860 there is a smattering of references to its use in Halifax, Northampton, Bertie, Nash, Pitt, and New Hanover, but very small numbers seem to have been involved.[18]

The only area of North Carolina where a substantial body of planters did apply marl was Edgecombe, an inland tidewater county towards the north of the state. Three subscribers to the *Farmers' Register* started applying it around 1840. "Their success," wrote Ruffin, who had visited the county out of curiosity, "induced others to follow their example," and a distinctive combination of marling and composting helped bring about a notable improvement in agriculture. "The principal material used in this county for improving the lands," observed one local farmer in 1850, "is Marl, of which there are almost inexhaustible beds in different parts of the county." Ebenezer Emmons also noted extensive applications there when preparing his geological survey of the state in the early 1850s. Edgecombe, he claimed, was agriculturally the most advanced county in North Carolina, and the success had been "secured chiefly by her marl beds."[19]

Overall, however, the farmers of North Carolina displayed little interest.[20] As in Virginia, marling was not practiced in the piedmont or mountain areas, nor in the lower tidewater counties. It seems, too, that hardly any applications were made in the tidewater counties to the south of the Neuse and Trent rivers. In North Carolina generally, "where the marl beds are rich and extensive . . . ," observed Ruffin in 1844, "little use had been made of them." One of the "great wants" of the lower parts of the state, he wrote in 1860, was the "proper use of marl." In the Carolina-Virginia border country in 1857 he examined a number of farms and spoke to their owners, declaring afterwards, "I did not see a man who appeared ever to have heard of me before, or who cared whether he ever heard of me again."[21]

Experiences of that sort were a little less likely to befall him in South Carolina. In December 1842, as previously mentioned, he accepted an invitation to conduct an agricultural survey of the state. James Hammond, the governor, had already begun marling, and he knew about the success of the practice in parts of lower Virginia. A few other planters had also experimented. William Scarborough, a Barnwell landowner, had found marl by accident while digging a ditch sometime around 1820 and made successful use of it. Another early user was Morton Waring, who applied it to good effect on his plantation on the Ashley River. By the late 1830s a number of planters in the districts of Colleton, Charleston, and Williamsburg, along the Edisto, Ashley, and Santee rivers, had started trials. But such individuals were few. According to Dr. Joseph Johnson of Charleston, writing in 1840, there were only about six planters in the whole state who were making extensive use of calcareous manures, with another six or so operating at a modest experimental level.[22]

When Hammond began, in 1841, he felt entitled to claim that his was probably "the first serious experiment with marl in South Carolina." A man from Georgia put the idea into his mind, making him question his initial prejudice against it.[23] In the summer of 1841 he read through *Calcareous Manures,* and in the fall he had marl transported from Shell Bluff, twelve miles down the Savannah River from his plantation at Silver Bluff in Barnwell District. "During the year ending on the 8th of November [1842], there were 85 trips made and about 93,000 bushels brought up," he recorded. "The labours of the week," he wrote in his diary in November 1841, "have driven politics entirely out of my mind and everything else but marl—marl." Six years later he had treated more than 2,300 acres. By the early 1850s it could be said of him that he had "marled more land than any other gentleman in America."[24]

It would be difficult to assemble many more than a couple of dozen additional names of marling farmers from plantation records and from the letters and articles available in the journals. Most of them, as in Virginia, were men of rank and substance. The impression one gets is that there were three principal pockets of improvement: one tiny one at Silver Bluff in Barnwell where Hammond was at work, a second around the city of Charleston, and a third farther north on the Pee Dee. "From the very few notices which have reached me of any other marling . . . ," Ruffin wrote Hammond in 1845, "I fear that on you, almost alone, still will rest the whole burden of establishing by practice in S.C. the truth of my doctrine." The practice, Ruffin declared in Charleston in 1852, had "languished, if not ceased, in general, after a few faint efforts."[25] When he visited some old marling acquaintances upcountry from Charleston in 1861 he discovered that one of them, Dr. St. Julien Ravenel, was burning marl to lime and selling it to neighboring planters "whom I urged, in vain, formerly to use the rich marl which underlies and is easily accessible on almost every plantation. . . . It is astonishing, and would seem incredible, that highly intelligent men, as are many of these proprietors, should not have used this manure, in its crude state as marl, and over all their land."[26]

In Georgia, discussion of marling was almost purely exhortatory or antic-
ipatory in nature. Ruffin observed in 1835 and again in 1844 that he had
heard of no case of marling in the state, and although journals like the
Southern Cultivator and *Soil of the South* published occasional pieces on marl,
these had no impact on practical farmers. Daniel Lee, the *Cultivator*'s editor,
thought in 1852 that the time was "not far distant when calcareous matter
will be rightly appreciated in the planting States."[27] A more perceptive comment came a couple of years later from *Soil of the South:* "We want to see the
attention of our planters who have such facilities, directed to this improvement. . . . There ought to be a mighty host, but 'tomorrow, next year, and at
a more convenient season,' have entombed so many good resolutions, that
we dare not hope for large success, while there is space to multiply acres, to
supply the deficiencies of production."[28]

Marling never became a commonplace activity in the Old South prior to
the Civil War. From the evidence of farming journals and manuscripts, it
was practiced on a noteworthy scale in small patches of Maryland around
Chesapeake Bay, in the central tidewater area of Virginia (about a dozen of
the state's 137 counties), in Edgecombe County, North Carolina, and on the
Hammond plantation by the Savannah. Elsewhere, enthusiasm was confined to insignificant numbers.

II

What then of lime, Ruffin's "kindred improvement"?[29] This was of importance only in Delaware and Maryland and in one or two spots in Virginia
along the James and Potomac. Lime, as it happened, presented planters with
a number of difficulties. In the first place, unlike most marl, it required
processing. Second, having a higher proportion of carbonate of lime and
being of low weight it did not bring many fertilizing impurities or much
body to a soil. Third, its concentrated character meant that it could work
very rapidly on vegetable material in the ground, often exhausting the supply in a year or two, and in the long term weakening a soil's productive
capacity if unaccompanied by applications of manure, compost, or other
sources of plant food. Fourth, *Calcareous Manures,* while establishing that the
case for liming was basically the same as that for marling, was not particularly forthcoming with advice on the use of lime. Likewise the *Farmers'
Register.* Fifth, and largely in consequence of these other factors, lime had a
much higher failure rate than marl. Journal reports of deleterious consequences, or of no change, or of modest benefits barely justifying increased

effort and expenditure, were numerous. Marl, by contrast, seemed to please almost all who used it.

Lime's main advantages over marl were its speed of action, when judiciously managed; its light weight in relation to volume, rendering it transportable at lower cost; and its high concentration of calcium carbonate, reducing the amounts that had to be applied to a given area. Shells or limestone rock could be ground into small particles and put straight onto the soil, but the normal way to make them fit for immediate work on the land was to burn them. The resultant "quicklime" was readily soluble in water. It was also highly absorbent, a feature which produced fine crumbling, even under exposure to the atmosphere. This was known as "slaking" and it promoted easy incorporation with the soil. On the other hand, excessive moisture in the lime could turn it into an awkward paste.[30] Burning, ideally, was done at or near the quarry or the shell-bed since it reduced weight and therefore unit costs of carriage.

A good many farmers in the Old South appear to have done their own burning. The process was commonly conducted in the open air, with stones or shells being piled up in layers with long green pine logs and the heap set afire. Fielding Lewis of Weyanoke in Charles City County—identified in his day as the principal pioneer of liming in Virginia—began burning shells in this primitive fashion in 1816 and was still doing so in the 1830s.[31] A number of other planters on the James who were unable to get marl at low enough cost followed his example, importing the shells from beds on the lower reaches of the James and the York. Hill Carter at Shirley was tempted to do the same, but was unable to because of a shortage of timber on his plantation. In Ruffin's view this outdoor method of preparing quicklime was relatively trouble-free, but the burning was "imperfectly performed at great expense of fuel."[32] Michael Tuomey found a few stone or brick "closed" kilns in South Carolina, but declared that there was not a single well-constructed one in the whole state, those presently in operation involving "a vast and unnecessary expenditure of time and fuel."[33] Kilns were widely distributed throughout the towns and cities of the South—principally, one would surmise, to serve building needs. A growing number were appearing in Maryland and Delaware to meet agricultural requirements.[34] One gets no sense whatever from journals and official reports of any substantial, technologically sophisticated industry such as that in operation in Pennsylvania, New York, and Maine.

Liming in the Southeast was only vigorously pursued in Delaware and

Maryland. In Delaware, by the 1850s, it was common in all three counties. Antony Higgins of Newcastle reported in 1853 that it was "universally used, and . . . regarded by our farmers as the principle [*sic*] element in the success already attained." It came in, "in vast quantities," as both stone and quick-lime, from the Schuylkill by way of Philadelphia and the Delaware River. In 1852 George Fisher wrote of its extensive use in farming in Kent County, and in the same year S. P. Houston referred to widespread application in Sussex. Slaked lime in the latter case was bought from both the Schuylkill and the Hudson.[35] For Maryland, Joseph Kennedy cited its use in twelve of the twenty counties, and in many of these—as in Delaware—it filled in for marl. Only two—Montgomery, upstream from Washington, and Worcester, in the southeastern extremity of the state—appear to have used neither ameliorative agent on any noteworthy scale.[36] By the Civil War, Maryland and Delaware were the most calcareously "corrected" states in the South.[37]

Unlike Delaware, Maryland relied heavily on its own resources—in particular, beds of oyster shells from around Chesapeake Bay.[38] Quicklime could also be obtained from kilns "thickly dotted" in and around Baltimore, fed by rail from nearby limestone quarries. The northern part of the state generally was rich in suitable stone, and this no doubt assisted progress in counties such as Carroll and Frederick.[39] There was, however, some buying from the North as well. An 1841 report speaks of a large lime trade up the Chester River which had been boosted by the transpeninsular Chesapeake and Delaware canal. Stone lime was also "very largely employed" in Dorchester County, farther down the Eastern Shore, and some of this may also have been imported.[40]

Only an impressionistic picture can be drawn, but it does suggest that the two most northerly states were well supplied with lime—from within and without—and that it often served as a substitute for marl where the calcareous earth was absent. It is also probable that lime was directed in the main towards increased grain, clover, and, indirectly, livestock production; that it was frequently laid on the land in compost form; and that it was commonly accompanied within improved systems of farming by applications of barn manure, plaster, and guano.[41]

In the four states to the south its substituting, compensatory function was much less pronounced. In Virginia it was largely confined to the James River and to Fairfax and Stafford counties on the Potomac. Ruffin remarked in 1842 that while marl was applied to only one-hundredth of the area where it might have been used, the fraction for lime was a mere ten-thousandth.[42] Fielding Lewis's disciples on the James have familiar names: John Selden of Westover, John Minge of Sandy Point, George and William Harrison of the Brandons, and Hill Carter of Shirley. They appear in the earlier list of grandee marlers and either were using both ameliorators or were varying their practice. Oyster shells were collected from various beds by Norfolk and other points in and around Chesapeake Bay and delivered at planters' landings. Burning took place on the plantation.

Even in the 1820s and 1830s there were complaints about inadequate supplies. There were also worries, as on Shirley, about fuel supplies.[43] As virtually no stone or quicklime was coming down from the Virginia mountains, attention inevitably turned to Northern producers. "Until our stores of lime-stone in the upper regions are unlocked," wrote J. H. D. Lownes in 1839, "we must look abroad for the present and future supply." Hill Carter brought in five hundred casks from Maine—seven hundred miles or so distant—in the late 1820s. John Selden was having New England slaked lime delivered at Westover at around 10 cents a bushel in the early 1840s.[44]

According to Ruffin in 1842, imports made it feasible for liming to spread to a much wider range of farmers. His emphasis, however, was as much on possibility as on specified achievement. There is no evidence to suggest that it was widely practiced along the James by middling to small planters, or by men other than those who already had access to marl. There are odd references to applications in Norfolk, Nansemond, and Southampton, but these do not appear to have been extensive. Elsewhere in lower tidewater it was likewise a case of only small numbers at work.[45] The Potomac basin seems to have been the only rival to the James as an area of occasional liming.[46] One or two instances were cited in Stafford County in the 1830s and 1840s. Some Fairfax men were using oyster shells in the 1820s and 1830s (one estimating costs per acre at up to $12). In the mid-1830s stone was coming downriver to Fairfax from above Harpers Ferry and bought by a man whose total application of lime by 1839 amounted to 35,000 bushels, on over 650 acres. Imported supplies were also available from Georgetown, in the District of Columbia.[47]

Piedmont Virginia had neither marl nor lime in any significant quantity, and lacked the transport facilities to provide either resource at a feasible cost. One or two of the lower counties, such as Nottoway, could get hold of some shells and Northern stone, and there was some sporadic use of lime from Richmond in counties between the capital and Charlottesville, but the general agricultural consequences were usually negligible.[48] "We have no right," declared the president of the Mecklenburgh Upper Corner Club, in

1843, "to expect that marl, lime, plaster, poudrette, or any other substance of foreign growth or manufacture can ever be obtained here sufficiently cheap, to justify their general and extensive use."[49] In the mountains the situation was hardly any better, despite an abundance of stone and timber and a few closed kilns. A handful of farmers were liming in Rockbridge in the early 1840s—but very sparingly. Throughout the whole Valley of Virginia, according to a postwar report, "very little lime has been used . . . as a fertilizer."[50]

The general shortage of lime in the state seemed an absurdity to the *Southern Planter* in 1849. "Vast as are the resources of Virginia for the manufacture of this article . . . it is, nevertheless, a fact that but a small proportion of what is used is burned in the State. Virginia coal is shipped to the North, used there in the lime kilns, and the lime itself sent to us. . . . We have heard it stated that there are many chimneys in the upper country built partly of limestone rock collected abundantly in the vicinity, whilst the mortar which holds the rock together is made of lime transported from Thomaston, Maine."[51]

There was much less limestone available in North Carolina, though one writer observed with dismay in 1834 that a quarry close to Raleigh lay abandoned while all the lime required for the building of the new State House had to be brought in by a thousand-mile voyage from the far Northeast by way of Wilmington, at a total cost of around $12,000.[52] Reports of agricultural liming suggest scattered use, mainly in tidewater, but nothing approaching general application, even in a single county. Before 1850 J. C. Burgwyn was using it in Jones and Isaac Taylor in Craven. Another farmer up near the Blue Ridge was hauling it twenty-seven miles and applying it in minute doses of two bushels to the acre. Ebenezer Emmons suggested in 1852 that lime had always been "too expensive to warrant its employment for agriculture." Similar rock in Wilmington was likewise being ignored.[53] Burgwyn continued to lime in the 1850s. A Burke planter, James Greenlee, was burning in a kiln in 1854—but apparently for building purposes. Stephen Norfleet took delivery of quantities of oyster shells and lime at his river landing in Bertie in eight different years between 1853 and 1861 at a total cost of around $700.[54] But it all adds up to very little. Liming was largely an irrelevance in North Carolina. This was a serious omission in a state that was short of good marl. In 1860 almost all the land remained as acidic as it had been when Ruffin published his *Calcareous Manures* nearly thirty years before.

The story is much the same for South Carolina, despite the traditional use of lime in the indigo industry. A few planters tried it out in tidewater, and in the York-Spartanburg-Laurens stone area (where eight roughly built kilns were in operation in 1844). There was more activity than in North Carolina, but it was still confined to a tiny minority. Michael Tuomey pointed the finger at uninterested planters and the lack of rail access to the state's limestone beds: "Until a permanent demand is created little can be done, and the cost of transportation is yet too high to admit of supplying the market, beyond the immediate neighbourhood."[55] Much of the lime that was used came, again, from the Northeast. Charleston and other coastal towns, it was reported in 1840, "continue to be supplied with Thomaston lime," despite the availability of cheap fuel and large pockets of calcareous material. A little Southern enterprise and a few kilns on the main rivers, it was suggested, could supply all that was needed at half the Maine price. Tuomey also drew attention to the abundance of fuel for lime production, adding, "Yet the market is supplied from the North." For Ruffin, in the 1850s, such imports were "unprofitable and . . . absurd."[56]

There is virtually nothing to be said about Georgia. Thomaston appears to have provided most of what was needed, and the size of the market was probably determined much more by building activity than by agricultural improvement.[57] Some hope was placed in the possibility of railway companies allowing low freights on limestone carried from the interior, but it is not certain that that would have helped matters very much. Even with reduced charges, C. W. Howard of Kingston was still having to pay $10 to transport $6 worth of stone along the fifty miles or so from his quarry down to Atlanta. Freights to Augusta stood as high as $25.25—a 420 percent addition to prime cost.[58]

The predicament of many of the improvement-minded Southern planters was summed up by James Peacocke of Jackson, Louisiana, in 1846. "Some of our northern friends recommend from 50 to 300 bushels of lime per acre," he wrote. "This might do among those who have the carbonate of lime within 100 yards of their doors, and get it calcined there; but those who have to import it and have it re-shipped as we do, until a barrel of lime is worth as much as the land, would find it rather an uphill work."[59] By water, his plantation lay about two-and-a-half-thousand miles from Maine. Payments for lime imports, according to Ruffin, had become part of the "enormous amount of annual tribute" flowing from the Southern to the Northern states. "We of the South," he commented, "have no right to blame any but ourselves."[60]

In explaining the narrow extent of marling in the Southeast, therefore, we cannot introduce lime as a significant factor. If we attempt to fill in some of the gaps in the marl map, we can certainly shade fairly vigorously over Delaware and Maryland, and rather more cautiously along parts of the Potomac and James in Virginia. Elsewhere we need only add a few well-spaced dots. What this means, of course, is that North Carolina, South Carolina, and Georgia were almost totally unaffected by amelioration—as was the entire area of the Old South lying above the fall line. It was a very extensive neglect.

III

Finally, there is the issue of diversification—for Ruffin, the final stage of a comprehensive improvement program. The exercise, of course, was not one of standardized range and sophistication. The term is used in a number of different ways. First, there is subsistence diversification as practiced on small farms and slave plantations to keep labor employed, meet immediate consumption requirements, and counter defects in supplies from the market (while at the same time, perhaps, selling a large portion of the product). Second, there is staple diversification, in which the farmer may alternate two or more cash crops to spread his risks and take some monocultural pressure off his land. Third, there is forage-and-livestock diversification, in which a relative shift occurs from staple onto animal and fodder products, with mutually reinforcing benefits. Fourth, there is area diversification, in which variety increases over a region, though monoculture may persist within separate units of production.

The category of relevance here is the third—and it may have elements of the first and second within it. Of all those cited, it is the most wide-ranging productively, the most dynamic, and the most sophisticated. The first category could, by contrast, be very crude indeed and add up to little more than a cotton, corn, and hog regime with no base whatever in soil amelioration.

Forage-and-livestock diversification posed a number of very obvious questions: 1. Would the new crops grow? 2. Did the planter know how to grow them? 3. Could new livestock be properly looked after? 4. Could livestock products be easily sold? 5. Could additional manure be effectively collected and applied to the soil? 6. Could any loss of staple income, resulting from reduced corn and cotton acreages, be easily made good? 7. Could the farmer work out a rotation appropriate to the physical conditions of his region? 8. Could he get his overseers or foremen to cooperate? 9. Could his slaves acquire the skills necessary for clover cultivation, haymaking, and cattle feeding? 10. Could a functionally diversified labor force be effectively supervised? 11. Could new month-by-month schedules be devised to accommodate the large number of differently phased operations on the farm? 12. Could the farmer work the potentially risk-reducing flexibility of the system as market circumstances changed?

Questions such as these must have given much cause for doubt and timidity. Their answers effectively appear in concentrated, aggregate form in the table below.

The Old South compared badly with the much smaller mid-Atlantic region in the value of its livestock in 1850,[61] and extremely unfavorably in the quantity of its clover and grain production. On an area-by-area comparison it led only in peas, beans, and swine. Equally revealing is the split between the upper and lower Southern states. Forage-and-livestock diversification, it is clear, was almost entirely confined to Delaware, Maryland, and Virginia. The Carolinas and Georgia produced a mere 2 percent of the Old South's clover, 6 percent of its grass, and 25 percent of its hay. The preference there was for the traditional fodder (and foodstuffs) of peas and beans, with livestock often roaming semiwild in search of food.

On the specific links between diversification and amelioration, one very general truth is apparent and there is no need to document it by further assembling of county-by-county detail. It is that marl and lime contributed

Table 4. *Livestock and Fodder, 1850* (Census Data)

	Area (1970)	Swine (Nos.)	Neat Cattle (Nos.)	Livestock ($ Value)	Clover Seed (Bushels)	Grass Seed (Bushels)	Peas & Beans (Bushels)	Hay (Tons)
Del., Md., and Va. as percentage of Old South*	35	31	34	47	98	94	12	75
N.C., S.C., and Ga. as percentage of Old South	65	69	66	53	2	6	88	25
Old South as comparative percentage of Pa., N.J., and N.Y.	+114	+216	+21	−29	−80	−86	+429	−88
Old South as percentage of U.S.†	7	24	21	17	10	7	47	5

*Excluding D.C.; including West Virginia.
†Including all present-day states except Alaska and Hawaii.

to the success of diversified farming in areas where that practice was already well established, and that they totally failed to promote it in parts of the Southeast where staple farming prevailed. Although amelioration helped remove impediments to successful rotational, mixed farming, it hardly features as a *cause* of such advance. Despite strong chemical and bacteriological links between calcareous manuring and diversified agriculture, the former seems to have worked in the main as a permissive factor. Probably most of the farmers responsive to proposals for amelioration were the sort likely to be interested in the other plans for improvement then in circulation. The main variables were entrepreneurial and environmental.

In the border states, mixed farming was already quite widespread, though not all that profitable on acidic soils. The old staple, tobacco, had been hit by periodic overproduction, poor prices, and soil deterioration, and was confined to what Craven terms "a greatly restricted area" in lower Maryland and south-central Virginia.[62] Unable to grow much cotton, farmers were effectively stapleless. Slaves, moreover, were being progressively replaced by free laborers, especially in Delaware and Maryland and in Virginia above the fall line.[63] Major centers of urban demand—and of outlets to overseas flour and grain markets—were provided by Baltimore, Washington, and Richmond. Northeastern ports were also accessible. Wheat and corn were the principal crops, and increasingly in combination with legumes, grasses, and stock. Dairy farming was developing close to the cities, and truck gardening, located particularly in eastern Virginia and the Maryland counties of Anne Arundel and Baltimore, yielded produce whose value more than quadrupled between 1840 and 1860.[64]

An adventurous marling farmer who spread out into mixed agriculture in these areas would not have been doing anything very unusual, although there was a good chance that by combining amelioration and diversification he would have been faring rather well. Calcareous applications would have benefited his clover, helped him feed his livestock more generously, enlarged his supplies of farm manure, and fixed additional nitrogen in his land for the use of succeeding grain crops. Judicious amelioration was probably a decisive factor in guaranteeing the profitability of forage-and-livestock diversification—as Ruffin consistently argued, and as the figures and observations cited in earlier chapters strongly suggest. A very large number, of course, chose to ignore it. Just as marling could be conducted without any subsequent changes occurring in the pattern of production, so, likewise, could mixed farming proceed without any resort to marling. In both instances, farmers would usually be settling for decisively submaximum returns.

In the Carolinas and Georgia there were only two significant centers of marling: Edgecombe County in North Carolina and the Hammond plantation on the Savannah River. Here, once again, planters acted as they deemed fit by their own perceptions and habits. In these instances, the outcome was an avoidance of diversification. Ruffin noted in Edgecombe that on marled cotton land there was "rarely a change to any other crop. . . . There is no such thing attempted as any rotation of crops. . . . Owing to the wide extent of cotton culture, and the small extent of forage crops and products—and the entire want of grass culture and of meadows, even on the lands admirably suited for grass—there is a frequent scarcity of hay. To supply the deficiency, northern hay is imported. . . . This is a shame—a disgrace to the agriculture of Edgecombe."[65] James Hammond in South Carolina was very much a cotton and corn man. In 1850, after the completion of his main marling operations, he had eighty-nine head of livestock at Silver Bluff, of which only two were cattle. He had no sheep. Hogs and work animals predominated. He insisted a few years earlier that it was "impossible to make anything but corn & cotton with our agents, white & black. And to vary our crops etc. materially, it is specifically necessary to break our gangs of negroes into squads of 10 to 20 and place them in separate farms, each squad under a manager. The managers will not pull together on one place, for anything, but corn & cotton."[66] So even the greatest of Ruffin's disciples, and an eloquent advocate of diversification, considered himself unable to capitalize comprehensively on his massive marling labors.

Part Four

Slavery and Agricultural Improvement

Chapter Eight

Operations and Skills

------··◆◆◆··------

AVING established that marl and lime were not widely used in the Old South, and having seen that soil, resource, and crop factors cannot explain very much of this neglect, we are now in a position to move on to considerations of a more institutional nature. Given the social realities of the South and the preoccupations of Edmund Ruffin, we come in particular to the issue of slavery. Was slavery, one way or another, the prime cause of the Old South's failure to engage in extensive, successful land amelioration, and in the various improvements which could follow from it? Must we rest finally on some identification of the institution's adaptive inefficiency? The answer will be decisively, if imprecisely, in the affirmative.

It should be stressed at the outset that most of the area under examination relied heavily on slavery for its labor right up to the Civil War. In 1860, 35 percent of its population was slave. For South Carolina the percentage was as high as 57. Marling operations, moreover, were almost entirely confined to tidewater, and along that wide strip of coastal territory slavery had proved especially tenacious. Lower Virginia, in the words of one observer in 1833, was "peculiarly the slave region" of the state.[1] The broad universality of this feature can be demonstrated by a randomly selected score of tidewater counties and districts from Delaware to Georgia.

Narrowing the focus further by selecting half-a-dozen counties or districts

Table 5. *Slave Population as Percentage of Total*
Population, 1830, 1860: Sample Tidewater
Counties/Districts (Census Data)

	1830	1860
Sussex (Del.)	7.1	4.5
Dorchester (Md.)	26.8	20.2
Calvert (Md.)	43.8	44.1
St. Mary's (Md.)	45.9	43.0
Westmoreland (Va.)	45.7	44.7
Essex (Va.)	60.9	64.0
King and Queen (Va.)	55.9	59.4
Middlesex (Va.)	51.9	54.4
Warwick (Va.)	58.0	58.6
Halifax (N.C.)	55.2	53.2
Greene (N.C.)	44.8	49.8
Lenoir (N.C.)	50.7	50.3
Duplin (N.C.)	39.3	45.1
Georgetown (S.C.)	89.2	85.0
Colleton (S.C.)	78.8	77.1
Barnwell (S.C.)	44.2	56.6
Burke (Ga.)	56.1	70.2
Bullock (Ga.)	25.1	38.1
Wayne (Ga.)	28.7	27.4
Decatur (Ga.)	33.9	49.7
TOTAL	49.1	51.4

where marling was conducted rather intensively, we find an even stronger preponderance of slaves. There is no evidence from printed or manuscript sources to indicate that marling farmers were any sort of modernized minority in these parts, operating reformed relations of production within the free interstices of slave society. Some did use wage or family labor, especially in Maryland and one or two places in Virginia,[2] but they were not numerous.

The most elementary questions on the relationship between slavery and land amelioration concern matters of skill, application, and versatility. What sorts of demands did marling place on slave workers, and how did they respond? Different authors provoke differing expectations. Ulrich Bonnell Phillips suggests the likelihood of improvement foundering on an intrinsic

Table 6. *Slave Population as Percentage of Total Population, 1830, 1860: Sample Marling Counties/Districts* (Census Data)

	1830	1860
King William (Va.)	64.3	64.8
Prince George (Va.)	55.0	59.4
Charles City (Va.)	53.8	52.5
James City (Va.)	51.7	44.6
Edgecombe (N.C.)	47.4	58.2
Charleston (S.C.)	64.3	53.2
TOTAL	58.5	54.8

and extensive black incompetence.[3] Eugene Genovese writes of low-quality labor, grudgingly given; the slave's "poor work habits retarded those . . . economic advances that could have raised the general level of productivity."[4] Kenneth Stampp, however, notes that some contemporary observers were impressed by "the success of many masters in training field-hands to be efficient workers,"[5] and Lewis Cecil Gray suggests that in daily farming operations slaves "frequently displayed considerable skill."[6] The list of observations on the subject is almost endless and certainly inconclusive. There is, in fact, little to be gained here from any general examination of the complex interplay of fear, incentive, education, dexterity, organization, and supervision. Farming systems and their skill requirements varied considerably. The same can be said for improvements. Our approach must be one of precise specificity.

Of the two forms of calcareous amelioration, marling was easily the more onerous. The basic functions were digging, hauling, and spreading. It can be noted at the outset that the most common complaint was not so much that these tasks were too difficult for those engaged in them but that they were arduous and time-consuming. "Our experience in marling," wrote a Virginia planter in 1833, "suffices to convince us that it is not one of the expedients to become rich without trouble."[7] Ruffin himself admitted that it was invariably a "heavy business."[8] "My plan of improvement," wrote James Hammond, "is extensive, labourious and costly. Can I continue it?"[9] In 1842 he calculated that he needed about 4,500 tons a year, boated twelve miles up the Savannah from Shell Bluff and then shoveled into carts for hauling onto the fields.[10] At Coggin's Point between 1851 and 1854, Edmund Ruffin Jr. had 13,573 cart loads moved from his pits: nine a day on average, for four years.[11]

I

The heaviest labor was the digging, and although no great skill was required from the laborer, marl pits often had to be opened and their working organized with considerable care. Basically, it was just a question of removing the topsoil with shovels and then digging a pit from which the marl could be shoveled and thrown into carts. These apparently simple jobs, however, were beset by a number of difficulties. The ground above the marl was likely to have a number of sizable plants, including trees, upon it and a tough tangle of roots. It might be very stony, thereby causing damage to digging implements. Since the surface material stood on marl, it was also liable to have poor natural drainage, and if the soil was at all heavy it could be sticky and unyielding. There was the question of depth: of just how much earth had to be removed before a good pit could be established. Francis Holmes, near Charleston, opened a pit 70 feet by 20 feet in the early 1840s, and remarked on the considerable labor involved "in removing the soil, which was from 4½ feet to 7 in depth." Another of his pits required a 13-foot dig to get well into the marl.[12] Ruffin wrote of a pit on his Coggin's plantation which involved a preliminary and highly problematical clearance of 10 to 12 feet of earth.[13] There could be further difficulties in digging the marl itself. Much of it came away easily, and crumbled as it was moved, but some marls were quite tenacious, with the consistency of soft sandstone or compact clay, and any wetness in the pits could greatly add to the effort of removal.

The biggest problem came from inundation. Water oozed through pit banks and trickled onto the marl. Rain during a storm, or sea water at high tide, could cause sudden flooding. "My soil is so wet in winter," wrote a Virginia farmer in 1833, "that a pit dug, without an outlet, will generally remain full of water."[14] Edmund Ruffin Jr. noted in his plantation diary in March 1851: "*Marl pit* (a large one) which had been dug about 10 feet deep and left in beautiful order last night is now filled with water & caved earth— I shall lose the bottom 4 feet of marl with all the sides—this is a great loss."[15] In February and March 1852 he was much troubled by another pit, the walls of which fell in on 25 February, had to be cleaned out on a very wet day to prevent it from filling up with rain water, collapsed again on 11

March, was flooded by heavy rain on the seventeenth, and was finally brought into effective operation on the twenty-second. Two weeks later another pit on the side of a stream was inundated by rain. "Started to baling," Ruffin recorded on 6 April.[16] Dr. John Palmer, of Balls Dam on the Santee in South Carolina, reported in 1843 that his marling program had been much reduced as a result of "frequent interruptions from freshets."[17] Francis Holmes had one of his larger pits flooded by a high tide. Six of his hands had to work for nearly two days with scaffolding, a pump, and buckets attached to long poles to remove an estimated 4,500 cubic feet of water.[18]

For obvious reasons, problems such as these were much less acute, and often not apparent at all, on riverside cuttings. James Hammond wrote that he had no experience with the widespread difficulties of pit-digging (resulting "chiefly from water") as his marl was simply "cut from the face of the cliff at Shell Bluff."[19] Some could shovel it straight onto flatboats or other small vessels.[20] Corbin Braxton had his marl dug alongside the Pamunkey, wheeled on to a lighter in barrels, and carried eight miles downstream to his landing.[21] A perpendicular bank running straight down into the water could, however, present difficulties, as on one farm on the Rappahannock where the planter had contrived to use a combination of rail track, wheeled vehicle, rope, capstan, and oxen.[22] Generally, however, waterside exposures seem to have posed few problems. A great deal of marl, therefore, must have been removed with elementary skills and a minimum of difficulty.

Even the problems connected with pit-digging could be substantially alleviated if, as Hammond suggested, people took the trouble to follow the advice offered in *Calcareous Manures*.[23] Ruffin considered it no serious matter if marl lay a substantial way below the surface. The depth of the digging could be a positive advantage when the excavation was conducted so as to make use of gravitational force. If the digging was angled to create overhangs and undermining, the earth would come down by its own weight, crumble through impact, and then be shoveled out. Stones and plants would drop in the same fashion, and roots could help initially by supporting the earth and letting it fall gradually. All that was needed for such a labor-saving method of digging was some extra time to let nature assist at its own relatively slow pace. Effective drainage, on the other hand, required the application of a good deal of well-directed manpower. Ruffin suggested that a ditch be cut, with its bottom on the same level as that of the pit itself, lowering it progressively as the pit was deepened. If this could not be done, water should be led into a small basin and bailed or pumped from there into the nearest channel.[24]

How many planters constructed the optimum pit one cannot tell. It is likely that a majority of planters found it laborious enough simply to open a digging without going to the extra trouble of providing an adequate drainage system. If pits filled with water, that was just too bad; either they would be abandoned temporarily or men would be set to work with buckets and pumps. In 1854 Ruffin passed through Edgecombe County in North Carolina where a great deal of marling and accompanying agricultural improvement was going on. "In every case observed," he wrote, "there were serious defects in the manner of working the pits, causing great loss of labor, and in some cases of marl also." If only the planters had taken note of the directions in his book, he commented, many of the difficulties would have been overcome.[25] It may be concluded that since many planters enjoyed relatively trouble-free digging by streams, and since many others, even in advanced counties, opened pits in a rather casual and slipshod manner, the skills required from slaves and overseers were kept to a minimum.

It is doubtful if the carelessness in itself was primarily a consequence of slave labor: planter directives were more crucial. And once the pit was opened, whether crudely or intelligently, the removal of the marl entailed little but the shoveling of heavy earth into the carts, if they came into the pits, or up onto the surface. A premium was set on physical power. "Strong labourers are required in the pit for digging," wrote Ruffin.[26] Francis Holmes reckoned that his prime hands could throw the marl up eighteen or nineteen feet "with a single toss of the spade." On a causeway, where it was shoveled into carts, he kept "an old fellow (a half hand) to assist in loading, and while the carts are away, he breaks up the lumps with the butt of his hoe, and hauls the marl into a heap."[27] No one suggested that simple tasks such as these were adversely affected in any way by the prevalence of slave labor, or that onerous supervisory functions had to be performed. "I rarely staid an hour at the pit," wrote Ruffin at Marlbourne in 1844, "& my overseer never attended to this work when I was at home. . . . But the kind of supervision given, however small in point of time where the work was going on, prevented any considerable loss of work, or omission in filling."[28]

II

As for the next stage—carting from the pits to the fields—not a great deal need be said. No unusual training was required for taking an animal and wagon along a track. "Boys who are too small for any other regular farm labour, are sufficient to drive the carts," Ruffin wrote. "Horses or mules kept at this work soon become so tractable, that very little strength or skill is required to drive them."[29] In June 1844 his main marling team comprised one digger, Joe, and three drivers: Edmund, sixteen, on an ox cart, and Daniel Byrd, fifteen, and Amos, twelve, on mule carts. In July he added another cart and placed a young girl, Phillis, in charge of it.[30] There could be initial difficulties if animals were unaccustomed to carrying heavy loads or if the condition or slope of the roads were awkward,[31] but Ruffin's point about the basic simplicity of the task was one that no one seems to have questioned at the time.

Frequently there was a short boat trip after the digging, as on the Hammond, Minge, and other riverside plantations where there were good exposures some distance along streams, but that too seems to have been fairly straightforward, with questions of cost rather than navigational skill the main concern.[32] Most commercial planters on the rivers, moreover, already had landings at which to receive cargoes. After unloading, the marl might have to be carried a good distance. Hammond was marling a large field three miles from his landing in 1843,[33] but on most other smaller plantations the normal trip was much shorter than that. Even Ruffin at Marlbourne, taking his earth on fifteen different pit-to-field routes from the Braxton plantation next door, had an average hauling distance of less than one mile in 1844.[34]

Discussions on hauling in the literature centered on track construction and upkeep, the sorts of carts that should be used, and the number of oxen, horses, or mules required for pulling them. Ruffin suggested that roads should be led down into the pits, with plenty of turning space provided, and cut through ravines as well to get as close as possible to natural exposures in low-lying parts of the farm. Grubbing hoes would have to be used to clear the way if there were many trees or other strongly rooted plants around, but if the land was relatively clear, then the work could be done with a plow. The track, once cut, could be firmed up by running empty, and then lightly loaded, carts up and down it.[35] Rain was always likely to be a problem, however, especially on clayey soils where the roads could quickly become heavy and mirey in wet weather. The solution here lay in the use of small, lightweight carts with broad treads. Vehicles of that sort could be pulled by a single animal, with loads of five bushels or more.[36] An official report on Virginia marling in 1868 referred to carts of this sort being custom-built,[37] but there is no evidence of such special construction being at all common before the Civil War. Many farmers simply diverted their large ox carts from other operations on the farm.[38] Most also seem to have hauled the marl away as soon as it was dug, and often this meant a lot of water being carried as well, thus adding to the effort required.

III

Before it was put on the fields marl was, ideally, in a fine and thoroughly disintegrated state, so that the soil could gain evenly and quickly from its application. Normally this posed very few problems. "Whether the marl is hard or soft," wrote Ruffin of the principal South Carolina deposits, "it breaks into lumps or crumbles more or less as it is dug."[39] Stephen Norfleet of Bertie County, North Carolina, noted that the shell marl from his pits was "for the most part thoroughly decomposed and ready for immediate use."[40] Lumps could usually be broken by hand or with simple implements.[41] Only in rare cases were they hard enough to require special grinding or crushing.[42] Generally, the marl needed no processing before it was put on the land. The most that scientists asked for was that it be exposed to the atmosphere for a long interval before it was applied to the soil, or perhaps left spread out on the field before being plowed in.[43] "Probably," wrote Emmons, "it is always important to give the marl air."[44]

Another aid to subdivision was composting.[45] Usually, however, this was recommended for quite different reasons. If marl or lime were applied to exhausted soils with very little organic matter present, then they could accelerate the exhaustion by quickening the decomposition of the organic residues. There might be higher crop yields for a time, but in all probability these would collapse within a year or two. Accordingly, suggested Emmons, "marls should be composted with organic matter, [such] as leaves, straw, and weeds . . . or anything which has lived."[46] Such practice is recorded throughout the Southeastern states. One of the very first marlers, the Reverend John Singleton of Maryland, observed in 1817 that his marl did better if combined initially with manure.[47] Ruffin suggested dried marsh earth and salt as valuable materials.[48] Farmers used a variety of soils from uncultivable corners of their plantations, and leaves, pine needles, and other surface litter as well.[49] Ruffin did object, however, to the habit in Edgecombe—a county famous for its composting—of adding excessive amounts of inferior soil which was not worth the effort of hauling.[50] Another combination in the more southerly states was with cottonseed, a valuable fertilizer in its own right. James Cook, for example, used the two together in Georgia, claiming, "It makes the richest looking manure I ever saw."[51]

No one seems to have gone to the extreme suggested to the North Carolina State Agricultural Society in 1869 of combining the marl with fish refuse, peat, and possibly guano and gypsum to make a marketable fertilizer.[52] No doubt there were combinations here and there with one or more of these and other materials, but there was almost certainly no commercial production of compound marl fertilizer in the antebellum period. Composting, when attempted, was done on the plantation. Dr. John Lawrence Smith of Charleston, a scientific associate of Ruffin's from Carolina survey days, suggested that the composts should be "allowed to become old, protected from the rain by a shed."[53] Most planters, however, probably adopted a shorter-term approach and left the heaps in the open. This, according to Ruffin, was normally what happened in Edgecombe, and he recorded the practice without criticism.[54] Exposure of the marl to the elements, after all, served to accelerate the desired process of subdivision into small particles.

Once again, one can detect little that was demanding on slave skills and knowledge. Processing, if required at all, involved only simple crushing and grinding. Composting was just a matter of gathering, heaping, and turning, some of which could be done by children. Nor does there seem to have been a great problem about calculating the proper proportions. Insofar as rules had to be set out, that was a matter for planters and overseers.

IV

The final task was the application of the marl, composted or plain, to the fields. This was a very straightforward, if tedious, business, requiring no notable new talents from workers or supervisors. "The spreading of marl in the field," Ruffin observed in 1832, "is a job that will always be ready to employ any spare labour."[55] Francis Holmes used women. He had little heaps piled at regular distances over the land to "insure equal distribution of the marl, which is too heavy to spread far with wenches."[56] James Hammond reported in 1842 that he laid his land off in squares and dropped a load of marl in each. It was then "spread by hand; each negro taking his square, and carrying his marl on a board or in a small tray. A prime fellow can spread an acre in a day. But it is a hard task, and counting the gang round I have not averaged over half an acre for each worker."[57]

Depositing the marl initially in small heaps was fairly general practice.

James Semple of York County, Virginia, had his foreman measure out seven yard squares, with a bushel deposited in each.[58] A visitor to some of the Virginia counties on the north side of the James in the mid-1830s was impressed by the large number of fields he saw dotted over with four- or five-bushel heaps.[59] Ruffin noted the same sort of thing in Edgecombe, with just one pile to an acre. On his own plantation in February 1844 he counted 942 five-bushel heaps set 30 feet by 40 feet apart.[60]

Marl was normally broadcast over the land and then plowed under.[61] "Scattered all the Marl that has been hauled into the field at Savages in advance of the Plows," recorded Stephen Norfleet in his diary in December 1858.[62] In 1844 Ruffin was spreading "on the fresh ploughing."[63] Francis Holmes took up a rested field for potatoes in 1844, put some manure from his cow pen on it "and the compost and marl broadcast over also; after which, on 13 March, it was all listed, and a furrow run on each side of the list, with the barshear plough covering up the same."[64] The greater the quantity of marl applied, the greater of course was the effort required to set it in the soil.

This sequence of procedures, however, was not universally adopted. Some Edgecombe farmers had their heaps placed at a distance from the fields and carted them on in the spring after plowing had been completed—obviously an awkward operation on soft, freshly broken ground.[65] In York County, Virginia, in the early 1830s, many planters ran furrows eight yards or more apart and dropped their marl into these.[66] Thomas Stubblefield of Gloucester County in the same state scattered his marl and his pen manure or wood litter in alternate rows up and down the fields.[67] Francis Holmes, although broadcasting in the orthodox manner for his corn and his potatoes, preserved the irregular surfaces of his old cotton fields and spread his marl in the alleys.[68] Joseph Johnson, the Charleston physician, waited until his corn plants were in the ground before he put the marl on, applying half to the roots and half at the first hilling.[69]

These, however, all seem to have been deviations from a simple, general pattern of marking-out, heaping, spreading, and plowing. Quite a lot of care, no doubt, was required to ensure that the heaps were properly spaced and the marl evenly spread, but if Ruffin was prepared to assign the work to any spare labor available and Holmes was happy to leave it with his "wenches," they at least must have regarded the work as fairly straightforward. Ruffin had Jem Sykes, six men, two women, and a number of children engaged in spreading work for three days in the spring of 1849. They succeeded in moving more than 1,300 bushels. This, wrote Ruffin, was "more than I had expected. I was not with the hands half an hour of either day, & only to look across the rows, to observe whether equally spread. The foreman was required to watch closely the distribution, & I believe it is as even as can be expected. I did not give any task, nor indicate what work would be expected—nor say a word to stimulate exertion."[70]

The term *laborious* was the one which contemporaries most commonly applied to marling—and clearly there could be difficulties in getting teams of slaves (as well as free laborers) to sustain satisfactory work rates. There were also awkward problems, particularly in digging and hauling, and many planters no doubt either failed in their attempts to minimize these or chose to ignore them altogether, abandoning the whole exercise if it became too troublesome. In terms of the skill, knowledge, and interest required from the labor force, however, marling was probably about as undemanding an exercise as any in the agricultural South. And there was nothing peculiarly rough and unsophisticated about Southern practice—to match what Phillips called the "crudity of the labor."[71] Marling, wherever resorted to over the centuries, had customarily been a ponderous and labor-intensive affair. The issue of slave ability, therefore, seems largely irrelevant to any explanation of restricted amelioration.

What may have been more important as negative factors were problems concerning the amount of manpower, animal power, and equipment that could be *released* for marling operations within plantations where resources were often very modest and, in quantitative terms, relatively fixed. There could have been difficulties to do with bending existing farm schedules, minimizing opportunity costs, and securing an adequate degree of task specialization. We can, therefore, pass on from the abilities of the slave worker to the flexibilities of the slave plantation.

Chapter Nine

Factor Diversion, Schedules, and Costs

I

*I*F there were problems having to do with the release of plantation resources, their scale obviously bore some relation to the amounts of marl that had to be applied to the acre. These varied substantially between one plantation and another as a result of differing notions concerning the respective virtues of liberality and restraint. They were also much affected by physical considerations such as soil depth, organic content, the proportion of carbonate of lime in the marl, and the climate.

"Depth of soil," observed James Hammond, "and the amount of vegetable matter in it must chiefly regulate the quantity of marl." The greater the depth and the higher the organic content, the larger the amount of marl that could be safely applied. Hammond also held that in relatively hot regions, such as his own, much caution was required, especially for the first dose.[1] "As regards the quantity of marl to be employed upon our lands," wrote Lawrence Smith, "it is difficult to come to any positive conclusion, even after knowing its strength." He advised planters to experiment for themselves and arrive at their own estimates.[2] Ruffin persistently argued the point about organic content and the dangers of plowing too much marl into exhausted land without accompanying applications of vegetable matter for the carbonate of lime to work on. "The experience of planters," wrote

Ebenezer Emmons in 1852, "is, that very poor soils are injured for a year or more by the application of marl, except in small quantities. One hundred bushels is regarded as sufficient for sandy exhausted lands."[3] He advised staggered doses on such soils. Better land, however, could take a large quantity all at once, and a decade or more might elapse before any re-marling was needed.[4] Ruffin and Hammond in fact believed that if damaging factors did not intrude, and if concomitant improvements were attempted, one good marling could do for all time.[5]

In Virginia it seems that the most common quantity applied to an acre was something between two hundred and three hundred bushels.[6] Farther south, the amount was usually less.[7] A rough guess, based more on impression than on arithmetic, might place the average overall at about fifteen tons or three hundred bushels per acre (using Hammond's equivalent of 105 lbs. to the bushel).[8] Usually this was the aggregate or the only dose. Making some allowance for possible later applications, however, a figure of fifteen tons might be suggested as the maximum likely average. Over a generation, that would represent an annual average of 12 cwt.: quite a small amount when compared with normal quantities for barnyard manure (and British marl), though a lot when compared with typical applications of commercial fertilizers.[9]

Such hazy figures obviously can have no more than a suggestive function here. If marling was largely a once- or sometimes twice-and-for-all operation, the central questions concern the ability of planters to find resources *for use in a relatively short, intensive burst* of amelioration. The assortment of statistics and observations available suggests quite strongly that factor diversion did not present serious difficulties. Marling would usually be fitted into the annual pattern of farm activity without causing excessive strain—and this was the case not so much in spite of slavery but in some measure *because* of it.

The normal habit was to use labor for marling when it would otherwise have been idle or engaged in work of little importance. Ruffin advocated and practiced a more specialized system, using a small force of designated marlers over a substantial portion of the year, but he was not at all typical. In 1841 he wrote of the common "transient and irregular labors" which were "always performed at great disadvantage. . . . . If, on the contrary, but one horse were kept regularly hauling marl from the pit to the field . . . the first year's manuring with that small force alone would amount to more than all that is done by a large farm force in the usual irregular manner, and at uncertain times. And neither would the regular employment of the small force preclude the using of the irregular and large—but would make it twice as useful, by making every thing ready for the employment whenever a leisure time occurred."[10] He did not say how many hands would be required to dig the marl, load it, and then lead the single horse to the fields. One might guess that between two and four would probably have sufficed, but on the normal, relatively small plantation even the minimum of two would probably be more than could be spared on any permanent basis. The 1860 census shows that slaveholders in the six states from Delaware to Georgia owned only 10.5 slaves on average. Given likely numbers of women, children, and old people, there could only have been at most three or four prime hands per farm. People owning more than ten made up a minority of 31 percent of the total; those with over twenty represented only one-eighth.[11]

Even Ruffin could not carry specialization to extremes. He cites a two-part operation at Coggin's Point in which marling was begun at the start of November 1823 and carried on until 31 May 1824. By the end of May he needed the horses for plowing work and in mid-June the entire labor force had to be employed in harvesting. Even in the marling period the job could be temporarily suspended if the weather was bad or there was "some pressing labour of other kinds" to be performed. Moreover, the special force of two men, two boys, two horses, one mule, and three carts was only used for digging and hauling. The preliminary work of removing the covering earth and exposing the marl was done by a larger body of workers: for one of the pits, nine ordinary hands, one old man, six women, two boys, and a young girl. Spreading on the fields was also done by spare labor when available.[12]

Table 7. *Slaveholding in 1860* (Census Data)

State	Average Number of Slaves Owned	Percentage Owning Fewer than 10	Percentage Owning Fewer than 20
Delaware	3.1	95.7	100.0
Maryland	6.3	81.3	93.7
Virginia	9.4	72.1	88.9
North Carolina	9.6	70.7	88.3
South Carolina	15.1	60.7	87.6
Georgia	11.3	66.2	84.5
TOTAL	10.5	69.4	87.9

In 1828 marling work was confined to five days in January, the whole of February and March, and from 5 August to 27 September: less than a third of the year.[13] Similar irregularity was in evidence at Marlbourne. In 1846 Ruffin had 43,259 bushels dug and hauled by the end of July, and only an additional 5,527 by mid-December.[14] Harvesting, plowing, and wheat sowing had intruded. In 1849 he had 30,527 bushels out by 17 May. Over the following four months a mere 5,625 bushels were moved.[15]

One ought, therefore, to talk of partial specialization. Some planters were prepared to follow Ruffin's advice, but they were not very numerous. In Virginia, John Dickinson, in an address to the Fredericksburg Agricultural Society in 1833, recommended that farmers put two or three hands, an ox-cart or tumbril, and two good mules aside for marling—"separate and distinct from the crop hands."[16] Collier Minge reported that he made continuous use of two men and a boy between 15 May and 25 December 1834 for digging marl on Ruffin's land at Coggin's Point and carrying it fifteen miles by water to his own plantation where a single cart, with horse and hand, was waiting to haul it to the fields.[17] In 1834 the same work force (with the boy missing for the first few weeks) dug and transported 17,000 bushels between late March and late December, with a twenty-day break in October for boat repairs.[18] In 1841 Bolling Jones of Surry County, Virginia, declared himself dissatisfied with the slow progress of his marling, which had been going on since 1834 "at leisure times," and announced that he had just "allotted a separate force for the especial business" so that he could complete the treatment of his arable land by 1842.[19] Edmund Ruffin Jr.'s plantation diary shows him digging and hauling between January and 30 April 1851 and again between 16 January and 13 May 1852. "Main job of work has been marling," he recorded for the month of March 1852. The number of loads moved—2,405 in the first year and 4,410 in the second—suggests a substantial degree of specialization, with a good number of men and carts involved. On 4 March 1851 he noted that digging and loading alone required four men. The same number, or more, were needed for hauling: on 1 April 1852 he had as many as five carts at work. But even he confined his operations to about one-third of the year. "Marling for the season stopped today from press of work," he recorded on 13 May 1852.[20]

"I shall put in 18 hands & six carts & hope to marl at 200 bushels to the acre," wrote Hammond to Ruffin in November 1841.[21] In the event he too settled for specialization on a somewhat smaller scale, he would need eleven prime hands to dig, transport marl up the Savannah, and unload at the plantation, and an additional two hands with two carts to haul from the landing place to the fields. There were "thirteen hands and two mules lost to the crop," the slaves representing perhaps more than a fifth of his total work force. This loss appears to have been sustained throughout the year. The carts, he reported, were "constantly engaged in hauling" and the boat, usually making two trips a week, had brought in as much as 93,000 bushels in the year up to 8 November 1842.[22] This is probably the largest and most extreme instance of specialization in the South. It was abandoned, however, once the fields were reached. As on Ruffin's plantations, spreading was work for a variety of hands.[23]

Specialization, therefore, was probably confined to only a handful of large plantations, and on these it was not normally sustained throughout the year or applied to every stage of marling work. There are, moreover, indications that even on these farms it was not always easy to implement. Hammond with his large field force of over five dozen seems to have experienced few problems.[24] He reckoned in 1842 that since he was not opening any new land he could get his marling done "without interfering with other plantation work, or lessening the number of acres planted per hand."[25] It is interesting to discover, however, that Ruffin's operations of the mid-1820s at Coggin's, referred to above, were partly conducted by hired laborers.[26] So too was Collier Minge's digging and boating from Ruffin's land in 1833 and 1834, and the marling work of Corbin Braxton in King William County around 1840.[27] Ruffin made no general habit of resorting to the slave-hiring market, but it seems likely that he and others periodically experienced the sort of problem alluded to by an intending marler: "A few laborers must be hired," he wrote, "for I have not more than sufficient to work my land."[28]

Ruffin, Minge, and Braxton may have had to use hired labor on occasions simply because they wanted a relatively specialized task force. Had they been prepared to proceed somewhat more casually, confining marling to periods of relative inactivity on their plantations, there might have been no great difficulty. Generally, planters ignored Ruffin's perfectionist and often impractical advice. He took note, and disapproved, of the apparent casualness over tidewater Virginia as a whole, and in King William, Gloucester, and Prince George counties specifically, as well as in Edgecombe County, North Carolina.[29] There were, wrote a planter from Surry County, Virginia, in 1837, "not more than one or two farmers" there "who allot a separate force for marling."[30] Francis Eppes of Prince George told how he began marling in September 1839, treated forty acres, abandoned it when crop sowing and subsequent activities absorbed the energies of his entire labor force, but was ready to start again in the late summer of 1840.[31] A Gloucester planter wrote in September 1839 that he had been able to harvest his wheat earlier than usual that year and had released his whole labor force of sixteen or seventeen hands with four tumbrils for more than a month of digging and carting marl and marsh-mud before having to stop to pull fodder. In that time he had managed to treat fifty acres.[32] W. C. Jones of Surry County reported that he had started marling in 1836, the work being "only done at leisure times, after finishing the crop." In the course of five years he had lifted and spread about 40,000 bushels over 210 acres.[33]

Stephen Norfleet, a major improving planter in Bertie, North Carolina, had about sixty field hands and arranged for his digging, hauling, and spreading in 1858 to be done between 3 and 11 September and off and on between 13 and 30 December. Cotton picking, significantly, began on 22 September. In all, marling occupied twelve days. On eight of these there was digging, on five carting, and on two spreading. Digging involved 33 hand-days and hauling, a total of 17 cart- and 17 hand-days.[34] No indication is given of the labor force needed for spreading. Norfleet was engaged in a variety of other improvements, with manure, compost, guano, plaster, clover, and peas, and when he was at work on these he made much use in his diary of the term "Balance of Hands." A variety of tasks was being performed, and men and women were moved around according to the needs or the slack of particular days and weeks. It is notable that on the dozen days of 1858 when he recorded marling operations he made no reference to any other activities, apart from the plowing that took place immediately after the marl was spread on the land. Presumably these were "leisure days"—on either side of the busy periods of cotton and pea picking and wheat and clover sowing.[35]

Dr. John Palmer on the Santee began digging in September 1838. "In two wet days," he recorded later, "I had about two thousand five hundred bushels heaped ready to be hauled the winter following."[36] Francis Holmes estimated in 1844 that to dig and cart between 900 and 1,000 bushels for seven acres he needed two prime hands for five days for the preliminary digging, two prime hands for two days and three prime hands for three days of throwing out and loading the marl, half a hand (an old man) to help with the loading for five days, and two drivers and two mules for five days to cart the marl six hundred yards to the field. Digging and hauling were confined to a very short space of time, the work starting on 26 February and ending around 7 March. Spreading began more or less right away and was followed by corn, potato, and cotton sowing.[37]

In 1849 James Hammond marled roughly twenty-two acres with just over 4,300 bushels. By that time he seems to have abandoned his specialized marling force. If attention is confined to the days when marl work was specified in his Plantation Book, the following sequence is apparent:

1 Sept.	3 hands hauling (total number of hands available, 63)
4 Sept.	3 marl carts running (total hands, 63)
24 Oct.	49 hands scattering dirt and spreading marl (total hands, 61)
25 Oct.	32 hands spreading marl (total hands, 61)
26 Oct.	32 hands spreading marl (total hands, 61)
27 Oct.	32 hands spreading marl and scattering dirt (total hands, 61).

As cotton picking began in the last week of September, marl work in October represented a clear diversion (with forty hands picking on 10 October, but only seven doing so on the twenty-fourth, twenty-fifth, and twenty-sixth).[38] However, the work seems to have been slotted in fairly conveniently, and overall it involved only a small fraction of the labor force available to Hammond in 1849. Assuming an average of sixty-two undifferentiated hands (from a total slave population of seventy-four) and a working year of 285 days,[39] we have a total of 17,670 hand-days. Assuming too that the work on 24 and 27 October was evenly divided between dirt and marl, we can calculate that marling absorbed only 111 of these hand-days in 1849. We have no figures for digging and boating, but Hammond estimated in 1842 that eleven prime hands could move 2,200 bushels in six days; i.e., that 1 hand-day was required for 33 bushels.[40] Using this figure, we need 130 hand-days to supply the 4,300 bushels used in 1849. The grand total, therefore, comes to 241: 1.4 percent of the labor time available (and only 0.6 if one were to split the hands evenly into prime and half). He had completed the bulk of his marling by the end of the 1840s, but the 22-acre operation of 1849 was probably more in accordance with the normal scale of a planter's annual marling work than were the vast undertakings which he set in motion at the beginning of the decade. It may be countered that other farmers usually had far fewer slaves as well. Working with a prime force of ten, however, one would still—on the Hammond schedule—get a diversion percentage of only 8.5. It must also be remembered that Hammond had special problems in fetching his material from a point on the Savannah some twelve miles distant from his plantation.

Marling, then, could be fitted into existing schedules without too much trouble. Ruffin noted for Prince George, Virginia, that "the operation ceases on almost every farm from March until in August."[41] Most marlers in the more northerly states found the late-summer-to-early-spring half of the year quite sufficient for their purposes. It offered much relatively idle time, avoiding most of the onerous months of plowing, sowing, and harvesting. The pattern could, however, be complicated by the growing of legumes or winter grain, or by livestock raising. Improvement on a wide front led to additional labors with manure and compost heaps, commercial fertilizers, draining, and ditching. (Stephen Norfleet and the Ruffins present good examples of planters who could implement many of these concomitant advances and still find a good number of odd days to fit in their marling.) In the cotton belt there was no extended slack period between August and March. The cotton harvest might not begin until the fall and could continue into the subsequent year. Our examples above, however, show one planter selecting two wet September days one year and getting 2,500 bushels out, and another squeezing his marling in just before crop sowing in the spring. Hammond chose odd times before and during the cotton-picking season, and apparently found it no great inconvenience to divert labor from the picking for a day or two in October.[42]

There could, on and off throughout the year, be a good deal of spare time on a plantation, whether in the border states or in the Deep South. This was potentially awkward for the planter because slaves could not easily be shed in slack periods and reclaimed when the pace of work speeded up again. They had usually to be fed, clothed, and housed throughout the year. In terms of planter economics, therefore, it made sense to maximize the amount of productive labor a slave could be engaged in. This point has been strongly argued by Ralph Anderson and Robert Gallman. There was, they suggest, a systematic "desire to keep all hands busy at all times" within slave agriculture. "The pressures to produce a full work year were not felt only by slaveholders, but these pressures were felt with peculiar intensity by slaveholders."[43] They specify a distinct problem of seasonality, the main solution to which—given a reluctance to engage in multistaple production and the difficulties of developing local hiring markets among planters affected by the same irregularities—was diversification into food production for home use.[44] Crop variety by itself, however, did not use up *all* the slack. This is clear from an abundance of references to "leisure time" in the journals. Anderson suggests elsewhere that crop work seldom exceeded 220 days a year: "Between 70 and 80 days (in a 290-day working year) remained for secondary or non-crop activities such as ground clearing, construction, chores and maintenance, fencing, ditching and textile production." Plantation managers, he observes, "dovetailed crop activities . . . and also primary and secondary activities in such a way as to minimise idle time."[45]

Marling, of course, was an ideal secondary activity, as the digging and hauling could be done more or less at any time of the year. There might be odd days of heavy rain, frost, or snow when work was impossible, but there was no special season when the job had to be undertaken. It could be begun in one month and perhaps continued in another. Irregularity was no problem. Indeed there was a lot to be said for leaving the dug marl just lying around until it was possible to haul or spread it. This, as we have seen, could help dry it out and assist its disintegration into small particles. Marling did involve heavy labor for men and beasts, but there was nothing very unusual about this in the slave South. Anderson notes that a hand on the plantations he examined would be required to hoe on average two miles or more a day with heavy, awkward implements. The physical demands of ditching, fencing, planting, and harvesting were also very considerable.[46] Marling represented merely a further category of onerous work for the slave.

It would be difficult to argue, then, that slave farming stood in the way of marling because of the numbers of hands, animals, and carts required or because of the scheduling of the work within the various farm calendars. Indeed the presence of seasonally idle slaves on many plantations may almost have *induced* some planters to undertake marling. A few of the larger plantations engaged in partial team-specialization, but the majority seem to have ignored Ruffin's unrealistic advice and to have succeeded in fitting the work into whatever days or weeks of the year happened to be convenient. In the words of an official report on Virginia in 1868, by which time many of Ruffin's perfectionist notions had been long forgotten, "The work of removal goes bravely and systematically on; and with good, active drivers and sufficient teams, a large surface may be marled *during periods of leisure.*"[47]

II

The matter, however, cannot quite be left there. Additional comment is required on costs and returns, for it may well be that although many planters had numbers and time to spare for the occasional bout of marling, even a temporary movement of resources into this activity was difficult to justify in terms of the balance of effort and return. The evidence presented in chapter 6 suggests that this is unlikely: the impact of marling on crop yields and, to a lesser degree, on land values seems to have been quite pronounced. The emphasis there, however, was on benefits, often viewed in gross terms. Little attention was given to outlays.

Costs depended on three main variables: the extent and duration of digging, the distance the marl had to be transported within (and perhaps to) the plantation, and the amount applied to each acre. The question of quantity has already been considered and seen to be awkward as a result of wide differences in practice. Digging and transport expenses also varied enormously—to the extent that averages become virtually meaningless. Of all the costs it does seem that hauling was generally the largest one. The comparative advantage of using lime or marl, according to Willoughby Newton of Virginia in 1853, depended "mainly on distance, as the principal expense is incurred in hauling."[48] The reason probably was that carriage involved not only laborers but animals and carts as well.

Ruffin estimated for 1828 that a horse added more to marling costs than a hired prime slave: 33.1 and 31.2 cents respectively per day. Mules were considerably cheaper, at 5.2 cents. Carts were 5.0 and tools 3.0 cents. Women, girls, and boys were all reckoned at 17.4 cents. Applying these figures to a substantial marling operation, Ruffin worked out that the entire outlay amounted to $51.47 (for 3,680 bushels). Further calculations show that the initial preparation of the pit absorbed 46.7 percent of the total cost (the work being unusually onerous, involving eight oxen); digging, loading, and hauling, 49.1 percent; and spreading, 4.3 percent. Figures for a 4,036-bushel operation at about the same time give, in the same sequence, percentages of 38.1, 55.8, and 6.1.[49] Francis Holmes provided data for a small 924-bushel job in South Carolina in 1844. These do not include spreading, but if 6 percent is added to his total of $12.40 (Ruffin's increments in this respect being 4.4 and 6.5 for the two operations cited) we find that preparation took 11.4 percent of the costs, digging and loading 37.3, hauling 45.7, and spreading 5.6.[50] High carting expenses were not the consequence of particularly long journeys to the fields. Ruffin gave two averages of 997 and 847 yards, and Holmes one of 600.[51]

A correspondent of the *Farmers' Register* wrote in 1842 of a total cost of 99 cents an acre, excluding spreading. Adding 6 percent for the latter, as before, we get a figure of $1.05: potentially applicable to much of Virginia, in

Ruffin's opinion.[52] Holmes's estimate in South Carolina (again adding on probable spreading costs) came to $1.88.[53] Ruffin's operations in 1828 cost him $2.08 an acre, and in 1845 he wrote James Hammond that he had been economizing on labor at his pits "so that I am sure that my estimate made last year, of $2.70 for applying 300 bushels, would be now reduced to $2, at most, & perhaps to less."[54] Dr. Joseph Johnson in South Carolina reckoned on a range of $2 to $5 per acre in 1838, and Ruffin, writing of marling operations covering some 9,370 acres in King William, Virginia, in the years up to 1842, suggested an average of $4.[55] Professor Henley Rogers estimated greensand marling on a New Jersey farm in the early 1850s to cost $5 per acre, and in 1857 L. Y. Atkins of Fredericksburg, Virginia, wrote that the expense of restoring land by marl and clover totaled between $5 and $7.[56] Two of Ruffin's early operations in the 1820s were unusually expensive— one costing $5.34½ an acre (which he thought at a lower and more appropriate level of application should have been $3.57½), the other $7.36 (again, partly because of excessively high doses of 572 bushels an acre).[57] According to Solon Robinson, James Hammond was running up marling expenses of $10 an acre on swamplands on his plantation.[58] This was almost certainly a good deal higher than Hammond's norm, for he seems to have been applying very large quantities—1,000 bushels or more—to ground of this sort, rich in organic material. William Shultice of Mathews, Virginia, estimated his average costs at $8.12, but his marl came from the York River and delivery charges made up 75 percent of the figure.[59] Finally, we have an estimate of $12 an acre for Hill Carter's marling up to 1837 at the Shirley plantation in Charles City County, Virginia. According to Ruffin, this work had been done under exceptionally disadvantageous conditions.[60]

As to typicality, we may take some guidance from Ruffin's observations on King William County in 1842. A good deal of marling had been done there, and by that year Ruffin had become a very informed witness for Virginia as a whole. The cost of marling, he wrote, "varies with every operation: but it is probable that $4 the acre would be an ample allowance."[61] Certainly figures much higher than this can usually be explained by exceptional circumstances. Four dollars an acre—incurred perhaps only once— was a fairly small sum compared with the amounts spent on Peruvian guano or on marling in Britain.[62] It might also be noted that the *opportunity* costs must have been very low if, as suggested earlier, planters marled at relatively slack times of the year. It can be a little misleading to add up figures for, say, slave upkeep during a marling period if the people in question would otherwise have been relatively idle but still in need of shelter, clothing, and sustenance.

Hammond found his heaviest operations "very expensive; but . . . profitable, notwithstanding."[63] William Harrison of Upper Brandon estimated in 1833 that the increase in his very first crops of corn and wheat would repay the whole cost of his marling.[64] The editors of *Soil of the South* advised Georgia planters, in the light of the benefit yielded by marling in the more northerly states, that they "could well afford to encounter difficulties, and incur expense, for its accomplishment."[65] Marl and other improvements at Marlbourne brought Ruffin profits of $4,496 a year on average during the period 1845–48.[66] When he visited Hill Carter's Shirley estate on the James in 1837, he was concerned at the large outlay for marling work there, but believed that four years of rotation farming on the treated land would repay the costs and that with really good returns Carter might recoup in only two. Carter himself was sufficiently impressed by his results to want to get hold of another 5,000 to 10,000 bushels a year. The fields, moreover, would be permanently improved. "This cost of marling," as Ruffin wrote, "is about as much as every emigrant from Virginia to the west pays in labor, per acre, for the mere clearing the forest growth from his new land—though he may have bought the land as low as $1.25."[67] Following his investigation of Prince George marling around 1840 he suggested that corn crops were up in value by $10 an acre and wheat by $6, and that about three-quarters of the increased product could be regarded as clear, net profit.[68] In 1842, when he attempted to measure the improved productive value of land known to have been marled in King William County, he calculated the crop increase at over $31,000 per year, compared with an initial expense of over $37,000. The deficit of $6,000 was no cause for concern: most of the costs applied to one year only, whereas increased yields could be sustained for an indefinite period, and possibly enlarged as time went by.[69]

There is little need to continue on this point, otherwise there would be excessive duplication of material presented in chapter 6. Substantial advances in crop yields were cited there. It was also noted that individual planters gave figures such as 3, 3.5, 6.7, 7, 8, 8.5, 8.6, and 9.5 dollars for the product-value increase per acre. The land value was quite another matter. If, however, farmers were not too worried about selling, and were happy simply to receive the extra cash for their enlarged crops, it would seem that marling was broadly worth their while financially. Even if we say—

very conservatively—that the bottom end of the $3–$9.50 range for crop-value increase per acre is the correct one, and if we push Ruffin's $4 per acre for costs up to a notional $6, the fact remains that a planter marling in the spring of one year could break even by the harvest of the next and, if careful and attentive, could look forward to many years on the higher-yield plateau without any additional applications. Adding the point made earlier about low opportunity costs, there seems little doubt that marling could be a very rewarding improvement.

Two final qualifying observations must be offered. First, most of the evidence on net returns comes from Virginia. We cannot be certain that the benefits of marling in, let us say, South Carolina consistently and substantially outweighed the costs. This is a matter we shall return to. For the moment it can simply be recalled that marl did well on cotton. With relatively low opportunity costs on single-staple plantations, land amelioration was almost certainly a profitable undertaking. Second, as noted earlier, the agricultural journals had an inevitable bias towards success. A marler who had made big profits would generally have been more eager to communicate the fact than a man who had met with depressing failure. All the same, had there been a widespread conviction that marling was unprofitable, some of this would have seeped through into the farming literature. This certainly happened with liming. As it was, there were virtually no negative voices to be heard. The same thing is true of the manuscript sources: a planter who had grave doubts would have expressed these with little hesitation in his private diaries and plantation books.

It seems fairly clear, then, that marling was not particularly demanding on slave skills, that it could be slotted into slack periods in the plantation calendar, and that short-to-medium-term returns seem generally to have outweighed the costs. There were problems, of course, and their aggregate force will have to be considered later. They seem insufficient, however, to explain why the vast majority of Old South planters chose to ignore Ruffin's prescriptions. The focus of analysis, accordingly, must be widened from the individual plantation unit to the slave economy and society at large.

Chapter Ten

Transport Facilities and Farm Inputs

THE main forces restricting the geographical range of Ruffin's reforms lay within Southern society at large. The two most potent were poor transport and negligent entrepreneurship. Both were, in considerable and ironic measure, functions of the institution which Ruffin was so determined to protect. Transport becomes an important issue for the simple reason that planters usually lacked accessible marl or lime-producing materials in and around their own properties. The marls of the Old South, though rich and abundant, were unevenly distributed, and limestone rock was typically an upcountry resource. Farmers wishing to ameliorate their lands usually had to import. In tidewater counties movement of marl could be a matter of only a mile or two. Inland from the fall line, however, with marl absent and lime only patchily available, carriage had usually to extend over much longer distances.

The question was not just one of shipping inputs to producers—and that in itself was rare enough in the early years of American farming; it was also one of moving an unwieldy commodity of very low value-by-weight. Calcareous earths like marl were particularly heavy, and in circumstances of poor transport-provision their prime cost could be doubled or trebled in the course of a very short journey.

Transport amenities were bound to be key determinants of success or failure in any reform scheme necessitating the use of outside commodities.

No special sophistications from development theory need be introduced by way of elucidation. F. M. L. Thompson has identified a mid-nineteenth-century agricultural revolution in Britain based on "purchased raw materials." These had to be brought in from beyond the farm along existing channels of interregional and intraregional communication.[1] Facilities for carriage of bulky inputs were also available in the United States in parts of the North.[2] British and Northeastern experience is helpful in demonstrating that there was nothing intrinsically untransportable about calcareous materials.

I

There are a small number of recorded instances of Southern planters using rivers to transport marl, and there is fragmentary information on costs as well. Some men bought or constructed their boats, some hired, and some resorted to the services of professional lightermen. Usually the cheapest way was to run one's own vessel. Collier Minge's cost him $300 in the 1830s and he calculated total annual operating expenses at $168. Corbin Braxton estimated that his decked lighter cost about the same to build, but thought the annual outlay (excluding manning costs and including sinking fund) to be a good deal lower, at $63. By using their own vessels, these men, in Ruffin's view, were able to avoid "the exorbitant charges and unfaithful operations of lighter-men."[3] Braxton had the marl dug and moved eight miles along the Pamunkey for a total cost of only 0.6 cents a bushel, his vessel contributing 17 percent to the figure and labor for digging and manning making up the rest. Minge carried it fifteen miles on the James and calculated the total cost for delivery at 1.9 cents in 1833 and 1.6 in 1834, the boat (ignoring manning costs) being responsible for 16 percent of the expense. He also brought marl into his Charles City plantation from exposures seventeen miles distant in Surry County.[4]

Hill Carter of Shirley began by using imported lime but in the early thirties decided that it would be cheaper to ship marl a dozen miles upriver from Prince George and was proved correct, despite the fact that his costs up to the point of unloading were around 5 cents a bushel. Digging and transporting for an acre, assuming an average application of 250 bushels of marl, would have cost Braxton $1.25, Minge $4.83, and Carter $11.25. William Harrison of Upper Brandon, Prince George, found the costs of transporting marl twelve miles down the James quite supportable in 1833, as did Benjamin Harrison of Berkeley and John Minge of Weyanoke in Charles City, who took several free vessel-loads from Ruffin in the 1820s and 1830s.[5] Southampton planters were lightering marl down the Nottoway in the mid-1840s, and in 1841 Richard Baylor of Essex County had it delivered at his landing on the York River from Urbanna in Middlesex. The distance was at least a dozen miles and the cost 4 to 6 cents a bushel. In 1838 some Mathews County farmers on Chesapeake Bay took delivery of 3,000 to 4,000 bushels from a source on the York, the marl costing 2 cents a bushel, the freight 3.5, and landing operations 0.5, giving 6 cents in all. It was estimated that a total of 12,000 to 20,000 bushels had been brought into the county by water.[6] There is also evidence of Virginia marl being exported north to Maryland and to Connecticut.[7]

Little movement occurred elsewhere. James Bryan of Craven County in North Carolina purchased a small area of marl land in neighboring Lenoir around 1840 for the purpose of boating the earth six or seven miles downstream to his plantation. A couple of farmers near Charleston moved it to their properties "in boats and flats from the marl banks some distance above" for a brief spell in the early 1840s.[8] There was also some traffic on the Pee Dee, and of course James Hammond used the Savannah to bring in marl to his plantation from an exposure twelve miles downriver, estimating in 1843 that it cost him about 2 cents a bushel. His slave-built pole boat cost around $600. In 1846 another larger vessel had to be constructed, the first having been *"eaten up"* by the marl.[9]

The following ton-mile figures (for slightly different periods) can be calculated, with a deduction where necessary of 1 cent per bushel for digging expenses.[10]

Minge (Va.)	1.3 cents
Ruffin (Va.)	1.5 cents
Hammond (S.C.)	1.8 cents
Mathews farmers (Va.)	4.0 cents
Baylor (Va.)	5.3–8.9 cents
Carter (Va.)	6.2 cents
Oakes (Va.)	22.4 cents

It would be pointless to estimate an average, but if the mid-range 4 cents for the Mathews farmers is in any way typical it suggests that the total value of the commodity could be consumed in journeys of less than fifteen miles. Rates of this sort, however, compared very favorably with costs on the roads. These, it has been suggested, lay between 30 and 70 cents per ton-mile nationally in 1800–19 and were still around 25 or so in the late 1830s and early 1840s.[11] They also bear comparison with railway charges. Charles Turner, dealing with Virginia lines, gives rates of 2–6 cents per ton-mile on the Virginia Central in 1857. In 1860 the Richmond and Petersburg was charging 2.5 cents for coal, but as much as 9 cents for wheat.[12]

In relation to canals, however, rivers (if our figures are broadly typical) seem to have been quite expensive. In 1854 average rates on all but one of the country's main artificial waterways were less than 2 cents per ton-mile, and in the case of the Ohio and Erie, as low as 1 cent, and the Erie, 1.1 cents. Coal was being carried for less than 1 cent in the 1840s, and in the 1850s the Chesapeake and Ohio in Maryland was charging as little as 0.50, including toll.[13]

Whatever the cost comparisons, it is clear that the natural waterways of the Old South were very rarely used for the transport of marl. The small list of names given above makes the point adequately enough. It is doubtful if there were many other shippers who escaped the attention of the journals. "Marl," wrote a James River planter in 1839, ". . . is not everywhere to be had, and is a heavy and expensive affair when both land and water carriage have to be encountered." A report to the Prince George Agricultural Society in 1842 noted that marl had only "to a small extent" been "carried by water to some of the neighbouring counties." Water transport, according to Ruffin, was a "much dreaded operation": few planters had gotten marl by river.[14] William Gresham of King and Queen County, Virginia, wrote in 1852 about the efforts that were being made there to set up a company to purchase vessels and deliver marl anywhere around the shores of the Chesapeake,[15] but no such enterprise was ever in fact launched. Ebenezer Emmons noted in the same year that certain greensand marls on the Cape Fear River could easily be loaded onto small craft but that no movements had as yet been attempted.[16]

For Ruffin it was profoundly frustrating that traffic in marl was conducted on only a very paltry scale in Virginia and hardly at all in the other Southeastern states. In 1841 he suggested three possible explanatory factors: demand, supply, and transport facilities on the rivers. As for the first, there was, he thought, no real problem. There were enough farmers who wanted marl. Unfortunately, they could not be easily and cheaply satisfied. There were an insufficient number of proprietors prepared to dig marl and make it available to vessels on the riverbanks. More serious still was the difficulty of finding "water transport to be properly and certainly performed . . . at other than exorbitant rates." There were quite a few people in the lighter business, carrying a variety of goods on the rivers, but because of what Ruffin saw as a universal laziness and ignorance among hands manning the vessels, their operations were inefficient and their charges much too high. The solution was for the marl buyers to construct their own large boats. He asked farmers "to take the proper course (by building and navigating lighters for themselves) to make their supply cheap."[17] In order to achieve economies and tempt marl owners into selling, they should also combine forces to place large, regular orders.

Ruffin himself had held back from providing marl on a commercial basis, partly because that might raise suspicions over his advocacy of its use. However, he declared in 1841 that as he had waited for almost a decade for others to do the job and virtually nothing had happened he was now willing to offer his marl, on board at Coggin's Point, for 2 cents a bushel and 1.5 cents for orders of 30,000 bushels or more.[18] The gesture proved abortive. There is no evidence of any notable response to this or to any of his other proposals on transport. Cooperative action in the cause of agricultural advance was well beyond the capacities and inclinations of the great mass of tidewater planters.

There is very little sign, either, of widespread trafficking in materials for lime production within the region. Resources, as observed earlier, were unavailable in any general abundance. This, combined with high internal freights, underlay the much-noted preference for oceanic importations of the manufactured article from the North. Even relatively high-value, low-weight lime could be costly to move around in the interior. Unlike marl, it could travel by rail and steamboat, but it was exposed to arbitrary discrimination in charges. It was, wrote a Georgia planter in 1853, "now so high in its freight that it amounts to a prohibition for agricultural purposes."[19]

II

The most central problem to which there was no satisfactory indirect solution was the urgent need for transport improvement in the Old South. Fogel and Engerman, in line with a number of other historians, suggest that such a need was significantly moderated in the South by the endowment of an "unusually favorable system of navigable streams and rivers."[20] This has some relevance to the Mississippi basin but is questionable for the Atlantic states. Partial adequacy for the export of high-value staples, moreover, had little bearing on the needs of bulky trades.

The figures already given suggest that there may have been substantial, if localized, cost benefits to be gained by a switch from rivers to canals. Rivers had the irregularities of natural landscape features and were exposed to the uncertain influences of weather. There could also be impediments in the form of fallen trees, loose logs, and fish dams.[21] Terminating inland at the spring line and often separated by extensive watersheds, they could not form a comprehensive network as railways and canals could. Long-distance transport, therefore, might involve much costly transshipment and wagon haulage. And although substantial fingers of sea—these "so-called rivers," as Ulrich Bonnell Phillips called them[22]—penetrated the coastline and permitted ocean vessels to move right up to plantation landings, these were largely confined to the border states and the northern part of North Carolina. They were not of noteworthy scale to the south of Cape Lookout. In any case, they did not guarantee easy passage for the small craft used in local trade. The going could be very rough on deep, wide stretches of water affected by tides and other strong currents and frequently whipped up into dangerous turbulence by high winds.[23] There is, moreover, the very elementary distinction that has to be drawn between rivers themselves and the transport facilities available upon them.

Navigability varied a great deal between one river and another, even in the relatively privileged tidewater regions. Thomas Jefferson cited a number of streams in the coastal counties of Virginia which in the 1780s offered very limited passage: the Chickahominy, the Appomattox, the Piankatank, and the rivers of Mobjack Bay and the Eastern Shore. J. F. Hart has noted how soil erosion in Maryland led, over the centuries, to the deposit of great quantities of sediment in "many former navigable channels," turning these into mud flats. J. T. Ducatel observed in the 1830s how soil deposition in the coastal areas of Somerset and Dorchester counties in Maryland was blocking once-navigable channels. The Cape Fear River in North Carolina lacked practicable navigation in stretches as low down as Black Rock when Emmons visited it in the early 1850s. In his study of the Santee River system in South Carolina, Henry Savage writes that in the early 1820s "transportation . . . was painful and unreliable at best. . . . Most of the time these rivers were either in freshet or too low to permit clear sailing."[24] When Ruffin was conducting his survey of the state in 1843 he gave up traveling by boat after only a month and bought a buggy. Moving by water, he found, was far too troublesome. Tides, rapid flows, looping channels, and swampy margins all posed problems. So many rivers, he observed, were "but the middle channels of wide cypress swamps . . . overflowed by every heavy rain." Luxuriant vegetation could create near-impenetrability.[25] The crossing of the 200-yard-wide Santee low down at Lenud's Ferry involved a tricky sail of a mile and a quarter to beat currents and deep water. Farther south, river traffic could get much closer to the fall line, but the middle country of the state—as of Georgia—was largely devoid of navigable waterways.[26] As a result, much of the Southeast had to make do with slow wagons moving along bad roads. The costs were very high. Radical improvements were needed almost everywhere: railways, canals, better highways, and deepened and straightened rivers.

Phillips, however, suggests that river schemes in Georgia and the Carolinas were of "distinctly minor consequence. . . . The chief reliance was upon the waterways as nature had provided them."[27] Savage observes how only a number of disastrous attempts to establish steamboat services on the Santee rivers finally persuaded South Carolinians "that their great river system would never be an artery of water-borne commerce."[28] Farther north, significant, small improvements were made on streams like the Roanoke, Staunton, and Dan, around the borders of Virginia and North Carolina,[29] but the record over the region as a whole was a poor one. It is instructive to look at the number of steamships at work on Southeastern rivers—a fair index of good navigability and commercial activity. An antebellum sampling of 3,000 from Lytle's *Merchant Steam Vessels* reveals that only 139 (4.6 percent) began their working lives in the Atlantic ports of the Old South. The Ohio River port of Louisville alone had a higher figure: 5 percent. Well over three-quarters of the tonnage was concentrated in Baltimore, Charleston, and Savannah, indicating that a large number of the ships were engaged in coastal trade rather than in upcountry freight and passenger work.[30] The triumphs of steamboat technology lay to the west: in the long-distance journeys up the Ohio, Mississippi, and Missouri.[31]

The Old South largely missed out on the two big advances which helped sustain life and growth in river commerce in the nineteenth century: channel improvement and steam. The area was left with relatively primitive carrying facilities: rafts, canoes, dugouts, flatboats, pole boats, lighters, schooners, and keelboats.[32] And if James Mak and Gary Walton's 1972 arguments on flatboat productivity apply in converse form, it is probable that even some of these services were particularly poor because of the relative absence of external economies deriving from steamboats and improved rivers.[33] The majority of planters in a position to use waterways had to rely on the irregular services of lightermen or make-do with their own small vessels. Caroline MacGill has written that "each well-organised plantation in the lowlands possessed its own boats, manned and superintended by the ablest negroes on the place."[34] It is worth recalling how the Minge and Braxton marl vessels in Virginia had cost around $300 each, and the Hammond pole boat (which lasted only five years) $600. The cost of a 75-ton flatboat for the Louisville to New Orleans run in the 1830s was usually little more than $100 (for a single but very long journey).[35]

In 1860 the Old South had a canal mileage less than a quarter that of the three mid-Atlantic states of Pennsylvania, New Jersey, and New York.[36] The great bulk of it lay with just two canals: the Chesapeake and Ohio in Maryland and the James River and Kanawha in Virginia, built to strike through the mountains to the rivers and commerce of the West. Both failed to get as far as the inland frontiers of their respective states and both proved notable failures. As far as one can tell, they did nothing whatever to help spread the practice of marling. Much the same can be said for the tidewater canals farther south: the Dismal Swamp, the Weldon, the Columbia, the Wateree, and the Santee. Some were well located in relation to marl deposits, but they were widely scattered, formed no system, and were usually short.[37] They could also be expensive. Writing of the Santee Canal in 1843, Ruffin noted that "the many proprietors of boats take the old river & coast-wise navigation rather than pay the canal tolls."[38]

Roads were notoriously bad throughout the region. Plank roads were extended, notably in North Carolina, but they proved expensive to keep in good repair.[39] "It is of deep sand," wrote Ruffin of a state turnpike near Charleston in 1843, "& I had to walk my horse nearly the whole way, & indeed walked myself for 4 or 5 miles to lessen the fatigue of the horse." A fourteen-mile stretch of road which he followed in the vicinity of Branchville passed through almost one hundred shallow ponds and swamps. At the end of his journey he was soaked, the water at one point having been six inches deep in his buggy.[40] Stories of this sort, of course, are legion. They are also of minor consequence, for even if roads had been extensively improved the costs of moving marl along them in slow wagons would have been very high. Their main function would have been to connect plantations to waterways rather than to act themselves as sufficient avenues of long-distance carriage.

There is no mention in the literature of marl being carried on the railroads, despite Ruffin's hope in the 1830s that an "immense amount of transportation of rich marl" would take place on new lines in Virginia.[41] "It is admitted by all," wrote a *Farmers' Register* correspondent in 1836, "that railways cannot compete in cheapness with moderately good navigation, whether as canals or rivers, for conveying the agricultural commodities of a country, or any heavy commodities, not of great value compared to bulk and weight."[42] Marl was not an item for which speed of transport mattered very much. Delivery, like digging, had no special season. What is more, the railways did not provide a very dense or busy network. In 1859 railroads in the Old South (with 104 million acres of farmland) took only 17.8 percent of the nation's total freight receipts, compared with 34.4 percent for the three states immediately to the northeast (with only 41 million acres of farmland). Maryland, one of the smallest, least slave-based, and most economically diversified of the region's states picked up, significantly, almost a third of the Southeast's total freight income.[43]

III

The defects of the natural transport system obviously cannot be blamed on Southern society. Failure to rectify them on any notable scale, however, is another matter. Improvements when they come are usually a reflection of expressed or latent demand. They normally also require recruitment of capital, labor, equipment, and materials, but the central, determining entrepreneurial perception is that of a community which lacks a useful service and will pay for one when it is supplied. Southern businessmen, and usually states as well, tended to shy away from internal transport improvements for the very good reason that the demand for them did not seem particularly pronounced. The South, of course, did a good deal of trading, but the emphasis was very much on external dealings, often in lightweight commodities which could bear high freight costs. The pressures for easier *internal* exchange were too weak in such a nonindustrial, undiversified economy to encourage the development of comprehensive, efficient, and competitive transport services.

Crops had to be exported and various supplies imported, and major avenues of export-import commerce had to be found or provided, but the economic structure overall was one of disarticulation. Hamza Alavi has discussed such patterns of exchange in his conceptual examination of the so-called colonial mode of production: "Segments of the colonial economies do not trade with each other; they are articulated only via their links with the metropolitan economies and they are subordinated thereby to the latter."[44] The agrarian South certainly experienced quasi-colonial economic pressure from the North and from Europe.[45] Ruffin's notion of "tribute," mentioned earlier, is very close to the early Indian nationalist notion of "drain."[46] The most basic, identifiable factor underlying the internal disarticulation, however, was slavery, and the same institution helped perpetuate some of the section's other well-documented colonial features.

The South's was an atomized economy, with the isolated plantation its principal feature. Robert McColley observes how settlement in Virginia was, from colonial times, diffuse and scattered. In early days, according to Wilbur Cash, "once the plantation was properly carved out and on its way, the world might go hang." P. J. Staudenraus describes plantations near the Savannah River in the late eighteenth century as being "like islands in a sea of forest."[47] In eastern Virginia in 1852 Frederick Law Olmsted wrote of "the isolated, lonely and dissociable aspect of the dwelling places of a large part of the people."[48] James Hammond's letters to Edmund Ruffin are imbued with the psychological malaise of a solitary and lonely man. "I have now lived so long by myself & in myself that I am utterly incapable of going into any crowd," he wrote in 1853. ". . . I have no one in 50 miles of me more sensible & companionable than my driver Tom."[49] Ruffin's excursions in South Carolina, especially in the inland districts, reveal an awkwardly wide separation of farms with bad lines of communication in between.[50] In Virginia, his old guardian and friend Thomas Cocke fell victim to the tribulations of an existence lived out in almost hermitical isolation. Ruffin's own plantations, for all their size and comparative sophistication, required, as we have seen, only the most occasional and simple contacts with the world beyond. Marlbourne he described as a place of "perfect seclusion."[51]

Another indication of economic disarticulation was the stunted growth of towns in many areas.[52] A region with small-scale internal exchange would hardly provide much of a base for flourishing markets. Williamsburg, despite its important educational functions, almost faded away in the early nineteenth century.[53] Guion Griffis Johnson notes that only a couple of North Carolina's census-listed towns in 1860 had populations of over 5,000 and thirteen were counted in hundreds. "Antebellum North Carolina was a *civitas sine urbibus.*"[54] Orangeburg, South Carolina, was described by Ruffin in 1843 as a small and pretty village.[55] Savannah, according to the novelist William Gilmore Simms in the 1830s, was "like most of our Southern townships and depots . . . stationary and has an air of utter languishment."[56] Cities such as Baltimore, Richmond, and Charleston could give an impression of urban grace and material achievement, but they were, so to speak, mere pebbles in the sand.

Such a fragmented economic and social structure, so unpromising for internal exchange, was the product of plantation self-sufficiency. That in turn was partly the consequence of slavery. Here, at last, we come onto a fairly definite negative link between the institution and agricultural improvement. The slave society did not ask for a wide network of improved communications. Eugene Genovese has observed how limited were the plantation's purchases, even of manufactured goods: cheap clothing, gins, rope, some implements, and not a great deal else.[57] For explanation, we return to the arguments of Anderson and Gallman. Their basic notions, it might be pointed out, are not particularly novel. Celso Furtado, writing about colonial Brazil, remarks that "it was only too obvious that, being unable to utilize slave manpower continuously in productive activities directly connected with exporting, the entrepreneur would have to find another series of tasks for this manpower during enforced interruption in the main job. The tasks thus adopted took the form of building work, opening of new lands, local improvements, and so on."[58] They also appear in Genovese, in Metzer, in Battalio and Kagel, and, in somewhat different form, in Wright.[59] Anderson and Gallman in fact identify at the outset what they term "Genovese's rule": namely, that "slavery requires all hands to be occupied at all times."[60] This, as already suggested, was fine for marling when deposits were available on the farm. None of the operations, with the exception of plowing-in, was much affected by seasonal imperatives. Digging and hauling could provide useful employment at any time of the year for comparatively idle slaves. Anderson and Gallman, however, also stress the effects on enlarged food production within the plantation—and this, through its exchange and transport implications, had a thoroughly deleterious effect on any land improvements dependent on bulky materials coming from *outside* the farm. "Fixed capital" which could not, in particular weeks and months of the year, be employed in cash-crop cultivation could be shunted into subsistence activities. With a slave labor force, they write, it was "sensible for planters to attempt to raise more than one crop and to fit their various activities into a pattern that placed fairly steady demands on their workers during the growing season." The widespread production of corn and pork on tobacco and cotton plantations led to a high degree of unit (and also sectional) self-sufficiency, and this inevitably "had effects on the structure of the southern economy, diminishing opportunities for specialization and trade." There was, accordingly, no "rich history of farm and village or town interaction." The internal diversification forced on the planter by fixed-cost labor "inhibited intra-regional trade" and therefore "worked against the development of an apparatus of economic growth."[61]

Part of the ideal apparatus, needless to say, was an extensive and modernized network of communications. No country has achieved sustained and broadly based economic advance without it. It was required in the South at optimal, abstract levels of judgment; it was not, however, much required by the physical units of production. "In each great economic province," writes Phillips, "nearly every locality was issuing the same sort of output, and there was little interchange of products between neighboring districts."[62] According to Gray, "the stimulus of personal contact and of a diversified commercial life was lacking."[63] The issue is not entirely one of slavery. It also concerns family farms, where a combination of modest aspirations and rigid labor costs often produced an even stronger orientation towards subsistence work.[64] These, however, tended to lie outside the tidewater regions where marling was most feasible. In the lower counties of the Southeastern states the labor force was, as noted, predominantly slave.

Lack of internal exchange was not only the result of a systemic proclivity towards self-sufficiency within the slave economy, but also of generally low consumption levels on the plantations. The slave in his capacity as proxy consumer was unable to stimulate lively flows of commodities. Expenditures on his behalf were, as Stampp puts it, mere "maintenance costs."[65] William Parker indicates that in the South Atlantic states these were no higher than $30 per capita in 1860 (compared with $674 for the slaveholder).[66] There is also the possibility that slavery in all but the slave-exporting regions competed with transport as an investment field. Observations on the constricted mobility of Southern capital have been offered by many historians. Extensive citation seems unnecessary. "Until the agricultural depression of the fifth decade," writes Gray, "there was a widespread belief that capital invested in land and slaves was more productive than in other lines of investment."[67] Wright comments on the South's "possibility of accumulating and speculating in slave property," this dampening interest in a variety of developments including transport improvement.[68]

IV

There can be no question whatever that a more extended resort to marling in the Old South was held back by defective communications. It was a matter of availability, cost, and convenience. Instances of marl's movement over notable distances are very hard to come by—in particular for areas beyond the vicinity of the James River. It might be suggested, however, that the issue is basically a false one—that whatever the need and the transport facilities, very little marl in fact would have been moved because of the sheer inconvenience and persisting high cost of carrying a commodity of such great bulk and such low money-value. Any such notion can best be answered with reference to experience beyond the South, which shows that where a range of commercial and industrial forces had created "an apparatus of economic growth" agriculturists could well take advantage of it, even with the weightiest of farm inputs.[69] A Virginia planter, visiting New Jersey in 1838, saw a depot on a canal near Princeton where marl was selling at 12 cents a bushel. It had been brought down to the coast from the interior of the state and then shipped forty miles up the Delaware to the distribution point.[70] In 1857 the New Jersey Fertilizer Company was advertizing greensand sales from its wharves at Raritan Bay, the price for delivery on board ship being 7 cents a bushel.[71] According to Hubert Schmidt, railroads in the state "made it possible to expand the use of marl, and commercial companies were formed to dig and sell it"; and Diane Lindstrom observes how Pennsylvania had a very extensive network of canals which permitted a wide range of primary commodities to be transported inexpensively. In 1830 lime had to travel around 250 miles before its wholesale value was doubled.[72]

The best evidence of transportability comes from the United Kingdom. Although the British definition of marl was somewhat looser than the American, the category did include many earths which Ruffin would have happily termed marl. In any case, the earths with little or no calcareous matter were often very heavy and clayey, making them costlier to carry than Southern marl. British farmers, moreover, usually worked with larger quantities. Comparisons, then, are quite in order. Marl, it appears, was moved over fairly long distances in Britain, despite the fact that it had been commonly regarded for centuries as an "exceedingly chargeable" improvement.[73] Ruffin took note of sizable trades in both Scotland and England.[74] James Robertson, in his 1813 report on the agriculture of Perthshire, wrote of its removal from the beds of old lakes and its purchase by farmers in the long valley of Strathearn for three pence a boll (about a cent a bushel).[75] In the late eighteenth century a canal was run from Carlingwark Loch to the River Dee in the county of Kirkcudbright, and marl from the loch distributed in flat-bottomed boats to farms as far as twenty miles or so upstream.[76] The

Reverend John Smith wrote in 1813 of a large trade in seashells from nearby Wigton Bay. "Many thousand tons of these shells are annually carried (by vessels constantly employed in the business) all round the coast, and sometimes even to the Isle of Man."[77]

Eric Kerridge, in his study of English agriculture in the early modern period, classifies marl as an "extraneous" manure, i.e. one brought in from outside the farm.[78] In Joseph Priestley's comprehensive *Historical Account of the Navigable Rivers, Canals, and Railways of Great Britain* (1831) almost a quarter of the new or improved avenues of communication cited had, in their respective Acts of Parliament, rates or exemptions stated for the transport of marl: thirty-six canals, twenty-eight rivers, and five railways. A great many others cited manures generally and these would frequently be taken to include marl. The Peak Forest Canal, which ran from Derbyshire into Cheshire and Lancashire, had no specific marl rate stipulated, but was welcomed by Henry Holland in 1813 for "the opportunity which is afforded of conveying marl at a slight expense to places where that valuable article is not met with."[79]

The part of Britain which engaged most widely in the commercial transfer of marl and like substances was East Anglia, a low-lying land with a long curving coastline and an abundance of slow-moving streams. In Norfolk there were also flooded peat diggings known as "broads" which added substantially to the range of available waterways. Most of the marl used probably came from thousands of small local pits,[80] but in east Norfolk, where deposits were usually absent, water transport was necessary if farmers were to get their supplies. Chalk and highly calcareous marls were taken from pits at Thorpe and Whitlingham close to Norwich and moved to farms downriver. Large quantities were carried as far as the coast at Yarmouth, a distance of roughly twenty-five miles, and then sent up the other streams that flowed into the North Sea.[81] Two other important sources were Horstead and Wroxham, a similar distance inland from Yarmouth on the River Bure. The scale of the east Norfolk trade is indicated by the size of the pits. Among those at Whitlingham are two very large excavations, 30 to 50 feet deep and 80 to 100 yards long, which had tramways running down cuttings to wharves on the Yare.[82] One of the Horstead pits, with a wet chalky marl at its base, curves back on itself and has an artificial channel from the Bure leading around the whole excavation to give small vessels direct access to the working face. Farmers in Woodbastwick, according to William Marshall in 1782, got most of their marl from Thorpe, and although the pits were only a few miles away by land they found it cheaper to have it brought "in boats round by Yarmouth, forty or fifty miles."[83] Arthur Young, writing in 1804, found Thorpe or Whitlingham marl in use at Langley (10 miles away by water), Caistor (30 miles), Hemsby (30 miles), Martham (45 miles), and Ludham (45 miles); and Horstead or Wroxham marl on the fields at Ludham (15 miles), Catfield (20 miles), and Horning (30 miles).[84] The trade was still flourishing in the middle of the nineteenth century. Agricultural produce, according to R. N. Bacon in 1844, went down the rivers to Yarmouth, and marl, oil-cake, coal, and other farm requirements came up, "in some places to the door of the farmer, while at other points the marl is laid up on staithes or wharves until required for use."[85]

To the south there was an even longer-distance traffic in calcareous material. Daniel Defoe wrote in the 1720s of Kentish chalk being loaded directly from cliffs onto vessels "and carry'd to all the ports and creeks in the opposite side of the county of Essex, and even to Suffolk and Norfolk, and sold there to the country farmers to lay upon their land, and that in prodigious quantities."[86] The trade was observed again at the end of the century by Charles Vancouver:[87] not only "rubbish chalk" was being imported by Essex farmers, but London muck as well.[88] In 1813 John Boys wrote that a "vast quantity of chalk" was being removed from the vicinity of Gravesend and carried over to Essex, and that quite a lot was also going 40 miles or so down the Thames to the eastern part of Kent.[89] The distances from Gravesend to Manningtree, Aldeborough, and Yarmouth—three of the receiving ports cited by Defoe—were about 70, 80, and 110 miles respectively.

British evidence, therefore, shows convincingly that it was possible to transport marl and similar materials economically over quite long distances by water, often along streams which would have been termed small creeks in the American South. Marling was widely viewed as an expensive improvement in Britain, but given that the Norfolk trade went on for more than a century it must be assumed that transport cost did not cancel out agricultural benefit. Kent was exporting chalk for at least the same length of time, and probably longer. In Britain, for centuries, there had been a large coastal shipping capacity available for the transfer of various commodities,[90] and this could be made use of in the chalk trade between Kent and East Anglia and in the shell-sand commerce between Galloway and other parts of southern Scotland and the Isle of Man. In Norfolk, marl was carried up and down rivers, navigations, canals, and broads on wherries, graceful, large-sailed oak and elm barges generally designed for moving in shallow water.[91] Even in a part of England which had become relatively inconsequential industrially by the nineteenth century, and where the water trade was to a substantial degree agricultural, there were great numbers of these boats at work. They did not have to be constructed by farmers themselves, but were made in special yards and usually owned either by the builders or by merchants, carriers, and others with capital to invest in river trading.[92] Elsewhere, on the numerous canals whose Parliamentary Acts had stipulated the rates (or exemptions) for marl, boats were usually the property of professional carriers, often operating on a very large scale, and, to a lesser extent, of individual captains or of the canal companies themselves.[93] As for improved rivers, we can note the example of the Aire and Calder Navigation which, according to Richard Wilson, had in 1797 "a fleet of nineteen sloops" and probably a number of fly-boats and keels as well.[94] Centuries of industrial development and expanding internal exchange in Britain had encouraged the proliferation of infrastructural amenities, making it possible, among other things, for farmers to receive bulky inputs at reasonable cost and minimum inconvenience. The Southern improver was much less well off as a consequence of the general context of economic disarticulation. The "fixed capital" laborer stood as a major impediment on the transfer of marl and lime.

Transport raised fairly straightforward issues of cost and availability. If calcareous materials were distantly located and expensive to procure, even the most sophisticated planter might decide that it would be appropriate to ignore them. Freight problems could both narrow and simplify economic options. Their absence, in the cases of farmers with good deposits on or around the plantation, could, conversely, widen and complicate. The location of resources and the state of transport were conditioning factors, coming into play only insofar as people adjusted their behavior to accommodate them. Strata and rivers by themselves made no decisions. In the last resort, the only central, dynamic variable at work was the planter himself—the man who identified, or failed to identify, the choices and the courses of action appropriate to them. The most interesting questions concerning the viability of an institution bear on the perceptions and preferences of those who direct it. Therein one finds human agency in its most purposive and coordinated forms.

Chapter Eleven

Farmer Entrepreneurship

------••◄∞►••------

I

RUFFIN held the Southern transport system in very low esteem, although he sought no systematic explanation for its shortcomings and certainly made no attempt to relate these to slavery. On Southern farmers his views were more frequently and more vigorously expressed, and can only be described as contemptuous. He occasionally accepted, moreover, the possibility of a connection between entrepreneurial sluggishness and some of the cultural and economic features of slavery. He would allow himself some moments of tactical politeness and even flattery when he addressed meetings of planters, and of course spoke in highly general terms of elevated Southern minds, but there can be little question that throughout his adult life he regarded the mass of the agricultural community as thoroughly unfit to discharge his plans for radical reform. This is clear from the expressions of abuse and despair scattered throughout his public utterances and private jottings, and it helps explain the irregularity of his interest after the mid-1840s in preaching the virtues of his "plan."

He knew that many farmers were making a very adequate living from traditional, destructive methods of farming, but for him it was not enough to be carried along by favorable market circumstances or by appreciations in slave values. A good farmer was not a man who was making a high income because the outside world liked what he was producing. He was someone alert to long-term dangers apparent in his methods and his markets, informed as to the possibilities of securing a permanently high-yield and low-risk base for his operations, and prepared to endure the discomforts of experimentation and diversification in order to break out of forms of agriculture that were potentially ruinous for his plantation and for the noble cause of economic, demographic, and political regeneration in the Old South.

Even allowing for the inevitably high standards by which he passed judgment, one cannot but be impressed by the sweeping range of his condemnation. From the 1830s to the 1850s he complained incessantly about the farming community ignoring, slighting, misunderstanding his advice. In 1852 the Southern scene as he saw it was one of "indolence and waste, and generally exhausting tillage and declining fertility."[1] Reforming practices usually petered out a few miles south of the James River. The planters of Edgecombe, North Carolina, while virtuously marling, were also limiting their own rewards by sticking to their old cotton and corn regime. The grandee planters of South Carolina were mostly shameless in their confessions of land killing. In Prince George, the very county where Ruffin had begun marling and where many neighbors had followed his early lead, there was not one good farmer to be found in 1840: without exception, there was "want of economy, of skill and management in practice, and want of general knowledge of, or regard to, the true principles of agriculture."[2] His own education, like that of most members of his class, had left him "totally ignorant of practical agriculture."[3] Ignorance, for Ruffin, was the principal source of bad practice and reluctance to change. This was to be explained in part by an excess of classics at school, but also by a complacency bred from honored tradition, by a lazy and casual mentality stemming from the widespread privilege of slaveholding, and sometimes by the rational calculation that with continuing profits, low land values, and high slave prices, there really was no particular need to learn better methods. Whatever the causes, the outcome was hundreds of thousands of benighted and unresponsive farmers. Defective agriculture, suggests Drew Faust, was seen essentially as "a failure of mind," both intellectually and morally.[4]

There is little in the work of modern historians to force one to question Ruffin's evaluation. Many of his observations accord with Genovese's and

Luraghi's ideas of a dominant planter class which, although highly acquisitive, was essentially cavalier in its dispositions and aspirations, with little regard for "steadiness, regularity and sustained effort."[5] Doubts about the general level of entrepreneurial worth also appear in the work of Gray, Craven, Gates, Cash, Cathey, Smith, Flanders, Moore, and many others.[6] Elsewhere I have argued that the men operating slave agriculture were very unimpressive as reformers, using partial and often misleading knowledge and working within an excessively narrow range of objectives.[7]

Even those who insist that the planter was an informed, calculating, and successful commercial operator have little to say about his long-term capacity for implementing adjustments and improvements in farming methods. Conrad and Meyer neatly combine "bourgeois" and "nonbourgeois" by suggesting that the very success of the planter-manager in effectively organizing his slaves and selling his products could encourage an "expensive image of himself as a *grand seigneur.*" Morton Rothstein declares, with specific reference to frontier farming, that there is little documentary support for the notion that planters lacked capitalistic, entrepreneurial drive. His evidence of that drive, however, lies mainly in bids for short-term profits from staple farming and in the flow of capital from the agricultural sector into industry, commerce, and finance. Jacob Metzer sees large planters achieving high degrees of efficiency through divisions of labor and economies of scale, but conveys no sense of any dynamic at work, of any ability to move out of one set of routines and into another. Nor do we know how many small to middling plantations—in the majority, overall—were in a position to secure the benefits of rational management. The same issues, begging the same questions, arise in Fogel and Engerman. Labor management was the key to success, although profits were boosted towards the end of the antebellum period by buoyant cotton and slave prices. Agricultural improvement, again, is not part of the picture. They write of "the extreme flexibility of the slave economy," but this appears to have been manifested not in any lively adaptability within individual production units but in the utterly different matter of their selective abandonment: in "interregional migration." Wright sees the financial value of slave property as "the essence of the profitability of slavery" and suggests that the slaveholder approached economic enterprise more as a speculator than an investor.[8]

These general opinions are of service in providing reference points and in establishing how the balance of judgment stands. They do not, however, indicate much that is precisely specific to the widespread reluctance to engage in marling, liming, and diversifying operations. One very basic problem is that there is no single, uniform entrepreneurial entity. The scale of operation varied greatly; so too did climate, soil, the availability of marl, and the cropping possibilities. Amelioration could be relatively easy and safe for one man and awkward and unrewarding for another. Lewis Cecil Gray splits Southern farmers into a number of categories: highlanders, lowland yeomen, small planters, middle-class planters, planter aristocrats, and plutocrats.[9] Facts concerning their behavior are usually inexact and difficult to accumulate in large, compelling aggregates. Profits and other accounting figures, where available, give some exactness, but they are only of limited value in measuring performance and long-term viability in production. Some of the fattest fortunes in the South were being made by the most reckless of farmers.

Once again, the issue of performance has to be approached with due regard for the specifities of land amelioration and some willingness to tolerate modest and sometimes uncertain conclusions. Definitive statistical pronouncements are quite out of order here. So are any efforts to cast the farmer entrepreneur in the role of sole and certain villain. Four points will be argued. First, that marling was a very bothersome and off-putting operation. Second, that the application of marl was not invariably a highly productive improvement by itself. Third, that the farmer received inadequate guidance. Fourth, that his weaknesses of perception, ability, and aspiration were heavily conditioned by the general social and economic environment within which he operated. On three of these arguments we return, imprecisely, to slavery and to the idea that the institution must carry some share of the blame for bad performance.

One must, nevertheless, avoid over-sharp distinctions between slave and "free" economies. Passive and unimaginative entrepreneurship was a common feature of conservative, agrarian societies, to some degree regardless of their relations of production. Ignorance, waste, dismissiveness over reforms, and lack of attention to fine commercial detail were not the prerogatives of the Southern planter. In British India, landlords, larger peasants, and moneylenders, who could draw good incomes from land on which private property rights and creditor power had now been clearly established, tended in the main to aim for an extension of the scale of their traditional functions rather than invest in modernizing improvements. "Agricultural implements and techniques," writes Barrington Moore, "did not change significantly between Akbar's time and the early twentieth century."[10] Alexander

Gerschenkron observes how the Russian gentry were rarely innovative in farming methods in the nineteenth century. Rotations, according to Alan Milward and Berrick Saul, were largely unknown in Russia, manuring was conducted on a thoroughly inadequate scale, and technology was primitive. Spanish agriculture before 1914 has been described as "under-capitalised and unmechanised," afflicted by absenteeism and productive of intense rural poverty.[11]

Even in industrializing Germany, where major agricultural successes were being achieved by the Prussian Junkers, Gerschenkron detects a strong survival of "preindustrial social values."[12] Britain, in spite of energizing intrusions by manufacturers and merchants and other stimuli emanating from an industrial economy, showed irregular patterns of agricultural advance. James Caird's county-by-county survey of 1850–51 reveals that improvements, though widespread, were in many places being impeded by landowner indifference and mortgage liability, by the incompetence of agents, and by ignorance and caution among tenants. Antiquated and modern farming frequently lay in close geographical juxtaposition. "The successful practices of one farm, or one county, are unknown or unheeded in the next."[13] It was a state of affairs very well known to Ruffin in Virginia— though hardly in the Carolinas and Georgia where the antiquated survived largely unmixed. One must, therefore, guard against exaggerated notions of the Old South being entrepreneurially freakish, even given its obstinate loyalty to acid-soil farming.

II

The first major point is that liming and, in particular, marling involved a good deal of bother. It is already fairly clear what the preliminaries were for a successful program of marl-based improvement. The farmer had to make some judgment concerning the acidity levels of his fields, getting clues perhaps from current yields and also from the sorts of weeds growing on the soil. He would then examine whatever ravines and river banks were present on the plantation, and perhaps bore as well, to see if there was any marl on his land. He would next resort to some form of analysis which could determine the exact calcareous content of his marl. Tests would have to be quite numerous to determine whether the deposits were standardized in character. Ruffin's *Calcareous Manures* might also be consulted for advice on digging and carting, especially if deep pits had to be prepared and if the deposits lay a long way from the fields. Long-term decisions had to be made about the best seasons for resource diversion into marling work; short-term decisions had also to be taken around changes in the weather. There had to be a general commitment to enlarging the degree of resource mobility on the farm—something that would widen the range of managerial responsibilities, directly or indirectly exercised. The most suitable hands for digging and hauling had to be identified and calculations made about the desirability of using the same people for the same jobs so that some measure of skill refinement might be achieved. Major programs could last for a number of years.

If marl was not on the farm, the planter would have to discover the site of the nearest deposits and determine whether he could have access to them. Distances for boating and hauling would have to be calculated and some measuring of expense attempted. Questions concerning the availability of a suitable plantation boat, the cost of constructing a specialized vessel, the manning of whatever craft was used, the possibility of recourse to light-ermen, the adequacy of plantation landings, the distance from river to fields, the transport-cost difference between marl and lime were all ones which might have to be considered. Finally there was the heaping in the fields to be attended to, followed by spreading and comparatively strenuous plowing. By this stage, of course, the farmer had to have decided how much to apply to the acre, this involving judgments on the strength and reaction of the soil, the composition of the marl, and the respective virtues of single and staggered doses.

When the crops materialized he could only measure the impact of the marl by taking into account other physical and human influences on yield in that particular year. These, in addition to marl's relatively slow speed of working, meant that a number of years had to pass before reasonably certain evaluations could be made. Once he was sure of his results he would then have to calculate aggregate costs, returns, and profits and set these against land values to see if it all made economic sense. He also had to keep an inventory, written or mental, of his mistakes to help him avoid repeating them.

Marling, therefore, although not expensive when material was available fairly close to the fields, and although not taxing on slave skills or farm schedules, was still an awkward and laborious business, requiring intelligence and perseverance from the planter. The principal challenges it posed, in short, were entrepreneurial ones. All the activities were relatively novel (although in hauling and spreading the work was fairly similar to that required for manuring). The farmer could go wrong at so many points: finding good marl, sizing up the needs of his land, keeping his pits drained, and costing the whole exercise. And, of course, on the question of costs he could come unstuck completely if the marl had to be imported into the plantation through a largely do-it-yourself transport system. The combination of external expense and internal effort would have made marling seem thoroughly unattractive to many thousands of farmers, however familiar they may have been with the numerous figures circulating on yield improvements.

III

With the second main issue, that of concomitant and sequent improvements, we come to the most serious problem of all. As it happened, marling as a self-contained activity—treating impoverished fields and then planting the corn and cotton as before—was sometimes a comparative waste of time and effort. Further labors often had to be undertaken alongside and subsequent to amelioration.

The most crucial of the concomitant improvements was the addition of organic matter to the soil before, during, or immediately after marling. As already discussed, marl and lime liberated such matter for plant nourishment, and if the existing supply was very slender it could be broken down and used up with a speed which served to intensify soil exhaustion after only a year or so. The problem was especially acute with quickly acting lime, but was apparent in marling as well, especially if the material had a high calcium content or was applied in very large doses. There were various solutions. The easiest was simply to rest the land before marling, keep livestock off it, let the weeds and natural grasses grow, and then plow all the greenery under. A second way was to apply the marl composted with vegetable matter. A third was to combine marling with manuring. A fourth was to grow green crops and turn these into the soil when the crop was sufficiently bulky. A fifth was to concentrate on soils naturally rich in organic matter, such as old-fields and drained swamps.

"I . . . believe," wrote Ruffin in 1824, "that the use of calcareous manures, will not be found very profitable, except on lands *not grazed*, or which are in some other way furnished with vegetable matter." The idea of, in effect, manuring as well as marling was not one which appealed to many planters. "Oh!" he imagined a reply, "if I am to manure in some other way all the land I marl, I cannot marl much; and for so much, the land could do very well without marl."[14] He should perhaps have acknowledged that many farmers, with their livestock roaming freely through woods, swamps, and abandoned fields, had very elementary difficulties in securing a manure supply in the first instance. Only a tiny minority could have equaled his achievement of carrying out 1,591 cartloads from leaf-littered hog and cow pens, stables, and cattle yards in the winter and spring of 1850–51. At Coggin's Point, Edmund Jr. had 32,054 loads of mud, straw, river grass, wood trash, and manure hauled out between 1851 and 1859—during which period he also applied 18,000 loads of marl and 3,024 of greensand.[15] "It would be leading you into error," James Hammond told the readers of the *Southern Cultivator* in 1846, ". . . to leave you to suppose that I rely solely on the marl to improve my lands. Rest, in connection with it, is indispensable, and manure becomes far more beneficial." Between 1848 and 1851 he manured 429 acres, using dung, stable scrapings, sawdust, corncobs, straw, and wash-house cleanings. Treating 82 acres in 1859 cost him a considerable $755, the bulk of the expenditure going on horse feeding, replacement of horseshoes, and wear and tear on wagons.[16]

On the eve of the Civil War the principle was still being enunciated. "The proportion of marl or lime to be added to a soil," wrote Thomas Clemson in a government report of 1859, "should be in accordance with the amount of organic matter already existing in it, or that may be contributed." The *Southern Cultivator* declared in 1861 that the man who expected to reclaim sterile soil by calcareous applications alone "need not be surprised if he has only his labor for his pains."[17] The point had to be made with great frequency for almost forty years because so many planters were paying scant regard to it. Those who had taken note, like the composting marlers of Edgecombe, were reaping considerable benefits.[18] Other prerequisites sometimes cited— of special relevance to heavier and possibly richer soils—were good drainage and deep plowing.[19] Viewed comparatively, however, they appear to have been side issues.

Failure to attend to the organic question was the main cause of marling damage (though more often than not it served merely to reduce the scale of yield improvements). Imbalance between vegetable matter and calcareous matter was bad enough, but large quantities of marl could also soak up a lot of the available moisture in the soil.[20] The most extreme manifestation of trouble was so-called marl burn, in which whole fields might, for a time, be unable to support even the barest cover of vegetation. Ruffin himself wrote of patches at Coggin's Point "so diseased by over-marling, as not to produce a grain of corn or wheat."[21] Heavy applications were also recorded as having damaged land in Prince George, James City, King William, and Nansemond counties in Virginia. Lucas Benners, one of North Carolina's experimental marlers, burnt up a field in 1818, and James Hammond noted in 1844 that while sandy cotton land marled with one hundred and two hundred bushels per acre was more productive than unmarled ground, fields treated with three hundred bushels proved notably less productive. There was, he observed, a clear "danger of heavy marling on worn land." In 1847 he found some evidence of marl burn on his plantation. He believed that hot climates necessitated particular caution.[22]

The planter thus faced the prospect of suboptimal returns or clear damage, and even if everything went well he might have to wait two or three years to witness any certain results. Some must have been put off by disappointment, others by reluctance or inability to try again and do the job properly. Many farmers in Gloucester County, Virginia, according to Thomas Stubblefield in 1836, "from an injudicious or ignorant application of marl appear to be prejudiced against its use entirely." One man's misfortune, moreover, could easily translate into another man's dismissiveness. Lucas Benners recalled that after his temporary failure in 1820 he was laughed at and ridiculed. Damagingly heavy marling in Nansemond, Virginia, had by 1842 rendered some land totally unproductive and, it was alleged, scared off a considerable number of potential improvers. Others could suffer from their own impatience. "Immediate and large returns from a single application of the material is almost universally expected," wrote *Soil of the South* in 1854. "Disappointment ensues."[23]

Planters trying to improve their soils, therefore, usually had to be prepared for labors additional to those of marling and had to be willing to accept at least medium-term perspectives to their improvement programs. If they made mistakes and suffered reversals they had to be prepared to consult the literature, identify their errors, and put matters to rights. These were tall orders. None of these points, it might be said, contradicts the conclusions of an earlier chapter that marling was a highly effective practice and that no farmers formulated any systematic case against its use. We have been looking here at badly conducted marling and at the possibilities of disenchantment. The best information on damage in fact comes from those planters—like Ruffin, Benners, and Hammond—who in the end gained most handsomely from marl.

IV

Even more demanding was sequent labor: the various postmarling improvements which the planter might undertake to capitalize on the efforts of
amelioration. The greater the latter, the greater the desire to see them fully
justified. Marl offered planters an invitation into diversified farming. For
many, as suggested earlier, it was a highly resistible one. As long as organic
levels in the soil could be maintained, there was still a good living to be
made from marling within the old restricted forms of staple farming. The
highest returns were being missed, but the work could be very profitable. It
is clear that a great many marlers settled for comparatively modest objectives. But it is also possible that a great many others, unimpressed by the
combination of laborious marling and moderate increments on income, and
thoroughly unwilling to embark on any of the logically sequential schemes
of diversification, decided to leave the whole thing alone. Why begin a difficult improvement if unprepared to see it through? The thoroughgoing ame-
liorator set his sights on goals which could be very awkward to achieve,
placing as they did a whole new complex of managerial, scheduling, and
labor demands on the plantation. And it was in this follow-through from
marling (and liming), as distinct from the original amelioration itself, that
slavery could exercise a number of direct and powerful negative influences.
Skills had to be more varied and the management more astute and informed. A further group, of course, might diversify *without* amelioration,
though probably at generally low levels of productivity.

The more northerly states of the Old South revealed most interest in diversified farming. This, as earlier suggested, was partly helped by marling
and liming and partly conducive to them. Many, we may presume, used
marl because they had the will and the opportunity to build upon it. Conversely, farther south, forces acting against diversification may have had a
discouraging effect on potential marlers. Such forces—acting to varying
degrees throughout the region—can be divided into physical, commercial,
and institutional categories. These, in turn, can be quite respectably nar-
rowed to climate, cotton, and slavery. (Soil, being already our basic datum,
need not be considered here). It should be noted that their influences
worked subjectively as well as objectively. If a planter thought, however
mistakenly, that his summers were too hot and his slaves too stupid for the
growth of a particular crop, then the chances were that he would ignore it.

Julius Rubin views climate as a basic determinant of the failure to diversify, in particular below the border states. Only a very limited range of green crops could be grown, he suggests, and these often needed extensive areas of farmland. Livestock were afflicted by lack of forage and by cattle tick. The lower South was consequently forced to stick with its old staples, assisted after the Civil War by large applications of commercial fertilizer. Radical changes in agricultural output had to await the scientific advances and government programs of the twentieth century.[24] This sort of physical (and in part institutional) determinism was shared by many contemporary observers, and it is interesting to note how even today a rich fodder crop such as alfalfa is largely absent from the Carolinas and Georgia. [25] Turnips, so vital to British agricultural progress, could not, in the view of one Southern farmer, be grown successfully "till our climate changes, and the summers become more cool and moist, and the winters less freezing."[26] Many thought the section generally too hot for clovers. Even Ruffin, in the relative coolness of Virginia, wrote of his "Providential clover," though it did remain the key crop in his various improving rotations and it received most of the manure that was available on his plantations.[27]

It is Genovese's contention, however, that the failure of livestock-forage diversification over much of the South had little to do with climate and everything to do with defective entrepreneurship and labor and a lack of large and accessible markets for animal produce. This is proved, he suggests, by the range of twentieth-century improvement.[28] Gray takes a similar view: people believed that the climate did not suit clover, but it is possible that in many instances "failures were due . . . to crude methods of sowing."[29] A number of official late-century reports, as noted in the first chapter, vigorously documented the South's capacities for mixed farming. Charles Wallace Howard, an editor of the *Southern Cultivator,*[30] declared in 1866 that clover, as well as a variety of grasses, could be grown anywhere in the state of Georgia as long as soil conditions were right. Hot summers, he argued, were certainly a problem in the section as a whole, but there was ample compensation in generally mild winters—in three-season growth. The adverse effects of heat could be overcome by suspending field grazing in the worst months. "This is not mere theory; the practical proof is found in every one of the cotton states."[31] Robert Somers complained in 1871 of the "want of herbage" and paucity of livestock in the South Atlantic states, but considered this was more to do with choice than with any climatic imperative.[32] Like Howard, Harry Hammond (James Hammond's son) stressed the importance of a reduction in grazing during the hot months to avoid the exposure of roots to the sun.[33] Average crops of clover and grass seed in Virginia were described as "very generous" in the 1880s.[34] W. J. Spillman suggested in 1906 that there were "few portions of the United States in which it is possible to produce a greater variety of agricultural products than in the territory comprising the States of North Carolina, South Carolina, Georgia, and Florida." Among the actual and potential forage crops mentioned by Spillman and the other commentators were sorghum; timothy; crowfoot; crabgrass; orchard, Bermuda, and Johnson grasses; red, crimson, white, bur, and Mexican clover; cowpeas; vetches; velvet beans and soybeans; cottonseed; potatoes; peanuts; and peaches.[35]

Monoculture and primitive rotations, as condemned by Ruffin, may of course have represented strictly market-determined choice. Stampp suggests they were popular because they "seemed to promise the largest returns on capital investments."[36] The most powerful impulse came from the desire to produce the largest possible quantity of cotton—something which could be intensified in periods of low as well as high prices, with farmers pushing for tolerable aggregate returns. This concentration on America's most successful cash crop was, according to Metzer, a feature of the "economic rationality of plantation management." Conrad and Meyer take a similar view.[37]

Commercial considerations were inevitably of the greatest importance. Ruffin could come along and properly insist that under a diversified system of farming reduced acreages of cotton could be more than offset by higher yields and a less precarious crop mix, but he was unlikely to get a sympathetic hearing. "The more Southern planter," he wrote in 1853, "might leave his field to be covered by its growth of weeds (or natural grasses) one year, (and also to be grazed,) and a broadcast crop of pea-vines to be ploughed under in another, for every three crops of grain and cotton. But the ready answer to this, (and I have heard it many times,) is 'What! Lose two crops in every five years? I cannot afford to lose even one.' "[38] The siren calls of the market and the comforts of habit were difficult to dismiss. The *periodic* profitability of cotton cultivation seems to have been a stronger impediment to postameliorative diversification, and therefore to amelioration itself, than were hot weather and drought. The main influence of climate, in fact, ran *through* that special crop which could do so well in the more southerly states. Entrepreneurial choice was more important than compulsions from the physical environment. And, of course, it was a choice much conditioned by short-term logic and a cramped appraisal of the options for sustained economic viability.

Can it also be argued that there were institutional rigidities and skill inadequacies on slave plantations which, regardless of climate or markets, made it difficult to branch out from the old routines? Almost certainly it can, though not exclusively so, given that the great bulk of ameliorating and diversifying farms in Virginia were run with slave labor. The problem was not so much that slaves were intrinsically unfit to look after the cows or cultivate the clover, or that the specific skills for each task on a diversified farm were especially taxing; it was, rather, that a considerably higher level of managerial flexibility, instruction, and control was required.[39] Was the planter, directly or through an overseer or foreman, prepared to show the slave what to do, move him around judiciously from one job to another (assuming a low degree of functional specialization on the typically small plantation), and supply an adequate degree of supervision? Ruffin's 1855 essay on clover cultivation nicely underscores the problems: the tasks themselves were basically simple, if sometimes troublesome, but they were also numerous and novel, and clearly required some diversions of labor away from more traditional work.[40] Metzer suggests likely enlargement of "coordination and supervision" difficulties in the event of significant diversification, and Aufhauser observes that "certain changes in technique were resisted by farmers" as it was considered unwise to break with old, familiar routines. John Elliott Cairnes made the same point in *The Slave Power*.[41]

Ruffin was well aware of the problem and saw the slave as very much part of it. "Improved processes and extended and varied culture," he wrote in 1836, "make it necessary to disperse the laborers on every farm, and greatly to vary their employments. . . . The ignorant slave who could well and profitably wield the how [*sic*] or the axe, under continual supervision, and the ignorant director of the work, who had only to see that it was 'kept moving,' become equally unfitted for the new and more perfect operations." Where the quality of manpower was not raised, improved farming often proved unprofitable. The system itself was fine: bad results came from "the unfit agents and means employed."[42] James Hammond, as seen, found it "impossible to make anything but corn & cotton with our agents, white & black." His overseers and foremen would "not pull together on one place, for anything, but corn & cotton."[43]

It may be objected that the strains of labor diversion apply as much to marling as to mixed farming, and that the argument here contradicts the findings in chapter 9. This can be easily answered. In the first place, the process of marling was fairly crude and without intrinsic seasonal restrictions. Second, there was a great difference between the demands of that single improvement and those of the variety of subsequent follow-through activities which were desirable within a thoroughly effective system of amelioration and diversification. It was at that second stage that land improvement, in its widest sense, ran up against serious institutional barriers. The problem was not strictly numerical. One could not easily pick and choose between the different elements of a diversified system, selecting ones which looked manageable and ignoring the rest. Many were interrelated to a high degree. Clover, for example, needed a good deal of manure;[44] manure, however, could only be supplied in large quantities if the plantation had a good livestock-carrying capacity; livestock, in turn, might be dependent on clover and other forage crops.

Two final points can be offered on restricted diversification. First, there was a debate in the late 1840s concerning the possible toxic effects of the lower South's principal green crop, the cowpea. Martin Philips, one of Mississippi's leading improvers, declared in 1848 that he had come across "a great number who know that peas have, and will *always* kill stock of any kind." Some provided substantiation. Others refuted the idea, or put the problem down to bad practice.[45] Whatever the balance of opinion, the exchanges could only have had a damaging effect on the enterprise of the more cautious planters. Second, farmers who grew cotton had an almost ingrained aversion to grasses. Because the crop had to be cultivated in a weed-free soil, a psychological block seems to have developed in relation to anything green. Willard Range describes how planters and overseers would go to the fields in the spring and, almost in anger, order their hands to "Kill the Grass!" or "Go for General Green!" C. W. Howard observed in the 1870s that "the whole subject of grass-culture is so new to them, it is so foreign to their practice, which has been to kill grass, that it is no wonder that they make mistakes." Many of the grasses—like crowfoot and Bermuda—happened to be good livestock feed. In 1906 the aversion was still at work: M. A. Crosby quoted an old saying, that "the southern farmer spends his summers fighting grass to grow cotton to buy hay with."[46]

V

Amelioration, when properly conducted and effectively exploited, was clearly a complex and demanding exercise. To understand it and to execute it the farmer needed a great deal of clear guidance. This brings us on to the key epistemic issue of instruction. Mere exhortation was totally inadequate, given the cash and opportunity costs and the novelties involved. That, however, was often all he got—mixed in with a mass of fragmentary detail on a variety of operations on a host of different plantations (frequently those of the very rich and comparatively leisured). It is surprising to discover that even James Hammond had to write to Ruffin in 1844 for some elementary information on clover. He had been told it was "the best thing in the world" and had sown some, but was ignorant about proper methods of cultivation and even wondered if he could reasonably expect his crop to grow.[47]

Ruffin's own inadequacies as a propagandist for improved farming are of obvious relevance here. His years of sustained, energetic campaigning lasted little more than a decade. His principal book, the *Essay on Calcareous Manures*, doubled in length between 1832 and 1852 to become a rather unwieldy and desultory volume of almost 500 pages.[48] His journal, the *Farmers' Register*, expired prematurely in 1842. In Beaufort, South Carolina, he was mortified to discover how ignorant planters were about marling and liming despite the wide circulation of his various publications on these subjects. In Edgecombe, his book was in most marlers' hands, but it was clear that instructions therein were not having the correct effect on some of their procedures.[49]

His prescriptions, especially on post-marling diversification, were easier to absorb in Virginia and Maryland than in the more southerly states. The hard battle against land-killing staple farming in Georgia and the Carolinas was one in which he chose not to engage with any sustained vigor or enthusiasm—not even during his survey of South Carolina in 1843. Generalized advice and denunciation were his main resorts. "You cannot influence us," a South Carolinian with an interest in marl told him in 1841, "so long as you speak only of its results on corn, wheat and clover." Another wrote around the same time: "I do not take Mr. Ruffin's work; it is too far north for me." More generally, as J. A. Turner of Georgia saw it in 1858, books and articles on agricultural chemistry "so overwhelm the ordinary farmer with technical terms that he finds it quite as difficult a matter to understand these, as he does to make new his old fields." The criticism was directed against the *Register*, despite Ruffin's efforts to write in fairly plain English. Most farmers, in the view of a North Carolina reader, found its language "unintelligible jargon."[50]

Ruffin did entertain some qualified belief in the virtues of "periodical publications, as a means of remedy" for defective agricultural practices.[51] Success was, of course, a function of circulation as well as of intelligibility and reception. At its peak his *Register* had a circulation of only 1,400. The journal apparently was highly spoken of in New Kent, Maryland, in 1833, but not widely circulated. A North Carolina correspondent surmised in 1834 that there was probably not a single subscriber in the whole of Halifax County.[52] In 1850 James Hammond announced his refusal to buy the *Southern Cultivator* anymore since the editor was an obvious abolitionist. He did, however, thank Ruffin for a copy of the Richmond *Southern Planter* (then in its tenth year), saying, "I have wanted to take that paper but don't know the price." Sometime earlier he had suggested that Ruffin come south and join with him and Michael Tuomey in the publication of a new journal, but the offer had been turned down.[53] There were certainly a fair number of periodicals available. Gray estimates that over eighty appeared in the section before the Civil War. The casualty rate, however, was high, and in 1860 the slave states together accounted for less than one-eighth of the national circulation of farming papers.[54]

Lack of information among Southeastern planters was also a consequence of the poor transport and stunted urbanization discussed earlier. Robert McColley suggests that "vigorous interchanges of ideas were much scarcer and slower than in northern provinces where wealth and refinement were so much more concentrated in the towns." Ronald and Janet Numbers stress the importance of urbanization for science and the problems of developing a large and vital scientific community in a land of dispersed plantations, small towns, and poor libraries.[55] Ruffin complained of a "want of intercourse and exchange of opinions among farmers,"[56] and was much impressed by the mentally beneficial effects of summertime fraternizing among the gentry in the low country of South Carolina as they escaped together from the heat and disease of their tidewater plantations. He had suffered himself from bad communications, having been initially ignorant of the early marling work of Singleton in Maryland, Hankins and Taylor in the Williamsburg area, and Benners in North Carolina.

Bad transport also impeded the growth and lively functioning of agricultural societies. These, as Ruffin saw them, usually performed pointless functions anyhow, and complaints were sometimes made about planters being reluctant to make verbal or written reports to their colleagues on matters of mutual interest.[57] When Ruffin offered to address the farmers in James Hammond's neighborhood in 1846, he was told he need not bother. The interest and the social habits were not there.[58] Hammond, despite all his improving labors, himself bore some of the self-paralyzing characteristics of the solitary farmer. "If I had anyone here, to urge me on," he wrote Ruffin, "I know I could do a great deal more in every way than I do. As it is when not on horseback I pass most of my time stretched on a sofa, dreaming or at best reading."[59]

VI

Thus far the Southeastern planter has been accorded very sympathetic treatment. He was, it has been suggested, part of a far-flung community of inefficient agricultural producers; his marling operations were likely to be laborious and troublesome; his subsequent follow-through into forage-and-livestock diversification was bound to pose the most daunting problems of adaptation; and he was only thinly supplied with clear directions to guide him safely through his pilgrim's progress. Slavery intrudes as pertinent to the matter of diversification, and of indirect relevance to the exchange of ideas.

Benefit of the doubt, however, can be overextended. The entrepreneur, in the abstract at least, carries the strategic function in "capitalist" economies of innovating his way through whatever serious difficulties the production process is encountering. However powerful the conditioning, he does remain a point of analytic focus. We come, therefore, to our fifth and last point: that concerning planter responsibility. Southeastern farmers, on the whole, showed a poor capacity for judicious adaptation, whatever the category of change. Their main adaptiveness, as Fogel and Engerman imply, may have lain in their ability to quit barren soils and move on to new land, either by extending their plantations or reclaiming within them, or emigrating. That, however, is not a flexibility of much interest in this study; it is feasible only with an open frontier, is essentially nomadic, and is thoroughly uninformative about the long-term viability of slavery. In any case, as was pointed out at the beginning of this book, millions of Old South planters stayed within the confines of their old states.

The propensity of these people to evaluate and practice farm improvement was adversely affected by a number of widely noted if unmeasurable traits. The first was a comparative lack of interest in agricultural education. The second was a partiality for diverting income into display rather than into investment. The third was a complex set of conservative instincts and attitudes which kept the farmer obstinately, and sometimes rationally, attached to traditional production, and reluctant to examine intelligently and imaginatively the full range of available options. These can be considered in turn.

Ruffin believed himself to have been quite typical of the Virginia planter class when he inherited Coggin's Point thoroughly untutored in the ways of farming. "The wealthy young proprietor," he told the Historical and Philosophical Society of Virginia in 1836, "is educated far from his future property, and receives instruction almost exclusively in dead languages . . . and perhaps afterwards he adds thereto more or less of study, (or the pretence of it), of law or medicine—and having arrived at manhood, he throws all aside to undertake the new business of farming." Small farmers, confined to daily toil, were even less well equipped.[60] By the 1850s he had detected no improvement, publishing an essay in which he argued that agriculture, being a highly demanding area of enterprise if taken seriously, needed the pedagogic support of state-funded educational establishments. Something had to be done fairly urgently to deal with "the enormity of the existing want of agricultural education" and counter the widespread scorn of scientific agriculture "under the contemptuous epithet of 'book-farming.'"[61] James Hammond took a similar line. "We have," he wrote to Ruffin, "Medical Colleges—Religious Seminaries—Law Schools etc. etc. in abundance—but no school to teach especially Agriculture. And what is more not one agriculturist in 100000 knows the least thing of Botany, Geology, mineralogy or chemistry. . . . His whole occupation is one of unmixed quacking!—But you are smiling & think me wild. I am only provoked to think how many years I was flogged & flogged through Latin & Greek & how carefully the keys of all this knowledge were withheld from me & are still withheld from those who ought to be as familiar with them as A.B.C." Others added their voices to the fairly standardized complaints.[62]

It would be futile to attempt to determine the balance of responsibility here between farmer demand and educational supply. The problem clearly had deep roots in the mores of Southern society. It was not, however, unique to the South. English university education at Oxford and Cambridge was, more than anything else, a system whereby the sons of gentry and gentlefolk became clerics and acquired some traditional graces in the process.[63] Even the worldly old University of Glasgow, with a predominantly middle- and working-class student body, was sending nearly half of its graduates into the church in the 1830s. Only a tiny fraction carried their education directly back to the land—where over a million still made their living and where the agricultural sophistication, especially in southern and eastern counties, was as high as any in Europe.[64] We are back with another of these points which, although highly important, are not peculiarly Southern. Farmers generally in Western Europe and North America rarely sought an agricultural education for their sons. They did not typically spend money and suffer loss of physical and managerial assistance to have their children instructed by others in the mysteries of farming science. Educational aspirations were usually conceived within a set of widely social rather than narrowly practical priorities. Boys for the most part were being turned into gentlemen with function and income rather than into scientists and mechanics—and such gentlemen, of course, while acquiring style, confidence, connections, and at least a veneer of learning, could also be, as Henry Barnard saw them at Charlottesville, "a set of pretty wild fellows generally."[65]

One or two agricultural professorships were set up before the Civil War, and 1858 also saw the establishment of the Maryland Agricultural College.[66] Achievement overall was insignificant. Ronald and Janet Numbers' recent appraisal of scientific education in the antebellum South contains no mention of agricultural work. By most measurable criteria, they claim, the South "lagged markedly behind the Northeast in promoting science" as a whole.[67] William Scarborough has lately identified a growing relationship between science and the plantation in the decades immediately preceding the Civil War, but stresses that only a small elite was affected and that its activities had very little impact on agriculture.[68] Ruffin formed, for him, the upsetting opinion that whatever the virtues of the case for change it could easily collapse if presented exclusively in the written word. It was not simply that planters did not read a great deal, though that was certainly a problem; it was also that they did not necessarily believe what they read. This in part reflected simple prejudice against book farming. "We must learn," declared one journal, "not to repulse information because we find it in books."[69] For Ruffin it was also a question of preference for visual over documentary proof. "It is true, and lamentable," he wrote, "that all that is said, written, or published . . . has scarcely any effect, even on those who hear and read all the facts and reasoning. But exhibit the same truths to the eyes of the same persons, and twenty of them will follow the example, where one would without such ocular proofs being presented." Improvements had to come before *"the eyes"* of the farmer to create any impression.[70] What was more, declared James Hammond, an advance had also to be *"decisive & established* before it will be admitted."[71]

Conspicuous consumption was another feature of Southern life which troubled Ruffin. It was a common characteristic of societies with much surviving "aristocratic" influence and pretension combined with relatively limited or narrowly conceived investment opportunities.[72] Insofar as it had hospitable, socializing dimensions it may also be seen as another consequence of isolated living—of the solitary farmer encouraging contact and making the most of it when it materialized.[73] Henry Barnard recorded his experience in the 1830s of "the princely hospitality of the *gentle* born families." At Hill Carter's Shirley plantation he enjoyed a huge feast at a splendidly appointed table, and washed it down with a variety of fine European wines.[74] Carter demonstrated that one *could* spend kings' ransoms on display and at the same time virtuously pursue agricultural improvement. Indeed, if queried, he might have asserted that the grandee style of life gave incentive, requiring as it did the sort of income that only intelligent farming could provide on Virginia soils.

The equation, of course, was of much less relevance lower down the class strata where the constraints of income and debt were tighter and where a single bout of extravagance might seriously compromise some improving investment. It could, in fact, be dubious at any level since scale alone did not guarantee wealth. Ruffin saw much extravagance when he moved among the summer houses of the tidewater gentry in South Carolina in 1843. John Manning's "palace" impressed him by its beauty. He could not, however, "but condemn the building, in its location, as a waste which even the great wealth of the proprietor cannot serve to justify."[75] He was in the country of the land killers and, although seigneurial himself, could only sense the essential fatuity of architectural display combined with agricultural ignorance. He was also offended by the celebrated "hospitality of Old Virginia." It had, he thought, been carried to great excess and had produced the "ruin of thousands of the kindest and warmest hearted people in the world." Among other things, it had attracted a host of gentlemanly spongers—men more capable of destroying a district than "clouds of Asiatic locusts, accompanied by the Asiatic cholera." The farmer who had the notion of improving his land was faced with a choice: either conform to the local display or be branded a "niggardly churl." Most preferred a bad farm to a bad name.[76]

What Ruffin failed to articulate with sufficient analytical force and clarity was the unsurprising fact that farmers, presented with any case for changing generations-old ways, were highly likely to prove resistant and uncomprehending. This was much more than a question of the novelty, difficulty, and time span of the particular reform program. It was also one of environmental condition, state of mind, and the interplay between the two. The man most in need of change, working a small farm of thin, unproductive fields, insecure and in debt, was likely to be the man with the least time, inclination, and risk-enduring capacity to undertake it. Few had the generous resources, spare hours, and experimental inclinations of the James River grandees.

As for slave ownership, this exercised influences at all social levels, intrinsic rigidities in the size of the labor force being compounded by noneconomic considerations of prestige, loyalty, and sheer dogged attachment to things as they were. In 1833, just before slavery became a closed issue, a New Kent planter wrote to the *Farmers' Register* about the institution being the "insuperable barrier" to improvement. "The owners barely can breathe, and not infrequently are compelled to sell one or more every year to square their accounts. But many would rather sell their teeth than their slaves."[77] Sales in Virginia, Ruffin suggested in 1832, were usually held up by "sentiments of humanity, and . . . false shame" until "compelled by creditors, and . . . carried into effect by the sheriff, or by the administrator of the debtor."[78]

Planters might also hold back from marling or greencropping because of aversion to undue contact with field labor. C. W. Gooch observed in 1833 that "the possession of slaves has had too great a tendency to make the owner and his family unwilling to take upon themselves any part of the drudgery of out-door business."[79] It was not fashionable for genteel Virginians to apply themselves to the details of practical work. The fault lay in part with the identification of work with slavery, and with the grand manners deriving from incomes which slave labor could support—manners which could be imitated quite a long way down the social scale. Such attitudes were perpetuated by the indulgence of the young—"idle, dissipated, vicious, with pistols in their pockets, and the fumes of liquor in their brains," in the Reverend George Pierce's words.[80] Ruffin's stern instincts found this thoroughly repellent. He insisted on having his own sons trained as "working men." Both Edmund Jr. and Charles were railway engineers in their early manhood.[81] Charles Yancey considered it "one great objection to slavery" that farmers should be able to survive almost entirely on the "reluctant labor of slaves . . . to the neglect of the important duty of rearing their sons to labor, either in the mechanic arts, or on the farm; to train them up to industry and economy, thereby lessening the inducements of vice and immoral practices."[82]

Emigration too had a major impact. Those who went were often, by their very departure, people of spirit. Virginia emigration, in C. W. Gooch's view in 1833, had "not only swept off the most enterprising portion of our people, but also much of the capital and moveable property of the state."[83] Resources which might have been directed to Southeastern improvements were being lost to the region.[84] Disrespect for Eastern soils greatly influenced those who remained upon them. Unsettling thoughts of emigration lingered on in many minds and could get in the way of long-term assaults on local problems.[85] Bad farming, combined with cheap Western acres, poor transport, and stunted urbanization, served to depress land prices in the Old South and, for the simpler minded, helped cast doubt on the very rationale of improvement. There was, noted Ruffin, a mistaken idea that the expense of marling ought to bear some relation to the selling price of the land. Many farmers, he wrote, "conclude that the improvement cannot justify an expense of six dollars on an acre of land that would not previously sell for four dollars." Low prices, moreover, tended to strengthen the old habit of survival by land purchase rather than by land improvement.[86] Objective circumstances were not changing sufficiently to alter traditional priorities. Despite the westward movement of the frontier, there were still patches of swamp and of fresh and abandoned land available around and within plantations, and of course the farms of the emigrants were there to be bought up at depressed prices. "How frequently," wrote a correspondent of the *Southern Agriculturist* in 1841, "do we hear the opening of lands alleged in excuse of neglect in many operations essential to good husbandry."[87] At the most simplistic level of all, there must have been many who simply did not believe that their fields, so battered by decades of crude, exhaustive farming, so thin and sandy to the eye, could ever be made to yield abundant crops.[88] Where the need was greatest, so also, very frequently, was the neglect.

The mass of farmers settled for low incomes and a simple life, unwilling to yield that "additional spirit of improvement" which Ebenezer Emmons called for in 1852.[89] Craven refers to powerful "forces of ignorance and habit" in the border states, and Moore to an agrarian conservatism which was "the natural result of employing slave labor in an atmosphere of impermanence engendered by progressive soil erosion." For Cash, the planters generally went through their lives in a state of paralyzing complacency and self-satisfaction.[90] Ruffin was clearly appalled by their blinkered view of the world they inhabited. In 1832 he observed that only promises of extravagantly high profits could get them to change their ways; in the 1840s he totally failed to influence farming practice in South Carolina through the labors attending his survey; and a day or two before his death he recorded that his teaching had been "mostly slighted & neglected."[91] Even his great disciple James Hammond succumbed periodically to the mental miasma, confessing to Ruffin in 1851 that he had not visited some of his fields for five years. His marling experiments, he recorded, had been laughed at by neighbors "who would enjoy every failure as a good joke."[92]

Marling, liming, and associated improvements were, in aggregate, troublesome and demanding—even for those who had deposits on their lands and could avoid transport problems. Because of this and because of their social and economic environment and their related mental dispositions, farmers found it extremely difficult to be responsive to Ruffin's proposals. Slavery exercised a number of direct and indirect influences, as suggested. But even if the entrepreneur were not adversely affected by the institutional context, slavery would remain at the center of the picture. The slave-owning planter was both function *and* component. The master was as intrinsic to the system as was the chattel laborer.

Part Five

The Inadaptability of Slavery

Chapter Twelve

Conclusions on the Failure of Reform

I

THE effort throughout has been to document and analyze Edmund Ruffin's experience as an agricultural reformer in order to gain some close, if partial, understanding of the capacity of slave agriculture to adapt and therefore to survive. Ruffin's case is a highly important and illuminating one. His period forces us to dwell on slavery in its final antebellum years; his location obliges us to examine the old, increasingly marginal areas of the institution, where the economic, social, and political crises were at their most acute; and his reforms constitute the single most radical yet rudimentary set of ideas ever laid before Southern farmers.

The principal conclusions must be about slavery, but it would be foolish to ignore other notions and clarifications that have emerged along the way. Generalizations can therefore be sought on both Ruffin himself and on Southern agricultural change, as well as on the central issue of institutional viability—differentiating not because the issues are particularly discrete but because the three categories have their own identities and relate individually to substantial bodies of historiography.

II

Edmund Ruffin, by his own high standards and periodically by his own incisive testimony, was a failure. His reform proposals had only minor effects on agriculture, and these almost exclusively in the border states. His political cause of secessionism ended in the nightmares of protracted war, family loss, and abolition.

The agricultural failure in particular needs to be stressed, since it is not well known. There was, most obviously, the premature demise of the *Farmers' Register*, the futility of the South Carolina survey, and the almost universal disregard of his proposals. Yet Avery Craven, J. Carlyle Sitterson, and Kathleen Bruce all refer to his contribution to an "agricultural revolution," and in his biography of Ruffin, Craven declares that "a new economic order had begun to rise on the foundations laid by this humble teacher."[1] Clement Eaton writes that Ruffin's labors helped bring about a "renaissance of agriculture in Virginia, Maryland, and the Carolinas."[2] William Scarborough, rather more circumspectly, claims that Ruffin "revitalized agriculture in the Upper South."[3] These observations are very misleading.

A successful reformer, busy persuading more and more of his compatriots, flattered and encouraged by the visible results of his labors, and honored for his contribution to the revival of sectional wealth and power, would hardly have pulled back from public service as Ruffin did just before his fiftieth birthday. His full-time professional "career" ended with the submission of his South Carolina report in 1843 and his retreat shortly after to the privacy of Marlbourne. Indeed, since this sustained commitment to reform had only begun in 1833, with the launching of the *Register*, it can be seen that for all but a decade of his life (and his final years) Ruffin was first and foremost a private farmer. Initially he had a youthful, experimental interest in improvement, challenging old ecological assumptions,[4] securing his family's continuing residence in eastern Virginia, and enthusiastically offering his fellow planters a plan for recovery. In later years, his wealth and position secured and his illusions exposed, he was attempting to capitalize privately on well-tested ideas and attend to the material future of the next generation, communicating with the farming public only irregularly and uncertainly. There is no evidence for the 1850s to suggest that he believed a fifth edition of *Calcareous Manures* would succeed where the *Farmers' Register* had failed ten years earlier. His late agricultural writings tended to be desultory in character and were probably in part a carry-over from past habits of inquiry and patrician pronouncement. He did have a local reputation, and vanity alone would have dictated some effort to remain in the public eye.

It is the case, however, that in his busy years with the *Register* and the Carolina survey he attached great importance to his public labors, occasionally entertaining hopes of a breakthrough in Southeastern attitudes and practices. The diary he kept during the survey reveals a typical combination of naive optimism and rueful skepticism. A year or two later the hopes had vanished, and in 1852 he ended a "plain and unvarnished" address to South Carolina planters with forecasts of "ruin, destitution, and . . . degradation." In it he also stressed the essential political perspective to his work.

> If Virginia, South Carolina, and the older slave-holding States . . . had been improved according to their capacity, they would have retained nearly all the population they have lost by emigration, and that retained population, with its increase, would have given them more than a doubled number of representatives in the Congress of the United States. This greater strength would have afforded abundant legislative safeguards against the plunderings and oppressions of tariffs to protect Northern interests . . . and all such acts to the injury of the South, effected by the greater legislative strength of the now more powerful, and to us, the hostile and predatory States of the confederacy.[5]

There is a thread in Ruffin biography—running from Craven through to Mitchell, and lying uncomfortably with common assertions of revolutionary impact—which conveys that Ruffin throughout his life was an unbalanced man, given to excesses of hatred, resentment, self-pity, and antisocial withdrawal and to foolish, injudicious behavior. It is largely a matter of emphasis and nuance, but it does sometimes seem as though historians start, in their minds, with the drama of Fort Sumter and the symbolically pointed suicide and then work back through the secessionism of the 1850s to the agricultural years of the 1840s and earlier, characterizing and explaining Ruffin's whole life by the intemperance and despair of his old age. Thus, for example, the wild foray into financial and political issues in the early 1840s, thereby bringing down the *Register*—a misconception, as has been shown above. Thus his premature resignation from the South Carolina survey late in 1843, when in fact he had more or less completed his contracted period in the state and written a fine 175-page report. Thus his denunciation of Virginia planters and his retreat to Marlbourne in 1844, as though that was some self-indulgent act of pique, unrelated to the condition of the reform movement in the state.

The experiments of the 1820s, the book of 1832, the journal of 1833–42, the state survey of 1843, the transformation of Marlbourne in the late 1840s and early 1850s—all show Ruffin to have been a man of great scientific insight and originality, of immense energy on behalf of causes in which he believed, and probably of more sophisticated judgment in agricultural matters than anyone else working in the section. At the same time he was a man who could exhibit ill humor, impatience, and other self-defeating peculiarities of temperament. When the agricultural cause faded after the mid-1840s, these found an ideal outlet in the anger and self-vindications of secessionism. But they should not be allowed to color the character and achievement of the agricultural work. That shows Ruffin at his most persistent, steady, and spirited.

The fact that he came increasingly to see his reforms as a means of rescuing the slave society of the Old South, and that slavery appealed to him mainly as a means of race control and class support,[6] is thoroughly blemishing by most modern perspectives. However, we have not yet had recourse to facile moralizing. Seen in historical and sectional contexts, his preoccupations were not particularly abnormal or extreme. Ruffin came from the class most likely to give bold and voluble articulation to widely held local anxieties. And unlike the great mass of his fellow Southerners he, for a while, had a solution, and a peaceful one at that. If there was any decent way to go about the protection of the institution which supported the white South, it probably lay more with the quiet processes of education and reform than with the excitements of secessionism and war. Ruffin's unique fascination is that he practiced the first well into middle age, and then quite dramatically succumbed to the second. This is highly instructive, in relation both to the reform capacities of slave agriculture and to the power of self-protective obsessions generated within a beleaguered slave society.

Despite the manifest virtues, Ruffin remains in many respects a defective reformer. It would be a mistake, however, to see this exclusively in terms of personality. One has to stress again the circumscriptions of Ruffin's class. His writings were directed in the main towards his fellow grandees: men of some literacy who had time and inclination to read books and subscribe to journals and who might be able to follow some simple science and elementary logic. The language and style of all his works was elegant, patrician, and uncondescending. One senses a wish to enter some Southern pantheon of letters: at the very least, a strong desire to impress the seigneurial population on the York, the James, and the Santee as well as the scientific community in Charleston. Despite the fact that most of his advice had to do with practical operations, he appears never to have considered the possibility of producing a handbook for the common cultivator.

One of the rare times in which he addressed the problem of humble-farm improvement was in the *Register* in September 1835. He inverted the issue on the one hand by declaring that an abundance of money never ensured improvement, and begged it on the other by asserting that the deprived farmer was usually much less responsive to new ideas than his wealthier neighbor. It was, nevertheless, the case "that many poor farmers have engaged" in marling "earlier than many of the rich" on the south side of the James. He did not cite numbers, naming instead the single case of John Moore of Prince George County, Virginia, who worked inferior land, had debts to pay off, and lacked both slaves and calcareous resources. With the help of his two young sons and a horse, Moore had succeeded over eight years in bringing marl onto his farm and spreading it on seventy-five acres, the labor being terminated by his death from cholera in 1834.

The tone of Ruffin's remarks suggests that Moore was highly exceptional, and the title of the piece—"Account of Marling Labors, Executed Under Great Disadvantages"—reveals that he saw little benefit in being a small farmer. "There was," he concluded, "not only the absence of spare capital, spare labor, and spare time—but the continued presence and pressure of privation and debt. Above all—there was want of information, and of any existing mode of general communication amongst farmers." Moore, Ruffin implied, was unusual and heroic.[7] Others of his achievement were unlikely to have been numerous. No one was trying very hard to explain to the hosts of small farmers how they might profitably proceed.

Ruffin's failure, then, should be interpreted in the context of the slave society and economy and, less consequentially, of his own elevated rank within it. He was, very literally and comprehensively, a victim of the institution he sought so desperately to protect.

III

On strictly farming matters, a number of general observations can be offered. This study, after all, presents detailed analysis of a very important category of agricultural advance. Too often in the past the question of improvement has been studied by static econometrics, by circumstantial surmise, by the aggregating of diverse and loosely coordinated data, or by close examination of small areas. On the Ruffin reforms specifically, there has to date been no significant attempt at measurement and no informed, extended discussion of the scientific principles underlying the proposals.

First, it should be noted that the whole category of farm improvement has been disaggregated here, with the focus resting squarely on what might be seen as one of its most basic components. The need for specificity in analysis of agricultural change is one of the principal assumptions underlying this study. Not only must differences be emphasized between the respective demands of land amelioration and other forms of advance. Amelioration itself has to be broken down into the dissimilarly taxing operations of marling and liming.

Second, there should be no doubting the validity of reform efforts in the Old South. The negative determinisms of the frontier, the soil, the climate, and the cotton market have been questioned, and Ruffin himself, despite intense frustrations, never viewed any of these four factors as particularly potent (though he knew that local perceptions gave them considerable *subjective* power). The successful minority who followed Ruffin's proposals would have thought it very odd to have been told that their labors had been pointless. If a man wished to remain resident in the Southeast and was able, through judicious marling, to increase his net income—and perhaps his social and political standing as well—then it was entirely sensible for him to assemble his laborers and carts and commence digging and hauling at the earliest possible date.

Third, it has been demonstrated by both theory and practice that Ruffin's ideas were sound and of fundamental importance for agriculture in the old states of the South. The results of marling and liming were usually very striking. Uncovered land in damp, temperate climates was almost universally prone to acidity, thus lowering yields through toxicity and reduced availability of plant nutrients. There may have been no Ruffin "revolution" in the Old South, but there does seem to have been some radical agro-demographic change in Ruffin's own Prince George County for a time in the 1830s and 1840s. Odd patches like that, where there was a high density of improvement and a check to emigration, showed the potential force of the reforms.

It is of course clear from the survival of hundreds of thousands of non-marling farmers that there could be economic viability on acid soils. This was so to a small degree because the best tobacco required that condition and to a larger degree because a great many people were prepared to put up with modest and frequently precarious livings, knowing nothing of marl or knowing enough about it to sense that it meant a lot of trouble. Income targets were mixed in with convenience, ease, and comfort targets. Many could have earned a great deal more, but spurned the opportunity. Some, with large plantations on good cotton lands, continued to do very well in years when prices were high. Many others, objectively quite capable of staying on, chose to conform to popular fatalism by abandoning their seaboard livings and moving off to new lands farther west.

Fourth, although the practices in question were European in origin, it would be nonsensical to suggest that they were somehow irrelevant for North America: that all European advances stemmed from a hunger for land and an abundance of labor and were, accordingly, unexportable to land-rich, labor-scarce America; and that agricultural reformers in the United States were bookish Europhiles, out of touch with the structural realities of their own economic environments.

Calcareous improvement was appropriate to parts of America because acid soils tended to be comparatively unremunerative and because it could be attended to in slack seasons by resident laborers at low cost and with minimal skill. Genovese has argued that Southern reforms were held back by high costs and ham-fisted, halfhearted workers, the problem only being resolvable by slave sales on a scale sufficient to open the way for free labor and raise the funds needed for improvement.[8] This is comprehensively inapplicable to marling. Existing laborers and budgets could cope. Moreover, the very idea of slave exports was one that Ruffin abhorred.[9]

British comparisons have been introduced, but it will be recalled that these concerned transport provision and not farming itself, the purpose being only to demonstrate crucial differences in infrastructural provision between two dissimilar economies. Strictly agricultural observations, however, would not have been entirely out of place, given the applicability of ameliorative practice to both countries and the fact that British farmers, working increasingly in an international economy and under awkward climatic and pedological circumstances, faced essentially similar choices between adaptation and emigration—to the cities, to the United States, or to the vast and growing imperial frontier. What is more, poor acid lands in Britain had frequently been areas of great advance, dramatically demonstrating the dynamic character of intelligent soil management. Ruffin often inserted extracts from British agricultural texts into the *Register*, probably intending them to prove practicability and help stimulate by example. The fact that planters took almost no notice is only partly explained by their being Americans.

Fifth, important differences of effort, understanding, and expense have been set out between basic amelioration and subsequent diversification. Genovese's remarks on reform difficulties have much more applicability to the latter, since these tended to be more demanding on management and labor, and often more costly as well. Post-marling diversification was uncommon in areas where there had not been some *prior* experience of breaking out from old, cramped ways, and this, as has been argued, owed much to the range and complexity of the new, varied operations and the sometimes awkward task of integrating them into a balanced farming year. Disaggregation is required not only to separate the crude from the sophisticated but to draw further distinctions *within* advanced rotational farming. There was no standardized set of problems. The rearing of dairy cattle and the growing of red clover, for example, made quite different demands on the financial and human resources of a plantation, despite the fact that the two operations might be in very close functional association.

Sixth, the significance of amelioration is not confined entirely by its own specifity. Its study may be irrelevant to an understanding of most operations in mixed farming, but it may yield hints on the application of commercial fertilizers. For many of these, the on-farm expense, skill, and schedule aspects must, as for marl, have been very permissive, thereby facilitating one highly important category of improvement. The transport-cost impediment must also have been similar, since such fertilizers were extraneous to the farm (though usually with easier value-to-weight ratios). Julius Rubin makes the general point that innovations likely to raise productivity among cotton growers were available only to a small elite: those who could practice deep plowing on rich alluvial soils and "those on thin soils but with cheap transportation which enabled them to buy large amounts of fertilizer."[10] Transport costs were a crucial variable and helped separate the small minority who could progress technically from the huge majority who could not. (Their inclinations, of course, were quite another matter.)

Genovese argues that high freights helped prevent widespread purchase of Peruvian guano, the best fertilizer marketed in the 1840s and 1850s. He criticizes Rosser Taylor and Weymouth Jordan for suggesting, with insufficient evidence, that there was major resort to the fertilizer immediately before the Civil War.[11] This is entirely appropriate. Jordan's talk of a guano "mania" greatly exaggerates its importance: a case of the practice being assumed from the idea. Southern imports only reached notable proportions in the early 1850s, and were already in serious decline before the end of the decade. Considering distribution between different ports, likely consumption hinterlands, and glutting followed by re-exportation to Britain in the mid-1850s, one can estimate the annual average Old South consumption at not very much more than 20,000 tons over the peak years 1851–57.[12] The equivalent British figure (excluding indirect imports) was just under 190,000 tons.[13]

Most of the guano was taken by Delaware, Maryland, and Virginia—states with 15 million acres of "improved" farmland in 1860. No more than 1 or 2 percent of that area could have been treated in these years of maximum interest.[14] In the Carolinas and Georgia, consumption was quite inconsequential. Taylor attributes meager purchases in South Carolina in part to "original cost plus cost of delivery," and notes how the Charleston agent in the centralized Peruvian trade had to pay $9 freight on each ton received from Baltimore in 1853.[15] Transport costs could be as high as $15 (adding perhaps one-third to wholesale prices) for other parts of the Southeast.[16] A Georgia planter pleaded in 1853 that "the managers of our railroads, river boats, etc." should try to bring down freights on guano in order to stimulate some interest.[17]

Even high-value manufactured items could be affected by poor transport. In 1849 Edmund Ruffin wrote to George Watt, a Virginia implement maker, telling him that his friend and kinsman Judge Thomas Ruffin of Alamance County, North Carolina, wanted to try out some plows. Carriage costs were so high, however, that there would be no possibility of sending back any that did not suit. They would therefore have to be of exactly the right sort for Thomas Ruffin's variously stiff and rocky soils, and accompanied too by clear instructions. "The long distance, and the expense and risks of transportation," Ruffin observed, "make the great difficulties of obtaining your implements here. It will be to your interest to lighten these difficulties, so far as you can."[18]

Seventh, the geographical range of this study is considerably narrower than the extent of slavery itself. Our region, however, is unquestionably the one in which the need for adaptation was most acute. A great many farmers to the south and west still had abundant land to spare, and Ruffin took little account of their affairs. Many, in any event, worked naturally calcareous soils, like the canebrakes of Alabama. This, however, does not mean to say that seaboard affairs were peculiar to themselves. Destructive practices were widely employed beyond the mountains, and in many localities yields were falling off after only a short period of settlement. John Hebron Moore writes of the "exhaustion" of lands around Natchez, Mississippi, before 1790. In the early nineteenth century: "Ten to twenty years of cultivation in row crops usually brought ruin to hill lands in all parts" of the state.[19] The frontier could not be extended forever. Natural limits would someday be encountered. Many of the problems of the Old South would progressively become the problems of the West.

The agricultural experience of the pressurized Southeast probably reveals more about the long-run economic prospects of slavery than do the successes of many of the large plantations of the Deep South and West where "rational management" was devising efficient systems of labor specialization and task interdependence, and perhaps achieving some economies of scale as well.[20] These conducted themselves by essentially static rules of accommodation to an external and ungovernable world cotton market. Their secular flexibility and adaptability have yet to be demonstrated. They may well have represented only a quasi-sophisticated structure of production, erected on a primitive, insecure base of exhaustive farming techniques, captive labor, costly credit, and temporary patterns of internal land availability and external raw-material demand, their managerial talents centering on elaborate routinism and timely nomadism.

IV

What final observations can be offered on slavery? In summary, it seems that it hindered agricultural improvement in three principal ways: through entrepreneurship, through transport, and through the impulse and spirit of reform.

The quality of entrepreneurial performance is extremely difficult to measure with precision, and the links between a complex slave society and the economic behavior of myriad planters within it evade anything more than impressionistic description. The issue, however, cannot be ignored. The farmer, after all, as owner and coordinator, performed the vital managerial roles within the slave economy. On his knowledge, foresight, imagination, and judgment rested much of the well-being of the system. He was the key internal, dynamic variable. Much of his activity has to be interpreted and evaluated in epistemic terms.

Knowledge was especially critical in consequence of its great *comparative* importance. Among other marling variables, labor and land were largely in position, and capital was not needed in substantial, additional quantities for on-farm operations. These factors of production themselves, of course, lay before farmers cognitively as well as physically. I have offered the conclusion elsewhere that the "controllers of slave agriculture were obstructed by combinations of resisted, partial, and misleading knowledge, and a pessimistic cramping of objectives."[21] And even if one were to insist that this defective behavior had nothing to do with slavery—that it had no connection with spoiling privilege, social display, indolence, contempt for manual labor, shortage of funds, isolation, and stagnant home markets—it would still have to be remembered that the planter was as intrinsic a component of the institution as were his black laborers. There could be no slavery without slaveholders. The possessed had to have possessors. When a slaveowner acted in a particular way, slavery itself was in motion. There is no conceptual or historical sense in separating slaveholder from slavery and agonizing over relations between the two.

In the matter of transport costs, slavery exercised relatively mechanistic and measurable influences. These could be very powerful and, being systemic, could not easily be willed away. Marl was rarely moved around commercially in the Old South, in sharp contrast to the mobility evident in the North and in Britain. Ruffin's concern here indicates how troubled he was by such compounding of the basic entrepreneurial problem. Planters were already mostly ignorant or dismissive, even when they had marl on or around their lands. When transport expense and effort were added to the other requirements for amelioration, the prospects for progress became bleak in the extreme.

The arguments on communications rest on Southern documentation, but also on three different bodies of scholarly work. First, there is that of Julius Rubin and F. M. L. Thompson, who separately claim—one for the United States, the other for Britain—that transport costs were, in the nineteenth century, becoming an increasingly important variable in agricultural advance; second, Ralph Anderson and Robert Gallman's notions of the atomized plantation economy being a consequence of the fixed-capital slave labor force; third, Samir Amin and Hamza Alavi's characterizations of disarticulated, lopsided economies, in which channels of commercial access to the capitalist metropoles are relatively lively while lines of internal communication are relatively moribund. Fragmentation persists, and what development occurs is largely skewed and agrarian. The economy retains pronounced colonial and dependent features. There is a fourth important point, concerning what might be termed geomorphological insufficiency. It is not enough to have a multiplicity of river and ocean highways. Since goods are not thrown into the water and allowed to float to their destinations, there can be no "natural" transport facilities worthy of comment in economic analysis. The most that one can cite is a decent physical basis for the employment of vessels, that latter provision being the key determinant of utility.

All four are reducible, practically, to questions of cost and convenience. If an improvement was dependent on off-farm resources, and if these were bulky and low in value and likely to have their initial worth doubled or trebled in the course of short, troublesome journeys, the planter was very likely to disregard it and continue with traditional ways.

Transport, of course, concerned sales as well as inputs. Whatever might be said about the scale and range of the internal market in the slave economy—and there is much disagreement on the issue—freight levels may well intrude as important determinants of that market's capacity to function. Whatever the potential level of consumption calculable from the material needs of a slave labor force and the food and raw material requirements of urban populations, it must be demonstrated that demand could become market, that buying power could be realized within a network of exchange. If transport costs were very high they would seriously impair the development of plantation-market relations. This would intensify the already strong tendency towards self-sufficiency, and damage the incentives to engage in diversified commercial production.

There is, lastly, the question of slavery and the articulation and pursuit of reform ideas. Politically, the institution had ambivalent effects: stimulating reform, as a protective and conservative exercise; compromising it, when discouragement and disillusion set in and alternative methods of defense were sought. The urgent issue of slavery's survival could pull attention away from the slow process of economic regeneration to the simpler strategy of secessionism. Ronald and Janet Numbers suggest that slavery also got in the way of scientific advance through "wasted time and energy devoted to its defense."[22] It was easier to hate Yankees than understand soil chemistry. The immodest, defensive spirit of the antebellum South was not conducive to critical self-evaluation.

Insofar as slavery encouraged social isolation, it impeded the circulation of literature and the verbal exchange of ideas, and, of course, provided

Ruffin with refuges into which he could retreat. His experience with the *Farmers' Register* in Petersburg is partly that of a man of rural experience unable to cope with the infidelities of town living. Unfortunately, he needed the urban world if his reform ideas were to be vigorously publicized.[23]

If one were searching for simple conclusions, one might find them in the idea that slavery not only hindered much reform but was itself intrinsically unreformable by the time Ruffin began his work. It was there to be protected and advanced by political action or by salvationist and revivalist appeal, but there were few thoughts of radically changing it. Even in the famous debates in the Virginia legislature in 1831–32, critical sentiment largely comprised wishing the institution away, and black men and women with it.[24]

Perhaps it was the typical predicament of people running an authoritarian system and fearing the sudden end of their control and the liberation of their victims. In imperialist government, any joys of conquest were quickly replaced by the insecurities of ruling uninvited in alien territory. Reforms therein had usually to do with fiscal solvency and army efficiency, the expansion of metropolitan economic interest, and the self-defeating accommodations of local nationalism. The worst moments came when the fragility of alien rule was, subjectively at least, exposed by indigenous revolt, unleashing pent-up excesses of racist reaction. The classic case in British imperialism was the Indian Mutiny. The classic case in American slavery was the Nat Turner uprising. In such tense, rigid systems, solutions come in the end not with adjustment but with removal: with colonial independence in the case of imperialism; with abolition in the case of slavery.

Imperialism and slavery, of course, were very different in that the imperialist ruled in generally foreign and unfamiliar land and had to cope with indigenous politics. The slaveholder, by contrast, lived at home, "knew" his slaves, and had no significant set of political demands to deal with. The dissimilarity, however, can be overstated. The imperialist, after all, had lines of escape to the mother country or to other colonies. And the slaveholder, though resident on his native or adopted turf, was governing people whom he might be choosing increasingly to view as biological and ethnic aliens; and who, by their very numbers and external support, seemed to be threatening the homeland.[25]

Ruffin certainly believed for a while that *agriculture* could be reformed, in some relatively neutral and technical manner, and that the benefits could spread to the institution. What he probably did not suppose, when he first took up the cause of economic advance, was that slavery itself might impede change and would consequently have to be placed on the agenda of any thoroughgoing reform program. He was not unique. There were many people who could talk about desirable developments in the section: tempering monoculture, keeping more livestock, improving the land, or building up a larger manufacturing base. But there were none around of any position who argued that such community objectives could best be secured by modifying or abolishing slavery. As long as the dominant institution remained inviolable, generalized appeals for economic and sectional recovery were, at best, windy and ill thought-out and, at worst, specious and self-serving. Ruffin's pleas belonged more to the first than the second, and his secessionism does at least appear to have had the virtue of honesty. If slavery was to be asserted, and comprehensive reform thereby denied, there were hardly any other options left. The popular one of issue-blurring and finger-crossing held no appeal for Ruffin.

The section was in the grip of race fear. The black man paralyzed the South not through his ineptitude but through the white man's contemplation of his presence.

V

There is always a danger in selective analysis of implying exclusivity in relationships: in this case, of conveying tight, closed interplays between slavery and farming. But it has never been posited here that there was any exact geographical correlation between slave densities and agricultural practice. We have instead been looking for slavery's regional, systemic influences through the aggregate economy and society, acknowledging a potentially wide range of impact on individual plantations.

Regression graphs for 1850, plotting slave population percentages county by county against: a) demographic change over the preceding decade; b) percentage of land classified in the census as "improved";[26] and c) acreage values for all tidewater down to the Savannah, and for Maryland, Virginia, and South Carolina individually, show a patternless mixture of positive and negative coefficients. Only one of the twelve is of clear statistical significance: 0.61 for slavery and Virginia improved land.[27]

Highland farms *without* slaves could operate by the most primitive methods; tidewater plantations *with* slaves could practice advanced forms of diversified farming. There was clearly no comprehensive incompatibility between slavery and farming progress. The history of the colonial and independent South is a long, if irregular, chronicle of expanding cultivation and growing wealth. The planters' talent was to occupy land which, by virtue of climate, location, and chattel labor, could give them powers of competitive production in a few subtropical and temperate commodities highly valued among European consumers and manufacturers. They had never been doomed to poverty. But could they adapt when they lost their old advantages?

The answer, of course, is that some could. Ruffin had numerous followers in Virginia, even though they formed a minute percentage of the farming population. Many of these men were slaveholders. This is partly the result of contiguity: all the marl and a high proportion of the slaves were found together in tidewater. It may also be a result of slavery itself, given that the institution nourished a good number of wealthy, literate, leisured, *Register*-reading planters, positioned by a river, owning water craft, and interested to discover for themselves what all the marl talk was about, and to keep their laborers busy on days when they had no other worthwhile work to do. Thus it was that Ruffin could claim of Virginia marling in 1852: "On the lands of our best improvers and farmers . . . slave-labor is used not only exclusively and in larger than usual proportion . . . but is deemed indispensable to the greatest profits."[28] Negative, restraining factors could clearly be transcended on an individual basis if entrepreneurship was lively and transport costs low. As it happened, however, only a comparatively small number enjoyed the right combination of will, ability, and good fortune.

Progress was by no means ruled out by slavery. Likewise, inertia was not necessarily the consequence of slavery. A preponderance of agricultural activity, whatever the relations of production, can have retarding effects on agrarian reform. It was, commented Joel Poinsett in 1845, "instructive to trace the improvement of Agriculture in Great Britain, growing out of the increase of manufactures in that country."[29] It is a simple, unperplexing paradox that agriculture is most easily stimulated within a vigorously industrializing society. Manufacturing requires transport improvements and these yield external economies to other sectors. Wealth accumulates and financial institutions are refined. Population expands, urban markets grow, modernizing ideas circulate, and traders and industrialists may carry capital and entrepreneurship back to the land. "Merchants," wrote Adam Smith, "are commonly ambitious of becoming country gentlemen, and when they do, they are generally the best of all improvers."[30] Although there are dangers of large appropriations of rural surplus by landed and urban groups, it is nonetheless usual, historically, for there to be mutually progressive relations between manufacturing and agriculture in advanced economies. Genovese's comment that "industrialization is unthinkable without an agrarian revolution which shatters the old regime in the countryside" is broadly true, and is certainly applicable to the South, but it is also reversible.[31]

One very specific difficulty for agriculture operating in a nonindustrial economy was that posed by the virtual absence of lime production in the South. Imports had to be taken, at high freight charges, from the far Northeast. Ruffin viewed this dependence on industrial states as a costly absurdity, but it was of course just one part of a wider structural weakness.

There can also be over-sharp distinctions between slave workers and free workers, and the arguments in this book have at no point rested on notions of special slave inability. British agricultural literature in the nineteenth century carries innumerable complaints about the ignorance and poor workmanship of the hugely exploited farm laborers—often in the style of planterly evaluation of slaves. "Cheap labour," in R. E. Prothero's words, "was bad labour."[32] *Metayage* in France, the *mir* in Russia, *ryotwari* settlements over much of British India, and of course debt peonage in the postbellum South, reveal how circumscribed the independence of agricultural producers could be in economically "free" societies. Whatever liberty they possessed did not have effects on aspirations, commitment, and motivation such as to make them yield an obviously higher quality of labor than that of the slave. Ruffin, although prepared to see the small American-style owner-occupier as perhaps the most vigorous worker, questioned the notion of the wage earner as being generally superior to the slave. The very concept of the free worker as formulated in capitalist societies was one which he approached with a proper degree of derision.

"Labour," write Hindess and Hurst with reference to slavery in the ancient world, "has a social form which determines its character and the character of the labourers who perform it. A slave vine-dresser, however well or ill disposed he is to work, has a determinate skill to perform in a determinate social process. This skill and this process are conferred on him by the system of social production and not by his 'motivation.'"[33] Frederick Bowser gives substance to the point in his study of slavery in colonial Peru. The institution was detached from the main export sector of silver mining, which was located in the mountains and used indigenous Indian labor. Slavery operated mainly in towns and cities, and in rural areas catering for diversified urban markets. It was the second body of captive labor in the colony and was required to provide a wide range of skills and a very high degree of occupational versatility.[34]

The above remarks are offered as cautions around the basic thesis and as counters to any simplified rendering of it. It would be carrying them much too far, however, to suggest that agriculture had total ascendancy over slavery as the prime determining category. Slavery, in the South, belonged to a broadly agricultural environment, but it was not wholly subsumed by it, or a mere function of it. The institution imparted its own very important peculiarities: the captive, largely immobilized, fixed-capital laborers; the highly uneven distribution of income; the huge masses of investment funds which it attracted and absorbed; the seigneurial pretensions of the larger slaveholders; the geographical association with hot, humid areas avoided by European labor; the fears and insecurities attendant, even among non-slaveholders, upon ethnic oppression and control; and what might, in North America at least, have been practical unreformability.

Slavery, established through agricultural calculation, itself helped perpetuate agriculture's dominance in the economy, blocking the ways towards a more varied, more integrated, more urbanized economy. As Gavin Wright observes: "The internal logic of slavery slowed the growth of non-agricultural economic activity in the South."[35] It was profitable enough to absorb the abilities of most men of material ambition; it impeded the development of an effective free labor market; it created a society generally unattractive to immigrants; and its work methods tended to constrict demand for manufactured implements. William Parker observes how labor and capital were locked away, but gives special emphasis to a pattern of consumer demand polarized at extremes of subsistence and luxury requirements. Missing, between the two, was a "middle-income market" of the sort likely to stimulate small-scale rural industry and accompanying institutional and infrastructural advance.[36]

If there is a simple way out of this interfusion of categories and circularity of logic, it would be to say that slavery had certain powerful, retarding influences on the reform movement while at the same time exercising looser, more indirect effects by its contribution to the persisting rurality of the South. The assault was mounted on a very wide front.

VI

Economic history tells us, if nothing else, that the material kingdom is inherited by those who perceive and adjust and reconstitute. "Rationality," writes David Landes, "may be defined as the adaptation of means to ends."[37] As ends change in accordance with an ever-altering pattern of problems, opportunities, and desires, the need for adaptation of one sort or another is a constant in the sphere of economic behavior.

Ruffin's proposals did not constitute any universal panacea, but they did concern the very fundamentals of agricultural recovery on Eastern soils, and as such were of the highest significance. Their almost total rejection by Southern planters shows a critical inability to engage even in the most rudimentary of adaptations. The British, on the other hand, had been going ahead with them for centuries, despite perennial complaints about costs and labor requirements. More gallingly for Ruffin, farmers farther up the Eastern seaboard were liming and marling with some enthusiasm, carrying supplies in on roads, railways, canals, rivers, and coastal waters. No doubt many of the Pennsylvania and Jersey improvers had been assisted by the advice abundantly supplied in Ruffin's own publications. Benefit had unwittingly been conferred on Yankees.

Concern with adaptation and change in the antebellum years is central to Genovese's *Political Economy of Slavery* and decisively absent from Fogel and Engerman's *Time on the Cross*. These two sharply contrasting works are worth citing at the very end to confirm some rather obvious historiographical perspective. In the central essay, "The Limits of Agricultural Reform," Genovese observes that while progressive farmers such as Edmund Ruffin, David Dickson, and Martin Philips "have rightly been honored by historians for their selfless efforts and genuine achievements, on the whole they failed. They assumed that the problem was one of evolution of better methods through the dissemination of information and that a thorough reformation could take place within the slave system." Such reform was beset by a number of inherent contradictions. Radical change in Southern farming "could not take place while slavery was retained."[38] The last remark is very close to the main conclusion of this book, although the underlying analysis is different on a number of important specifics.

By contrast, there are virtually no points of contact with *Time on the Cross*. Fogel and Engerman, both there and in their later writings, have little to say about agricultural change. Reform, racist insecurity, and political anxiety are not issues. Ruffin is not cited in the index. Slave plantations are seen to have enjoyed the benefits of a drilled labor force, economies of scale, and managerial modernity, thereby winning them generally superior efficiency in comparison with Northern family farms in 1860.[39]

Others have raised questions about some of the Fogel and Engerman findings, assumptions, and algebra, but there has been surprisingly little criticism of their basic approach. The equating of efficiency with short-term profitability is a matter of scholarly choice, but it does, as suggested at the outset, present us with something very static and partial. We are told little about the dynamics of slavery or about its long-term viability. The questions addressed are appropriate to the sophisticated mathematical techniques which have been developed in recent decades; but for other issues—such as those at the heart of this study—different methods are needed. It is not simply a matter of the relative imprecision of the data; it also has to do with the limited usefulness of neoclassical economics for the historian. Abstraction, equilibrium-staticity, and impersonality are not really in his trade. Fogel and Engerman themselves acknowledge that "cliometrics provides a set of tools which are of considerable help in analyzing an important but *limited* set of problems."[40]

It is essential, though, that the noneconometric historian avoids any return to complacent, philistine traditionalism. There is little modern appeal in accumulatory agricultural history, short on intellectual direction and careless of measurement. There are many areas of inquiry in Southern economic history that require neither cliometric nor catalogic treatment but, rather, the formulation of new questions and their pursuit with as much analytical vigor, quantitative precision, and imagination as the author can assemble. Final answers will not emerge, but, with charity from readers, there might result some extended sense of the ambiguities and ironies of the past.

Abbreviations

———··❦··———

Manuscript Sources

Boykin Papers	Papers of Alexander Hamilton Boykin, near Camden, South Carolina (Southern Historical Collection, University of North Carolina Library, Chapel Hill)
Burgwyn Papers	Papers of the Burgwyn Family, Northampton County, North Carolina (Southern Historical Collection)
Greenlee Diary	Diary of James Harvey Greenlee, Burke and McDowell counties, North Carolina (Southern Historical Collection)
Hammond Papers (LC)	Papers of James Henry Hammond, Silver Bluff and Redcliffe, South Carolina (Microfilm, Library of Congress, Washington, D.C.)
Incidents	Incidents of My Life, Papers of Edmund Ruffin, Prince George and Hanover Counties, Virginia (Microfilm in Southern Historical Collection)
Lamar Plantation Book	Plantation Book of John B. Lamar, Sumter County, Georgia (University of Georgia Library, Athens, Georgia)
Lawton Papers.	Papers of Alexander Robert Lawton, Beaufort District, South Carolina (Southern Historical Collection)
MFJ	Edmund Ruffin, Farm Journal for Marlbourne, Hanover County, Virginia, 1844–1851 (Virginia State Library, Richmond)
Mills Account and Letter Books	Account Books and Letter Books of Charles F. Mills, Savannah, Georgia (Southern Historical Collection)

Norfleet Diaries	Diaries of Stephen A. Norfleet, Bertie County, North Carolina (Southern Historical Collection)
Ruffin Papers (UNC)	Papers of Edmund Ruffin, Prince George and Hanover counties, Virginia. (Microfilm in Southern Historical Collection; originals located in and owned by the Virginia Historical Society)
Ruffin Papers (LC)	Diary of Edmund Ruffin, Prince George and Hanover counties, Virginia (Library of Congress)
SC Diary	Private Diary of Edmund Ruffin, Agricultural Surveyor of South Carolina, 1843. Papers of Edmund Ruffin, Prince George and Hanover counties, Virginia (Microfilm in Southern Historical Collection)
Edmund Ruffin Jr. Plantation Diary	Plantation Diary of Edmund Ruffin Jr. of Amelia, Charles City, Hanover, and Prince George counties, Virginia (Southern Historical Collection)
Ruthven Farm Journal	Julian C. Ruffin, Ruthven Farm Journal, Prince George County, Virginia, 1848–1858 (Virginia State Library)

Printed Sources

AA	*American Agriculturist* (New York)
AF	*American Farmer* (Baltimore and Washington)
BR	*Bank Reformer* (Petersburg, Va.)
CC	*Carolina Cultivator* (Raleigh, N.C.)
DAB	*Dictionary of American Biography* (American Council of Learned Societies edition)
DBR	*De Bow's Review* (New Orleans)
FJ	*Farmer's Journal* (Bath and Raleigh, N.C.)
FR	*Farmers' Register* (Shellbanks and Petersburg, Va.)
RCA	*Report of the Commissioner for Agriculture*
RCP	*Reports to the Commissioner of Patents*
Ruffin *Diary*	*The Diary of Edmund Ruffin.* Vol. 1, *Toward Independence, October 1856–April 1861.* Vol. 2, *The Years of Hope, April 1861–June 1863.* Edited by William Kauffman Scarborough. Baton Rouge: Louisiana State University Press, 1972, 1976.
Thomas Ruffin Papers	*The Papers of Thomas Ruffin.* Edited by J. G. de Roulhac Hamilton. Raleigh: Edwards & Broughton, 1918–20.
SA	*Southern Agriculturist* (Charleston, S.C.)
SC	*Southern Cultivator* (Augusta, Athens, and Atlanta, Ga.)
SFF	*Southern Field and Fireside* (Augusta, Ga.)

SP	*Southern Planter* (Richmond)
SS	*Soil of the South* (Columbus, Ga.)
THM	*Tyler's Quarterly Historical and Genealogical Magazine* (Holdcroft, Va. [?])
VMHB	*Virginia Magazine of History and Biography* (Richmond)
WMQ	*William and Mary Quarterly* (Williamsburg, Va.)
YDA	*Yearbook of the Department of Agriculture*

Notes

Chapter One

1. Fox-Genovese and Genovese consider the well-being of the slaveholders to be the main test. These were, after all, the people with the largest stake in the survival of the system and the greatest interest in identifying any threats to it. "Was their economy strong enough and flexible enough to support their pretensions and guarantee their safety as a ruling class?" they ask. *Fruits of Merchant Capital*, p. 41; also p. 39.

2. Ibid., p. 37.

3. Fogel and Engerman, *Time on the Cross* 1:192, Supplement, pp. 126–31. For comment, see David & Temin and Wright in David, *Reckoning with Slavery*, pp. 202–23 and pp. 312–16 respectively.

4. Furtado, *The Economic Growth of Brazil*, pp. 57–58, 69–71.

5. Shackle, *Epistemics and Economics*, p. 457; also p. 52.

6. Baumol, "Entrepreneurship in Economic Theory," p. 68.

7. For functionally "loose" definitions, see Cole, "An Approach to the Study of Entrepreneurship," in Lane and Riemersma, *Enterprise and Secular Change*, pp. 183–86; Soltow, "The Entrepreneur in Economic History," pp. 87–88.

8. Key texts here are Von Hayek, "Economics and Knowledge"; Kirzner, *Perception, Opportunity, and Profit;* Knight, *Risk, Uncertainty and Profit:* Von Mises, *Human Action*.

9. See Kilby, "Hunting the Heffalump," in Kilby, *Entrepreneurship and Economic Development*, p. 26.

10. Shackle, *Epistemics and Economics*, preface.

11. Conrad and Meyer, "The Economics of Slavery in the Ante Bellum South," in Woodman, *Slavery and the Southern Economy*, pp. 47–48; Fogel and Engerman, *Time on the Cross* 1:191–97.

12. Conrad and Meyer, "Economics of Slavery," pp. 82–83; Fogel and Engerman, *Time on the Cross* 1:4–5.

13. Wright, *The Political Economy of the Cotton South*, pp. 92–97.

14. Gray, *History of Agriculture in the Southern United States to 1860* 2:669. See also pp. 924–27, and Gates, *The Farmer's Age,* p. 143.

15. Flanders, *Plantation Slavery in Georgia,* p. 191.

16. Fogel and Engerman, "Explaining the Relative Efficiency of Slave Agriculture in the Antebellum South," pp. 275, 290, 293.

17. Wright in David, *Reckoning with Slavery,* p. 317.

18. Such strong precedent should be clearly established. See Morton, *Morton's Cyclopedia of Agriculture* 7:371; Darby, *A New Historical Geography of England,* pp. 92, 154, 216, 338, 408, 413–16, 456; Thirsk, *The Agrarian History of England and Wales* 4:167, 180; Prothero, *English Farming, Past and Present,* p. 10; Gardner and Garner, *The Use of Lime in British Agriculture,* pp. 12–25; White, *Roman Farming,* pp. 138–39; Gras, *History of Agriculture* p. 192; Kerridge, *The Agricultural Revolution,* pp. 241–50; Fussell, "Crop Nutrition in Tudor and Early Stuart England," pp. 99–100, 104; Prince, "The Origins of Pits and Depressions in Norfolk," pp. 20–27; *AF* 6 (April 1824): 9.

19. Fogel and Engerman, *Time on the Cross* 1:253. See also p. 199.

20. Wright, *Cotton South,* p. 17.

21. See Faust, *A Sacred Circle,* passim.

22. Quoted in Taylor, *Slaveholding in North Carolina,* p. 18.

23. Quoted in Bonner, *A History of Georgia Agriculture,* pp. 64–65.

24. *Returns of the Fifth Census; Report on the Eighth Census.*

25. *FR* 5 (July 1837): 186.

26. Ibid. 6 (November 1838): 454.

27. Ruffin, *An Address on the Opposite Results of Exhausting and Fertilizing Systems of Agriculture,* p. 23; also p. 22. *Proceedings of the Agricultural Convention and of the State Agricultural Society of South Carolina from 1839 to 1845,* p. 426. See also Elliot, *Address Delivered by Special Request Before the St. Paul's Agricultural Society,* p. 9: "To all of us, it is expedient to divert capital, by every available mode, from the superabundant production of cotton to other pursuits."

29. Otto, "Southern 'Plain Folk' Agriculture," pp. 31–36.

30. Bonner, *Georgia Agriculture,* pp. 61–65, 71–72.

31. See account of Hammond's farming by Solon Robinson, in which it is reported that ditching and clearing on a 600-acre stretch had cost three times as much as the subsequent marling (£30 to $10 per acre). *SC* 8 (1850): 37–38.

32. Ruffin, *An Essay on Calcareous Manures* (Sitterson ed.), pp. 122–23, 139.

33. Clipping in SC Diary (letter of 11 February 1843).

34. Ibid., Hammond Correspondence, James Hammond to Edmund Ruffin, 7 July 1844.

35. Quoted in Craven, *Soil Exhaustion as a Factor in the Agricultural History of Virginia and Maryland,* p. 159. See also *FR* 6 (November 1838): 454.

36. Chambers and Mingay, *The Agricultural Revolution,* pp. 54–65, 77–81, 201. They also note how "Flemish farmers had been steadily developing the intensive cultivation of their poor, sandy soils since the Middle Ages." For further comment on the United Kingdom, see Jones, *Agriculture and Economic Growth in England,* pp. 9–11, 162–64; Grigg, *The Agricultural Revolution in South Lincolnshire,* pp. 18–20, 47–

48, 162–63, 178–79; Riches, *The Agricultural Revolution in Norfolk,* pp. 3–5, 15–17, 33–34, 36–42, 77–81; Mingay, *Arthur Young and His Times,* p. 59.

37. Clay, Orr, and Stuart, *North Carolina Atlas,* pp. 193–94; Genovese, *The Political Economy of Slavery,* chapter 5; Hart, *The Southeastern United States,* pp. 36–40, 43; Smith and Phillips, *North America,* pp. 287–95, 308–15.

38. For this and the continuing problems where liming has not been used, see Foth and Shafer, *Soil Geography,* pp. 27, 38, 177–81, 183, 186, 192.

39. See below, chapters 8 and 9; also Mathew, "Slave Skills, Plantation Schedules, and Net Returns in Southern Marling," pp. 174–76, 185–86.

40. *RCA* (1874): 229.

41. *YDA* (1914): 266–67.

42. Hart, *Southeastern United States,* p. 39.

43. Haystead and Fite, *The Agricultural Regions of the United States,* pp. 77–79, 91, 97–98, 121–22, 126–27, 131–32.

44. Buol, Hole, and McCracken, *Soil Genesis and Classification,* pp. 276–78.

45. Flanders, *Slavery in Georgia,* p. 85.

46. Ruffin, *Exhausting and Fertilizing Systems,* p. 16.

47. *SA* (February 1828): 79.

48. The best known being *A Memoir on the Origin, Cultivation and Uses of Cotton* (Charleston, 1844).

49. *Proceedings of the Agricultural Convention of South Carolina,* p. 176.

50. *Reports and Resolutions of the General Assembly of South-Carolina Passed at Its Regular Session of 1843,* p. 90.

51. Ruffin Papers (LC), Diary 14, (16, 17, 18 June 1865).

52. Ruffin, *Diary 1,* editor's introduction, p. xvi, and Craven's foreword, p. xiii; Ruffin, *Calcareous Manures* (Sitterson ed.), editor's introduction, p. xix; Eaton, *The Growth of Southern Civilization,* p. 179.

53. For Virginia neglect, see Mathew, "Edmund Ruffin and the Demise of the *Farmers' Register,*" passim.

54. Newby, *The South,* p. 140.

55. Ruffin, *Address to the Virginia State Agricultural Society on the Effects of Domestic Slavery on the Manners, Habits and Welfare of the Agricultural Population of the Southern States,* p. 26 (my emphasis).

Chapter Two

1. All Virginia genealogical and historical detail on the Ruffins from *Thomas Ruffin Papers* 4:234–37 (F. G. Ruffin to P. C. Cameron, 1 June 1870); *Diary* 1:259 (27, 29 December 1858); *VMHB* 5:217–18; *WMQ* (1) 18:253; Ruffin Papers (UNC), Family and Private Letters, William E. B. Ruffin to Edmund Ruffin, 18 June 1846; Edmund Ruffin, Genealogical Chart, 1858 (in library of UNC); Materials in possession of Braden Vandeventer of Norfolk, Virginia, cited in letter to me from Professor William K. Scarborough, 18 April 1982; Materials in possession of James Gilliam and David Ruffin, shown to me in September 1985.

2. Scottish background from Arbuckle, *The Gowrie Conspiracy,* passim; Barbé, *The*

Tragedy of Gowrie House, pp. 75–76; Bruce, *Papers Relating to William, First Earl of Gowrie, and Patrick Ruthven,* pp. v–vi, 55–57; Burnet, *History of His Own Time 1: 32–33*; Cromerty, *An Historical Account of the Conspiracies by the Earls of Gowry and Robert Logan of Restalrig Against King James VI,* pp. 2–4; Donaldson, *Scottish Historical Documents,* pp. 153–56; Lang, *James VI and the Gowrie Mystery,* pp. 119–20, 143–44; David Mathew, *James I,* chapter 11: Thomson, *A Kind of Justice,* p. 54; Williamson, *Scottish National Consciousness,* pp. 57–58; Willson, *James VI and I,* pp. 35–43, 46–47, 50–51, 452.

3. Thomson, *A Kind of Justice,* p. 91.

4. There is no British surname of "Ruffin." The name "Ruthven," moreover, was largely confined to the House of Gowrie and some kindred families. Black, *The Surnames of Scotland,* p. 706; Ewen, *A History of Surnames of the British Isles,* p. 345 and passim; Johnston, *Place-Names of Scotland,* p. 209.

5. *Thomas Ruffin Papers* 4:237 (F. G. Ruffin to P. C. Cameron, 1 June 1870).

6. Craven, *Edmund Ruffin, Southerner,* p. 3. The *VMHB* gives a good deal of information on the Cockes. See, for example, 5:181–87, 38:232–33.

7. Craven, *Ruffin,* pp. 2–3.

8. Ruffin, *Calcareous Manures* (Sitterson ed.), editor's introduction, p. viii; Craven, *Ruffin,* pp. 3–4; *DAB* (American Council of Learned Societies ed.), 8 (1935), pt. 2, p. 215; *WMQ* (1) 5:16n.

9. Ruffin, *Calcareous Manures* (1842 ed.), appendix, note 6. There were a number of Ruffin plantations and houses south of the James River in Prince George County, and I have received much assistance from James Gilliam of Hopewell and Inge Walker Sonuparlak of Evergreen in sorting out confusions having to do with construction, ownership, and occupancy. Evergreen was the name of George Ruffin's main house and lands. On his death, the mansion and the immediately surrounding acres passed to his wife, Rebecca Cocke (Edmund's stepmother), and on her later marriage were lost to the Ruffins. Edmund's inheritance was the remainder, a large slab to the east, loosely known as Coggin's Point. He occupied a house south of the headland and this fairly modest dwelling bore the same name. It lay on a neck between Tar Bay and the swamps of Powell Creek, about three miles along from Evergreen. In 1829 the family moved to a more inland and more healthy part of the estate, the new house there being christened Shellbanks. It stood about three to four miles south-southwest of the Coggin's Point house. By the mid-1830s Edmund had effectively abandoned Prince George—for Petersburg, South Carolina, and Marlbourne. Edmund Jr., amassing the property into his own hands in the 1830s and 1840s, later built Beechwood (cottage, then mansion)—again near the river, on a high bluff, less than a mile southwest of the Coggin's place. An additional nearby Ruffin plantation was Ruthven, the property of Julian Ruffin, the house of which lay only a mile from Shellbanks. Across the James, and just visible from Coggin's Point, was another farm of Edmund Jr.'s, Evelynton, which stood on raised ground above Herring Creek.

10. Ibid.

11. For example, Collings, *Commercial Fertilizers,* p. 60; Craven, *Ruffin,* p. 60.

12. Emigration was seriously considered, however. See Ruffin, *Calcareous Manures* (1842 ed.), appendix, note 6.

13. See, for example, section 3 below and *SP* 14 (August 1849): 227–37.

14. Ruffin Papers (UNC), Undated and Miscellaneous Writings, Address to Agricultural Society of Rappahannock. See Ruffin, *Calcareous Manures* (1842 ed.), appendix, note 6. Colonel John Taylor of Caroline County, Virginia, was an agriculturist, a political writer of Jeffersonian persuasion, and three times a U.S. senator. He published essays on farming methods in a Georgetown newspaper in 1803 and reprinted them ten years later as *Arator: Being a Series of Agricultural Essays, Practical and Political, in Sixty-Four Numbers*. See also Craven, "John Taylor and Southern Agriculture." Sir Humphry Davy's *Elements of Agricultural Chemistry* (1813) was the product of more than ten years of research and lecturing at the Board of Agriculture in London. "The dawn of a new era," writes R. E. Prothero (otherwise Lord Ernle), "in which practical experience was to be combined with scientific knowledge, was marked by the lectures of Humphry Davy in 1803." *English Farming*, p. 216.

15. Ruffin, *Calcareous Manures* (1842 ed.), appendix, note 6.

16. Earlier read before a meeting of the Prince George Agricultural Society. John Skinner (1788–1851) had begun the *Farmer* in 1819 to publicize the ideas of John Taylor and others and promote improved agriculture in the border states. *DAB*, Pt. 1, 17:199–201. For more detailed treatment of these early years, see Allmendinger, "The Early Career of Edmund Ruffin."

17. Incidents 3, p. 241.

18. Millar, Turk, and Foth, *Fundamentals of Soil Science*, p. 146; Craven, *Ruffin*, p. vii; Gray, *History of Southern Agriculture* 2:780.

19. *AF* 3 (January 1822): 324–25.

20. Craven, *Ruffin*, p. 36 (also p. 39); Oakes, *The Ruling Race*, p. 206. See also *Diary* 1:619–20.

21. Craven, *Ruffin*, pp. 40–41.

22. Incidents 2, pp. 110–11. Cocke had done some unsuccessful experimental marling himself back in the early years of the century. By Allmendinger's presentation, he above all others was the man Ruffin wished to convince in his experimenting years. "The Early Career of Edmund Ruffin," pp. 130–32, 154.

23. Incidents 2, pp. 111–12.

24. Ibid., opp. p. 131.

25. Allmendinger, "Early Career of Ruffin," p. 149.

26. Paul Gates cites half a dozen successful Southern publications before the Civil War, two of which predated the *Register*. Beyond these there was only "a scattering of meagerly supported journals with small formats and a large proportion of articles cribbed from northern periodicals." *Farmer's Age*, p. 342.

27. Incidents 2, pp. 113, 138; below, chapter 7. For appraisal of the *Register*, see Hallock, "The Agricultural Apostle and His Bible," pp. 205–15.

28. Incidents 2, pp. 138–41, 144, 159.

29. Ibid., pp. 147–48, 156; *Thomas Ruffin Papers* 2:161, 145 (Edmund Ruffin to Thomas Ruffin, 21 July 1835 and 19 July 1836). See also Hallock, "Agricultural Apostle," p. 214, for evidence of additional circulation by reprint.

30. Incidents 2, pp. 149–53, 154b.

31. *Diary* 2:542 (20 January 1863).

32. *BR* 1 (September 1841): 1–3.

33. Sharp, *The Jacksonians versus the Banks*, p. 241.

34. Craven, *Ruffin*, pp. 66–71. See Demaree, *The American Agricultural Press*, pp. 79, 117–18, 118n; Sitterson, in his introduction to *Calcareous Manures*, pp. xxi–xxiii; Eaton, *Southern Civilization*, p. 179; Gates, *Farmer's Age*, p. 342; Mitchell, *Edmund Ruffin*, pp. 40–44.

35. The percentages exclude the lengthy "Westover Manuscripts" supplement of 1841 and the incorporated new edition of *Calcareous Manures* in 1842. Included, these lower the figures somewhat.

36. *FR* 9 (October 1841): 617; Incidents 2, p. 159; Sharp, *Jacksonians versus the Banks*, pp. 243, 246, 256–57, 265.

37. Incidents 2, pp. 138, 155; *FR* 6 (April 1838): 63; *FR* 7 (December 1839): 639; *FR* 9 (August 1841): 507; *FR* 10 (March 1842): 155n; Craven, *Ruffin*, p. 61; Demaree, *Agricultural Press*, p. 17; Gray, *History of Southern Agriculture* 2:915.

38. *FR* 7 (December 1839): 639. Demaree notes that "incredibly high unpaid balances . . . proved a major cause for many failures." *Agricultural Press*, p. 118.

39. *FR* 9 (August 1841): 507.

40. Ibid.; ibid. 7 (March 1839): 188; Incidents 2, pp. 146, 156–57.

41. *FR* 9 (August 1841): 507; ibid. 10 (March 1842): 155n. The language indicates that balances were still favorable. See also Incidents 2, p. 155.

42. Incidents 2, pp. 142–46, 158–59.

43. *FR* 1 (November 1833): 384; ibid. 4 (December 1836): 510. See also ibid. 1 (June 1833): 62; Demaree, *Agricultural Press*, pp. 101–2.

44. Incidents 2, p. 155. For a fuller account of these years on the *Register*, see Mathew, "Demise of the *Farmers' Register*."

45. *SA* (February 1844): 48.

46. Ruffin Papers (UNC), Hammond correspondence, James Hammond to Edmund Ruffin, 24 November 1842.

47. Faust, *Sacred Circle*, p. 16. *FR* 10 (1842): 39–40. "Ten years will fully test the experiment," he wrote in 1841, "and if it fails I have no hope but emigration. The labours of the week have driven politics entirely out of my mind and everything else but marl—marl." Hammond Papers (LC), Diary, 1841–1846, 13 November 1841.

48. See Merritt, *James Henry Hammond*, passim; Faust, *Sacred Circle*, pp. 95–98; Faust, *James Henry Hammond and the Old South*, pp. 238–39; Hammond Papers (LC), Correspondence and Speeches, Edmund Ruffin to James Hammond, 6 July, 7 September 1845; Ruffin Papers (UNC), Hammond correspondence, James Hammond to Edmund Ruffin, 16 June, 22 July, 23 August, 6 October 1846, in which Hammond invites Ruffin to move south and collaborate in setting up an agricultural newspaper. Ruffin thought Hammond had "unquestionably the most powerful mind in the southern states." *Diary* 1:75 (20 May 1857).

49. Ruffin Papers (UNC), Hammond correspondence, James Hammond to Edmund Ruffin, 18 December 1842.

50. *FR* 8 (April 1840): 243–44; Faust, *Sacred Circle*, pp. 100–101; Merritt, *Hammond*, p. 61.

51. Incidents 2, pp. 155, 159.

52. Details from SC Diary. Dating in text reduces need for footnoting. I am presently editing this diary for the University of North Carolina Press.

53. SC Diary, 24 April 1843.

54. Ibid., 7 June 1843.

55. Incidents 2, pp. 159–60. SC Diary, 12, 13 September 1843. His only writing in the fall was a page of notes concerning "small matters worth being remembered," such as the feeding of slave children. There are also brief references to Abbeville and Pendleton in the northwest of the state. SC Diary, Minutes (including entry for 20 October 1843).

56. Ruffin Papers (UNC), Hammond correspondence, James Hammond to Edmund Ruffin, 1 December 1843; *Diary* 1:55 (11 April 1857).

57. *Diary* 1:55 (11 April 1857).

58. *Report of the Commencement and Progress of the Agricultural Survey of South-Carolina* (1843); Incidents 2, p. 160.

59. SC Diary, 7, 9, 11, 13, 15, 17, 20, 25 February, 15, 17, 18 March, 13, 19, 24 April, 26, 29 May, 1 July 1843.

60. Ibid., 16, 17 March 1843.

61. Ibid., 13, 16 February, 23 February to 9 March, 28 March 1843; Incidents 2, p. 159.

62. SC Diary, 18 February, 1, 8, 23 March, 3, 15 April, 19 June, 4, 5 July 1843.

63. Ibid., 18 February, 1, 6, 8, 10, 20 March, 12 May 7, 27 June, 11 July (clipping).

64. Ruffin, *Survey of South-Carolina*, p. 3; Ruffin, *Exhausting and Fertilizing Systems*, pp. 3, 5, 16, 22.

65. *SA* (April 1844): 18, 125–26, 138–43, 224–26; (May 1844): 170–76; (June 1844): 221–23.

66. Incidents 2, pp. 160–62, 182; *SA* (February 1844): 45–49.

67. Incidents 2, p. 163; MFJ, introduction.

68. Incidents 2, pp. 141, 162–63; *Thomas Ruffin Papers* 2, Edmund Ruffin to Thomas Ruffin, 7 April 1844, pp. 225–26.

69. Incidents 2, p. 166; Craven, *Ruffin*, p. 86; MFJ, introduction, also entries for 5, 21 June 1844, 10 May 1845, 13 January, 7 July, 23 December 1848; Ruthven Farm Journal, 4 January 1848, 30 December 1858. (Note, by the way, how "Ruthven" revives the ancestral Scotch surname.)

70. MFJ, introduction; Sick list, 10 July to 10 December 1844, 22 April 1846, 13 January 1847, 30 September, 27 November 1848, 4 April, 9 August 1849, 5 January, 14 May 1850, 15 September 1851; Incidents 2, insert, pp. 27–28, 217.

71. *SP* 9 (August 1849): 227–37.

72. MFJ, introduction. To Ruffin's dismay, the privilege was withdrawn in 1851. He turned to another neighbor, J. W. Tomlin, who had deposits about a mile distant. Incidents 2, p. 214.

73. MFJ, 9 February, 15 March, 30 December 1844, 15 January 1846, 31 December 1847, 14, 23, 30 December 1848, 20 December 1849. See also figures in *SP* 9 (August 1849): 227–37.

74. MFJ, 15 September 1846, 13 May 1847, 22, 24, 26 August, 25 October 1848, 8 January, 29 April, 17 August 1849.

75. Ibid., 20 June, 8 August 1849.

76. *SP* 9 (August 1849): 227–37; Incidents 2, p. 216. See real estate figures in Inman and Inman, *Hanover County, Virginia,* pp. 55, 60, 84, 119, 159.

77. Incidents 2, pp. 215–16; *Diary* 1:xx.

78. Ruffin Papers (UNC), In Remembrance of Jane Dupuy, formerly Ruffin; *Diary* 1:xx, 5; *Diary* 2:xxv–vi; *Thomas Ruffin Papers* 2:512 (Edmund Ruffin to Thomas Ruffin, 18 April 1856).

79. Obvious from the *Diaries.*

80. Incidents 2, p. 155; Incidents 3, pp. 221–24.

81. Incidents 3, pp. 226–31, 246–47. The paper was *Exhausting and Fertilizing Systems.*

82. Incidents 3, pp. 233–35, clipping from *Fredericksburg Herald* on p. 243.

83. Ibid., p. 237, clippings on pp. 231, 238.

84. In the mid-1850s he also served as agricultural commissioner of Virginia and as the Hanover County delegate to the Virginia Farmers' Assembly. *Diary* 1:10–14; ibid., p. 352 (2 November 1859); Craven, *Ruffin,* p. 92; Mitchell, *Ruffin,* p. 86.

85. *Diary* 1:168, 239–40, 243–45, 247–48, 275, 351–53, 393 (16 March, 22 October, 1–5, 12 November 1858, 26 January, 2, 4 November 1859, 16 January 1860); *Diary* 2:546 (20 January 1863).

86. Ruffin, *Premium Essay on Agricultural Education.*

87. *Diary* 2:232 (10 February 1862). According to Mitchell, his tracts on slavery fared little better. *Ruffin,* p. 241.

88. See below, chapter 7.

89. Mitchell, *Ruffin,* p. 165.

90. *THM* 9 (1928): 271.

91. *Diary* 2:547–48 (20 January 1863).

92. Ibid. 1:238 (20 October 1858).

93. Ibid. 1:xxii; Craven, *Ruffin,* p. 107.

94. *Diary* 2:367 (4 July 1862). See also Stampp, *The Imperiled Union,* chapter 1; Incidents 3, pp. 250–52.

95. *Diary* 1:184–89, 195–97, 220–23, 361–71, 415–19, 433–39, 444, 448–69, 483–84, 495–502, 505 (6, 8–14, 27, 31 May, 11, 14 August 1858, 26 November–2 December 1859, 25 April, 7, 11 May, 17–26 June, 27 July, 11–31 August, 3–25 September, 6, 7, 14–22, 27 November 1860); Craven, *Ruffin,* pp. 160–63, 167–68, 178–80; White, *Robert Barnwell Rhett,* pp. 146–47; McCardell, *The Idea of a Southern Nation,* pp. 316–18.

96. *Diary* 1:512–13, 515–29, 570–71 (27 November, 20 December 1860, 24 December 1860–10 January 1861, 22 March 1861).

97. Ibid., p. 588 (12 April 1861). See also Craven, *Ruffin,* pp. 214–19. Ruffin's claim that he fired the first shot has been accepted by some historians and disputed by others. The matter is one of only symbolic and antiquarian significance and hardly merits detailed exploration. A lot seems to depend on what is taken to constitute "first." Boatner (*Cassell's Biographical Dictionary of the American Civil War,* p. 712) suggests that Captain George S. James started it all off with a signal shot from Fort Johnson and that Ruffin came in with the second shot. Ruffin himself acknowledged in his diary that "a signal shell was thrown from . . . Fort Johnson" at 4:30 A.M., but

considered that that was not in itself the opening of the attack: merely the indication that attack should commence from his own position at Cummings' Point (*Diary* 1:588 (12 April 1861). Meredith (*Storm Over Sumter,* p. 166) also views the signal as the first shot, credits Ruffin with the second shot, and mistakenly places him on Sullivan's Island on the north side of the harbor entrance. See also Sitterson, introduction to *Calcareous Manures,* p. xxx, n. 32; Wilcox and Ripley, *The Civil War at Charleston,* pp. 15–16; Pindell, "The Unrepentant Rebel," p. 42; Abbott, "The First Shot at Fort Sumter," pp. 41–45; Lee, "Who Fired the First Gun at Sumter?" [with reply from Julian M. Ruffin], p. 111.

98. *Diary* 2:548–49 (20 January 1863).

99. Incidents 3, p. 247; *Diary* 1:450 (25 August 1860).

100. *Diary* 1:349 (19 October 1859). See also 1:363, 364 (27 November, 21 December 1859); Franklin, *The Militant South,* pp. 242–43.

101. *Diary* 1:483 (7 November 1860). See also 1:482 (3 November 1860).

102. Ibid. 2:541 (20 January 1863).

103. Ibid., pp. 92–93, 229 (23 July 1861, 6 February 1862); Craven, *Ruffin,* pp. 237–39.

104. *Diary* 2:43, 595–96, 621, 658 (10 June 1861, 8, 9 March, 11 April, 16 May 1863); Craven, *Ruffin.* p. 249.

105. *Diary* 2:302, 307–8, 337, 350–51, 368, 401–7, 416–31, 474–75, 477, 504–5, 553–54, 600, 604, 624 (13, 19 May, 11, 22 June, 4 July, 3–6, 17–27 August, 28, 31 October, 5 December 1862, 23 January, 16, 17 March, 17 April 1863); ibid., pp. xv–xvi; Craven, *Ruffin,* pp. 254–55.

106. *Diary* 2:37, 112–13, 135, 310–11, 323, 323n, 330–31, 441–42, 468, 532 (28 May, 25 August, 23 September 1861, 21, 29 May, 3 June, 9 September, 20 October 1862, 5 January 1863); Craven, *Ruffin,* pp. 23, 253; Mitchell, *Ruffin,* pp. 206–7.

107. *Diary* 2:549, 573 (20 January, 8 February 1863).

108. Ibid., p. 531 (5 January 1863); Ruffin Papers (LC), Diary 14 (16, 17, 18 June 1865).

109. Ruffin Papers (LC), Diary 14 (16, 17, 18 June 1865).

110. Ibid., Memorandum for the instruction of my son Edmund Ruffin Jr., 18 June 1865.

111. Ibid.; Taylor, *Cavalier and Yankee,* p. 339. (Taylor uses Edmund Jr.'s account of his father's death in a letter to his own sons. This was later published as "Death of Ruffin" in *Tyler's Quarterly*).

Chapter Three

1. Ruffin, *Essays and Notes on Agriculture,* pp. 274–77. For more extended comment on agricultural entrepreneurship, see chapter 11. See also Mathew, "Planter Entrepreneurship and the Ruffin Reforms in the Old South, 1820–60," passim.

2. *FR* 3 (April 1836): 749.

3. Ruffin, *The Political Economy of Slavery,* p. 22.

4. Incidents 2, insertion, pp. 27–28; *Diary* 2:317 (26 May 1862); *FR* 3 (April 1836): 749.

5. *Diary* 1:87 (4 July 1857).

6. Genovese, *Roll, Jordan, Roll*, p. 302.

7. *Diary* 1:143 (9 January 1858); also p. 136 (5 December 1857).

8. Ibid., pp. 215–16, 240–41 (21 July, 26 October 1858).

9. Quoted in McKitrick, *Slavery Defended*, p. 29.

10. Ruffin, *Slavery and Free Labor Described and Compared*, p. 9.

11. Ruffin, *Political Economy of Slavery*, pp. 3, 8–9, 22; *Diary* 2:489–90 (14 November 1862); *FR* 3 (April 1836): 249, 748–49.

12. *Diary* 1:288 (23 February 1859). In Henrico and Dinwiddie counties (with Richmond and Petersburg respectively) free blacks made up at least 26 percent of the colored population and 10 percent of the total population in 1850. De Bow, *Statistical View of the United States . . . Being a Compendium of the Seventh Census*, p. 320. See also Berlin, *Slaves Without Masters*, pp. 174, 288.

13. Ruffin, *Political Economy of Slavery*, p. 3.

14. Ibid., pp. 3–4; *Diary* 1:287–89 (23 February 1859).

15. Ruffin, *Slavery and Free Labor*, p. 13.

16. Mitchell, *Ruffin*, p. 132; Ruffin, *Slavery and Free Labor*, pp. 10, 12.

17. *DBR* 26 (January–June 1859): 415–29. This contrasts with Genovese's argument that agricultural advance in the upper South depended on finance generated by slave sales. Genovese, *Political Economy of Slavery*, pp. 132–44.

18. Ruffin, *Slavery and Free Labor*, p. 9.

19. *DBR* 26 (January–June 1859): 415–29.

20. Ruffin, "Domestic Slavery," p. 10 (my italics). Briefer extract already quoted in chapter 1. All pagination from reproduction of pamphlet in *SP* 13 (1853).

21. Ruffin, *Political Economy of Slavery*, pp. 8–9; Ruffin, *Slavery and Free Labor*, p. 13; Ruffin, "Domestic Slavery," p. 16. For sympathetic treatment of Ruffin's ideas here, see Adams, "The Dilemma of Edmund Ruffin," pp. 321–35.

22. For example, Ruffin, *Political Economy of Slavery*, pp. 20–23. See Fitzhugh, *Sociology for the South* (Wish ed.), pp. 63–86; Fitzhugh, *Cannibals All!* (Woodward ed.), pp. 158–83.

23. Ruffin, "Domestic Slavery," p. 10. See also Hammond's "Speech on the Admission of Kansas," U.S. Senate, 4 March 1858, reproduced in McKitrick, *Slavery Defended*, pp. 121–25.

24. Ruffin, *Political Economy of Slavery*, p. 20. See also *Diary* 2:119, 288, 490 (1 September 1861, 24 April, 14 November 1862).

25. Ruffin, "Domestic Slavery," pp. 10, 11; Ruffin, *Slavery and Free Labor*, pp. 9–10, 13.

26. Newby, *The South*, p. 100.

27. Ruffin Papers (LC), *Diary* 14 (16, 17, 18 June 1865).

28. Ruffin, *Slavery and Free Labor*, p. 10.

29. See below, chapter 10.

30. Ruffin, "Domestic Slavery," p. 10.

31. Ruffin, *Agricultural Education*, pp. 6–14. See also Numbers and Numbers, "Science in the Old South," passim; Scarborough, "Science on the Plantation," passim.

32. Thomas R. Dew, "Review of the Debate in the Virginia Legislature" (1832), reprinted in McKitrick, *Slavery Defended*, pp. 27–29.

33. Ruffin, *African Colonization Unveiled*, pp. 17–32; Ruffin, *Political Economy of Slavery*, pp. 15–20; *Diary* 1:296, 324, 332–33 (9 April, 24 July, 22 August 1859); *The Free Negro Nuisance and How to Abate It*, reproduced in *Diary* 1:621–26; Craven, *Ruffin*, p. 135.

34. Ruffin, *Political Economy of Slavery*, p. 15.

35. *Free Negro Nuisance* in *Diary* 1:621–24. See also *Diary* 1:152, 205, 327–28, 340–41 (28 January, 29 June 1858, 3 August, 13, 15, 19 September, 31 December 1859).

36. *Diary* 1:341, 348, 388 (17 September, 1, 17 October 1859, 4 January 1860).

37. Ibid., pp. 102–3, 149–50, 176, 179, 271, 471, 577 (10 September 1857, 22 January, 18, 20 April 1858, 17 January 1859, 1 October 1860, 4 April 1861).

38. Ruffin, *Political Economy of Slavery*, p. 22. See also *Diary* 1:54, 149–50, 176–79 (9 April 1857, 22 January, 18, 20 April 1858).

39. *Diary* 1:96–99, 153, 179 (13 August 1857, 30 January, 21 April 1858).

40. Ibid., pp. 29, 181–82, 450–51 (30 January 1857, 26 April 1858, 28 August 1860).

41. Ruffin, *Political Economy of Slavery*, p. 22; *Diary* 1:52 (5 April 1857), 2:35 (26 May 1861).

42. *Diary* 2:226–29 (5, 6 February 1862); also editor's note on pp. 226–27.

43. Ibid., p. 277 (1 February 1859).

44. Ibid., pp. 114, 175 (17 October 1857, 18 April 1858).

45. Ibid., pp. 207–9 (4 January 1862).

46. Ibid., 1:557 (26 February 1861); also 2:35–36 (26 May 1861).

47. Craven, *Ruffin*, pp. 27, 29, 31–33, 35. See also *Diary* 1:xxxi–ii, and p. 254 (12 December 1858); *Diary* 2:487–88 (10 November 1862).

48. *Diary* 1:162–63, 344–45 (1 March 1858, 29 September 1859).

49. Ibid., pp. 307–8 (2 June 1859).

50. Ibid., p. 290 (28 February, 2 March 1859). On both sides of the slavery debate, Bachman suggested, there might be "room . . . for indulgence of a large share of mutual forbearance, candour, and charity. Southerners could proceed fearlessly in an unbiassed search after truth," given their knowledge "that nature has stamped on the African race the permanent marks of inferiority." *The Doctrine of the Unity of the Human Race*, p. 8.

51. See, in particular, Channing, *Crisis of Fear*, p. 26; Collins, *White Society in the Antebellum South*, p. 65; Genovese, *The World the Slaveholders Made*, pp. 103–13; Genovese, *In Red and Black*, pp. 58, 190, 306–7; Rawick, *From Sundown to Sunup*, p. 140; Roark, *Masters Without Slaves*, p. 72; Stampp, *Imperiled Union*, p. 241.

Chapter Four

1. Information on this complex subject has come in the main from survey texts on agricultural chemistry. As these for the most part make roughly identical points, they have not been given individual references as the discussion proceeds. Citation is

accorded only when direct quotations have been used or when an author makes a distinctive observation. The principal books consulted were Bear, *Chemistry of the Soil;* Black, *Soil-Plant Relationships;* Brady, *The Nature and Properties of Soils;* Cooke, *The Control of Soil Fertility;* de V. Malherbe, *Soil Fertility;* Millar, Turk, and Foth, *Soil Science;* Pearson and Adams, *Soil Acidity and Liming;* Russell, *Soils and Manures;* and Thompson, *Soils and Soil Fertility.* Articles on special aspects of the question have been examined and have been cited in the normal fashion. The procedure adopted by a nonscientist, studying the sometimes disputatious literature in the journals and unable to adjudicate, was to read to the point at which the relative scale of majority and minority opinion could be determined with some confidence. It may be noted by the reader how the broad characterization of acidity and amelioration in modern texts is very close indeed to that of Ruffin.

2. Millar, Turk, and Foth, *Soil Science,* p. 146; Robert S. Whitney in foreword to Pearson and Adams, *Soil Acidity and Liming,* p. vii; Bear, *Chemistry of the Soil,* p. 237; Brady, *Properties of Soils,* p. 404.

3. Russell, *The World of the Soil,* p. 51.

4. Liebig, *The Natural Laws of Husbandry,* p. 90.

5. Chernov, *The Nature of Soil Acidity,* pp. 5–6 (my italics).

6. Millar, Turk, and Foth, *Soil Science,* p. 126. See also Brady, *Properties of Soils,* p. 382.

7. Brady, *Properties of Soils,* p. 390.

8. Truog, "Lime in Relation to Availability of Plant Nutrients," pp. 2–3.

9. Moser, "Calcium Nutrition at Respective pH Levels," p. 339; Harston and Albrecht, "Plant Nutrition and Hydrogen Ion," p. 247.

10. See Pierre, "Hydrogen-Ion Concentration, Aluminum Concentration in the Soil Solution, and Percentage Base Saturation as Factors Affecting Plant Growth in Acid Soils," pp. 183, 205; Magistad, "The Aluminum Content of the Soil Solution and Its Relation to Soil Reaction and Plant Growth," pp. 181, 210.

11. Millar, Turk, and Foth, *Soil Science,* p. 139.

12. Hurd-Karrer, "Relation of Soil Reaction to Toxicity and Persistence of Some Herbicides in Greenhouse Plots," pp. 2–3.

13. Ogg, "The Revival of Liming," p. 356.

14. Midgely, "Lime—Its Importance and Efficient Use in Soils," p. 330. One dissenter from such views is Alfred Åslander, who advocated the practice of "standard fertilization," in which nutrient deficiency is recognized as the main problem on acid soils and is tackled, not by liming, but by the short-circuiting referred to. A fertilizer mix is worked out in relation to the missing or trapped ingredients in a soil. This recipe for success, however, does not appear to have been very effective in dislodging traditional notions. Åslander, moreover, does not claim that liming is useless. He recognizes its beneficial results and merely suggests that there are preferable ways of tackling acidity. Even if he is correct, his ideas have little relevance to the antebellum South, where commercial fertilizers were very expensive and in short supply. Few planters could have considered informed and well-judged "standard fertilization" as an available option (though many adopted crude and traditional versions of it by default). Åslander, "Standard Fertilization and Liming as Factors in Maintaining Soil Productivity," pp. 181–94.

15. *SC* 4 (July 1846): 99.

16. Ruffin, *Calcareous Manures* (Sitterson ed.), p. 22.

17. Emmons, *Report of Professor Emmons on His Geological Survey of North Carolina*, p. 80.

18. Ruffin, *Calcareous Manures* (Sitterson ed.), pp. 79–80, 159, 169–82.

19. Marshall, *The Rural Economy of Norfolk*, pp. 16–18; *Morton's Cyclopedia* 7:370.

20. Ruffin, *Calcareous Manures* (Sitterson ed.), p. 79; Ashley, *The Bread of Our Forefathers*, pp. 137–38.

21. Chambers and Mingay, *Agricultural Revolution*, p. 62.

22. Prothero, *English Farming*, pp. 10, 174.

23. Ruffin, *Calcareous Manures* (Sitterson ed.), p. 181.

24. *SA* (April 1844): 136.

25. For example, *RCP* (1856): 234.

26. Ruffin, *Calcareous Manures* (Sitterson ed.), pp. 80–81, 169–70; *FR* 3 (March 1836): 691.

27. See, among others, *SA* (April 1844) 136–37, (June 1844): 218; *SC* 4 (July 1846): 98; *SP* 10 (November 1850): 339; *FR* 8 (November 1840): 679–82; *RCP* (1859): 154–56; MFJ, introduction. (Ruffin used greensand marl at Marlbourne.)

28. *RCP* (1856): 234–36, (1859): 156–57.

29. Ibid. (1859): 156.

30. *FR* 8 (April 1840): 247. See also *RCP* (1856): 235; *RCA* (1868): 391.

31. *RCP* (1856): 212–15, 234–36; *SC* 4 (July 1846): 97–98.

32. *RCP* (1859): 156–57.

Chapter Five

1. Midgely, "Lime," p. 329; Hart, *Southeastern United States*, p. 19; Chapman and Sherman, *Oxford Regional Economic Atlas: United States and Canada*, pp. 159–60; Jones and Bryan, *North America*, p. 156; Craven, "The Agricultural Reformers of the Ante-Bellum South," p. 304.

2. Hart, *Southeastern United States*, p. 156; Gates, *Farmer's Age*, p. 142; Akehurst, *Tobacco*, pp. 141–42, 226–27.

3. See, for example, maps in Millar, Turk, and Foth, *Soil Science*, p. 264; Donahue, Shickluna, and Robertson, *Soils*, p. 278; Henderson, *The Soils of Florida*, p. 16.

4. Midgely, "Lime," p. 329; Millar, Turk, and Foth, *Soil Science*, p. 471; Pearson and Adams, *Soil Acidity and Liming*, p. 162. See also Bridges, *World Soils*, pp. 59–60.

5. Batten and Gibson, *Soils*, pp. 97, 164–85.

6. Bunting, *The Geography of Soil*, pp. 166, 183–84.

7. Henderson, *Soils of Florida*, pp. 43, 45.

8. Hart, *Southeastern United States*, p. 30.

9. Moser, "Calcium Nutrition," pp. 339–344.

10. Golden, Gammon, and Thomas, "A Comparison of Methods of Determining the Exchangeable Cations and the Exchange Capacity of Maryland Soils," pp. 154–55.

11. The Williamsburg readings were made by the author. See *FR* 8 (July 1840): 415–18.

12. Cummings, "Agronomic Problems in the Agricultural Reconversion of the South," pp. 14–15; Clay, Orr, and Stuart, *North Carolina Atlas*, pp. 140, 142.

13. Clay, Orr, and Stuart, *North Carolina Atlas*, pp. 138, 143, 148.

14. Stuck, *Soil Survey of Beaufort and Jasper Counties, South Carolina*, p. 47.

15. Fippin, *Address Delivered at the Summer Meeting of the Agricultural Society of South Carolina, July 14, Nineteen-fifteen*, pp. 9–10.

16. Walker and White, "Effects of Liming on Crop Yields and Chemical Properties of Tifton and Greenville Soils," p. 5.

17. Donahue, Shickluna, and Robertson, *Soils*, p. 279. West Virginia, as part of antebellum Virginia, has been included in the calculations.

18. Ibid., p. 289.

19. Cited in Thompson, *Soils and Soil Fertility*, p. 204.

20. Pearson and Adams, *Soil Acidity and Liming*, p. 176; Hart, *Southeastern United States*, pp. 45–46; Akehurst, *Tobacco*, pp. 28–29.

21. *FR* 3 (April 1836): 748.

22. Akehurst, *Tobacco*, p. 148.

23. Thompson, *Soils and Soil Fertility*, p. 205; de V. Malherbe, *Soil Fertility*, p. 169.

24. Pearson and Adams, *Soil Acidity and Liming*, p. 172.

25. Walker and White, "Effects of Liming," p. 19. See also Donahue, Shickluna, and Robertson, *Soils*, p. 289.

26. See below, chapter 6.

27. Paden and Garman, "Yield and Composition of Cotton and Kobe Lespedeza Grown at Different pH Levels," pp. 309–10.

28. Brady, *Properties of Soils*, p. 414.

29. Fergus, Hammonds, and Rogers, *Southern Field Crops Management*, p. 598.

30. Ruffin, *Calcareous Manures* (Sitterson ed.), pp. 32–33; Ruffin, *Notes on the Cane-Brake Lands, or the Cretaceous Region of Alabama*, p. 24.

31. Ruffin, *Cane-Brake Lands*, p. 2.

32. *SP* 13 (April 1853): 103.

33. Ibid. (December 1853): 354.

34. *FJ* 1 (May 1852): 51.

35. *SS* 4 (December 1854): 360.

36. *RCP* (1859): 153.

37. *RCA* (1868): 368–70; Chapman and Sherman, *United States and Canada Atlas*, pp. 54–55.

38. *SA* (August 1844): 306; *RCP* (1859): 157–58.

39. *RCA* (1868): 383.

40. Reviewed and quoted in *FR* 3 (May 1835): 36–43. See also (December 1835): 470, (March 1836): 664; *RCA* (1868): 383–85.

41. Kennedy, *History and Statistics of the State of Maryland According to the Returns of the Seventh Census of the United States, 1850*, pp. 12, 14.

42. *FR* 5 (May 1837): 50.

43. Ibid. 3 (July 1835): 187; Ruffin, *Calcareous Manures* (Sitterson ed.), p. 149.

44. *FR* 3 (September 1835): 269; ibid. 6 (June 1838): 142, (December 1837): 142–43; AA 9 (September 1850): 282; *RCA* (1868): 390.

45. *AA* 6 (April 1847): 118; *RCA* (1870): 270–71; *FR* 10 (October 1842): 461, (June 1842): 298; *FR* 4 (January 1837): 524; *FR* 9 (May 1841): 264; *FR* 5 (May 1837): 5–6; *FR* 7 (November 1839): 670.

46. *RCA* (1868): 391; *FR* 1 (July 1833): 108; *FR* 3 (November 1835): 414; *AA* 4 (April 1845): 118.

47. *FR* 5 (December 1837): 511.

48. Ibid. 1 (February 1834): 574, (July 1833): 108.

49. Ibid. 8 (November 1840): 679–82; *RCA* (1868): 391.

50. *FR* 9 (January 1841): 23.

51. Ibid. 1 (February 1834): 535, 555; ibid. 6 (June 1838): 183–84; ibid. 7 (April 1839): 209.

52. Emmons, *Survey of North Carolina*, pp. 41–42, 76; *RCA* (1868): 385–86; Ruffin, *Sketches of Lower North Carolina and the Similar Adjacent Lands*, p. 84.

53. Emmons, *Survey of North Carolina*, pp. 67–70.

54. Ibid., pp. 51–65; *RCA* (1868): 385–86.

55. Emmons, *Survey of North Carolina*, pp. 41, 65–66, 173; *RCA* (1868): 385.

56. See *FJ* 1 (May 1852): 50; *FR* 8 (May 1840): 257–58; Emmons, *Survey of North Carolina*, p. 51; *RCA* (1868): 385–86.

57. *FR* 8 (April 1840): 247; *SA* (April 1844): 126–27. See also *FR* 8 (August 1840): 500.

58. *FJ* 1 (April 1852): 29–30. See also Emmons, *Survey of North Carolina*, pp. 44–48; *RCA* (1868): 385.

59. For example, *FR* 6 (May 1838): 111; *SA* (June 1838): 297–99, (July 1838): 385–86.

60. *FR* 7 (February 1839): 79.

61. See below, chapter 6.

62. *SA* (March 1844): 113. See also (May 1844): 166–67, and Ruffin, *Exhausting and Fertilizing Systems*, pp. 7, 18.

63. *SA* (April 1844): 137.

64. Ibid. (September 1844): 353. See also *SC* 3 (February 1845): 21.

65. *SA* (May 1844): 170–74.

66. Ruffin, *Exhausting and Fertilizing Systems*, p. 19; *FR.* 6 (May 1838): 111; *SA.* (April 1844): 141–42.

67. *SA* (June 1838): 297. See also (October 1844): 399.

68. Ibid. (April 1844): 140.

69. *SC* 4 (June 1846): 81.

70. *SA* (February 1844): 47; Ruffin, *Exhausting and Fertilizing Systems*, p. 7.

71. Lyell, *A Second Visit to the United States of North America* 1:314, 338–39, 348–49; 2:41–42, 48.

72. Lewis, *Transactions of the South Central Agricultural Society,* p. 404.

73. Ibid., p. 402.

74. Jones, *First Report to the Cotton Planters' Convention of Georgia on the Agricultural Resources of Georgia.*

75. *RCA* (1867): 427.

76. Ibid. (1868): 369.

77. Ibid., p. 383; ibid. (1864): 27, (1868): 385, 393–94.

78. Emmons, *Survey of North Carolina,* pp. 51–52, 75–76; Emmons, *Agriculture of North Carolina,* p. 75; *RCA* (1868): 385.

79. *RCA* (1868): 386; *SA* (April 1844): 125; Ruffin, *Diary* 1:654 (11 March 1861).

80. *RCA* (1868): 388.

81. *SC* 11 (July 1853): 206–7.

Chapter Six

1. *FR* 3 (September 1835): 272.

2. Ruffin Papers (UNC), James Hammond to Edmund Ruffin, 7 July 1844, 7 August 1845, 26 September 1847, 1 July 1849, 11 March 1851, 19 December 1853, 1 May 1854; *SC* 4 (July 1846): 99.

3. Ruffin Papers (UNC), James Hammond to Edmund Ruffin, 20 July 1851.

4. *FR* 10 (August 1842): 386. See also Craven, "Reformers of the Ante-Bellum South," p. 311.

5. Ruffin, *Calcareous Manures* (Sitterson ed.), p. 127. See also *AF* 6 (March 1824): 5; *FR* 10 (August 1842): 385–86.

6. *FR* 8 (July 1840): 416.

7. Ibid. (March 1840): 170.

8. *SC* 1 (March 1843): 10.

9. De Bow, *Statistical View,* pp. 171–72.

10. Ruffin, *Calcareous Manures* (Sitterson ed.), p. 84; ibid., (3d ed.), p. 238. See subsequent chapters for comment on Singleton's experiments.

11. *FR* 8 (August 1840): 486.

12. Ibid. 9 (May 1841): 287. See also ibid. 4 (January 1837): 525.

13. Ibid. 10 (June 1842): 259; Ruffin, *Survey of South-Carolina,* "Tabular Statement of Marling Operations." See also *FR* 1 (July 1833): 108.

14. *FR* 5 (August 1837): 247.

15. Ibid. 3 (September 1835): 272.

16. Ruffin Papers (UNC), James Hammond to Edmund Ruffin, 1 June 1847.

17. For an early example, see *AF* 6 (March 1824): 5.

18. *FR* 8 (August 1840): 486–87. See also *AF* 6 (March 1824): 5.

19. *FR* 10 (June 1842): 259. See also ibid. (October 1842): 489.

20. Ruffin, *Calcareous Manures* (Sitterson ed.), p. 88; *SP* 14 (April 1854): 103.

21. *SP* 12 (February 1852): 56.

22. Ibid. 14 (April 1854): 102.

23. Helper, *The Impending Crisis of the South,* p. 69.

24. Emmons, *Agriculture of North Carolina,* p. 78.

25. *FR* 4 (May 1836): 53; ibid. 8 (September 1840): 528–29.

26. *SC* 2 (August 1844): 130.

27. Ibid. 1 (March 1843): 10; Hammond Papers (LC), Diary 1841–46, 13 November 1841.

28. Ruffin, *Survey of South-Carolina,* p. 50; *SA* (January 1844): 36–38; *SC* 4 (July 1846): 99.

29. Ruffin Papers (UNC), James Hammond to Edmund Ruffin, 13 May 1850.

30. Plantations of Robert Gourdin, Francis Holmes, Samuel Palmer, and Philip Porcher. Tuomey, *Report on the Geological and Agricultural Survey of the State of South Carolina*, p. 59; *SA* (June 1843): 220–21; *SC* 3 (February 1845): 21.

31. Quoted in Tuomey, *Survey of South Carolina*, p. 51

32. *FR* 4 (May 1836): 53; ibid. 7 (September 1840): 529.

33. *SA* (January 1844): 37. See also ibid. (June 1843): 223, (October 1844): 393.

34. *FR* 3 (April 1836): 748.

35. Ibid. 8 (August 1840): 500; ibid. 9 (January 1841): 27, (May 1841): 264.

36. Ibid. 10 (June 1842): 259.

37. *SC* 4 (July 1846): 98; Tuomey, *Survey of South Carolina*, p. 50.

38. *SP* 17 (June 1857): 346; *AF* 6 (April 1824): 9. See also *FR* 8 (November 1840): 682.

39. Ruffin, *Cane-Brake Lands*, pp. 24–25.

40. Ruffin, *Calcareous Manures* (Sitterson ed.), pp. 85, 110, 132. See also pp. 96, 104, 122.

41. *FR* 1 (July 1833): 17; ibid. 3 (December 1835): 477–78.

42. Ibid. 1 (March 1834): 607; ibid. 5 (May 1837): 5–6; ibid. 10 (October 1842): 461. See also *AA* 6 (August 1847): 246–47.

43. *FR* 10 (August 1842): 386. See also *SP* 13 (May 1853): 140–41.

44. *AA* 6 (April 1847): 118–19.

45. *FR* 8 (April 1840): 247.

46. Ruffin Papers (UNC), James Hammond to Edmund Ruffin, 4 November 1846, and final letter of collection, 1857.

47. *SC* 4 (July 1846): 98.

48. See, for example, *SP* 13 (May 1853): 141.

49. Ruffin, *Calcareous Manures* (Sitterson ed.), p. 127.

50. Cited anonymously in *FR* 10 (July 1842): 366.

51. *AF* 6 (March 1824): 5; *FR* 8 (May 1840): 320; *SP* 13 (May 1853): 141.

52. *FR* 3 (August 1835): 225.

53. *SA* (July 1844): 249. See also ibid., p. 245; *FR* 4 (June 1836): 109; *FR* 5 (May 1837): 51–52.

54. Quoted in Ruffin, *Survey of South-Carolina*, p. 50.

55. *FR* 3 (September 1835): 272.

56. *SA* (February 1844): 49.

57. In *SS* 2 (June 1852): 275.

58. *FR* 8 (August 1840): 491–97.

59. Ibid. (November 1840): 687–89; ibid. 11 (January 1841): 26–27.

60. Ibid. 10 (October 1842): 488–89.

61. Ruffin Papers (UNC), James Hammond to Edmund Ruffin, 10 July, 9 November 1849.

62. *SC* 2 (September 1844): 144.

63. *FR* 8 (August 1840): 491–97, (November 1840): 688; ibid. 9 (January 1841): 27.

64. See, for example, ibid. 3 (August 1835): 236; Ruffin, *Calcareous Manures* (3d ed.), pp. vi–vii.

65. *SP* 12 (February 1852): 56.

66. *FR* 1 (July 1833): 109; ibid. 8 (July 1840): 415–16.

67. *FR* 5 (May 1837): 6.

68. *AA* 9 (June 1850): 188.

69. Ibid. 6 (August 1847): 247.

70. De Bow, *Statistical View*, pp. 322–28.

71. Kennedy, *Agriculture of the United States in 1860; Compiled from the Original Returns of the Eighth Census*, pp. 154, 158, 162.

72. *FR* 7 (May 1840): 257.

73. *SC* 2 (September 1844): 144.

74. Ibid. 8 (December 1850): 185.

75. De Bow, *Statistical View*, p. 286; Kennedy, *Eighth Census*, p. 104.

76. *FR* 10 (August 1842): 385.

77. *SA* (February 1844): 45–49.

78. *FR* 8 (July 1840): 415–16.

79. *SP* 14 (August 1854): 243.

80. *FR* 1 (March 1834): 606.

81. *SC* 8 (December 1850): 185.

82. De Bow, *Statistical View*, pp. 284, 320, 326.

83. Craven, *Ruffin*, chapter 2. See also Bruce, "Virginian Agricultural Decline to 1860: A Fallacy," pp. 3–13 (an article which deals with a Virginia "agricultural revolution in the period before 1843").

84. Kennedy, *Eighth Census*.

Chapter Seven

1. Three complete runs of antebellum journals—the *Farmers' Register*, the *Southern Planter*, and the *Southern Cultivator*—were exhaustively scrutinized for this and other chapters concerning agricultural practice. The remaining ones cited in the foreword and the list of abbreviations were examined very extensively, but selectively.

2. *Delaware Journal* quoted in *FR* 5 (March 1838): 744.

3. *FR* (June 1842): 259; Ruffin, *Calcareous Manures* (3d ed.), pp. 237–39: Gray, *History of Southern Agriculture* 2: 780; Craven, *Soil Exhaustion*, pp. 94, 136.

4. *FR* 1 (February 1834): 535, (March 1834): 615; ibid. 2 (May 1835): 36–42; ibid. 5 (May 1837): 49–51; (June 1838): 144; ibid. 7 (February 1839): 105; ibid. 9 (February 1841): 100; Ruffin, *Calcareous Manures* (3d ed.), pp. vii, 237; Kennedy, *State of Maryland*, pp. 11–14.

5. Quoted in Cabell, *Early History of Agriculture in Virginia*, p. 32.

6. Gray, *History of Southern Agriculture*, 2:612, 780n; Ruffin, *Calcareous Manures* (Sitterson ed.), pp. 81, 81n–82n; (3d ed.), p. 236; *FR* 9 (January 1841), pp. 22–26.

7. *FR* 10 (June 1842): 258–59; also 1 (July 1833): 108.

8. Ibid. 8 (August 1840): 486, 488, 491–97; Incidents 2, p. 107; Ruffin, *Calcareous Manures* (Sitterson ed.), p. 5; *Calcareous Manures* (2d ed.), p. iv; *SP* 14 (April 1854): 102; Ruffin, *Survey of South-Carolina*, "Tabular Statement of Marling Operations"; *SA* (February 1844): 45–47.

9. *FR* 1 (July 1833): 108; ibid. 9 (May 1841): 264. See also *WMQ* (1) 26 (1908): 62.

10. *FR* 3 (December 1835): 478; ibid. 5 (December 1837): 511; ibid. 2 (November 1834): 389, (March 1835): 636–37, 644; ibid. 10 (November 1840): 679–89; Ruffin, *Survey of South-Carolina*, "Tabular Statement of Marling Operations."

11. *FR* 10 (June 1842): 259; ibid. 4 (January 1837): 524–27, (May 1837): 5–6, (May 1841): 264–66; ibid. 10 (June 1842): 289–99, (October 1842): 461–62; ibid. 6 (June 1838): 142; ibid. 3 (December 1835): 470; ibid. 1 (October 1833): 266; ibid. 2 (September 1834): 255; ibid. 7 (November 1839): 668–71; ibid. 9 (February 1841): 80; ibid. 10 (May 1842): 203; *RCP* (1848): 496; *AA* 4 (April 1845): 118, (September 1850): 282; Bruce, "Virginian Agricultural Decline Fallacy," p. 11; Ruffin, *Survey of South-Carolina*, "Tabular Statement of Marling Operations."

12. *FR* 1 (February 1834): 524; *SP* 12 (March 1852): 65–66; *SP* 15 (June 1855): 163–65. See also *SP* 16 (March 1856): 74, (May 1856): 131; *SP* 19 (October 1859): 612.

13. De Bow, *Statistical View,* p. 322.

14. Ruffin, *Calcareous Manures* (3d ed.), p. vii. See also *FR* 8 (July 1840): 418, (November 1840): 691; *FR* 9 (May 1841): 287; *FR* 10 (May 1842): 203, (December 1842): 523.

15. Ruffin, *Exhausting and Fertilizing Systems*, p. 9 (my emphasis); *RCA* (1864): 17.

16. *RCA* (1868): 64.

17. *FR* 1 (March 1834): 614; ibid., 3 (August 1835): 225.

18. Ibid., ibid. 1 (March 1834): 581; ibid. 8 (August 1840): 500–501, (April 1840): 253, (May 1840): 257–58; Emmons, *Survey of North Carolina*, pp. 51, 63, 66–67; *Diary* 1:52, 56 (6, 16 April 1857); *RCA* (1868): 76; Norfleet Diaries 4 (9–11 September, 13, 20, 30 December 1858).

19. Ruffin, *Lower North Carolina*, pp. 285–96; *SC* 8 (December 1840); Emmons, *Survey of North Carolina*, p. 53.

20. Lewis Cecil Gray's remark about marling being pursued there with "much enthusiasm" in the late 1850s seems to have little applicability beyond Edgecombe County. *History of Southern Agriculture* 2:805. See also Cathey, *Agricultural Developments in North Carolina*, p. 95.

21. *FR* 8 (April 1840): 248; *SA* (February 1844): 47; Ruffin, *Lower North Carolina*, p. x; *FJ* 1 (May 1852): 53; *Diary* 1:56 (16 April 1857).

22. *FR* 6 (April 1838): 689, (June 1838): 173, (August 1838): 265; ibid. 8 (March 1840): 178–81, (May 1840): 301–2; *SA* (June 1838): 297–98, (December 1838): 635–36.

23. *SC* 1 (March 1843): 10. Up to the summer of 1841, Ruffin recorded, Hammond has been a "scoffer & ridiculer." SC Diary, 7 June 1843. (The governor had also confessed to Ruffin that he had originally been strongly opposed to the idea of an agricultural survey. SC Diary, 18 February 1843).

24. *FR* 10 (December 1842): 522; *SC* 1 (March 1843): 9; *SC* 4 (July 1846): 99; *SC* 10 (August 1852): 228; Hammond Papers (LC), Diary, 13 November 1841 (also 20 August 1842). For an excellent account of Hammond's improving labors, see Faust, *James Henry Hammond and the Old South,* chapter 6.

25. *SA* (September 1844): 353–54, (June 1844): 214–17, (July 1844): 244, (October 1844): 393; *SC* 3 (February 1845): 21; *SC* 2 (September 1844): 144; *FR* 10 (August 1842): 190–91; Ruffin Papers (UNC), Hammond correspondence, James Hammond to Edmund Ruffin, 4 May 1844; Hammond Papers (LC), Correspondence and Speeches, Edmund Ruffin to James Hammond, 7 September 1845; Ruffin, *Exhausting and Fertilizing Systems*, p. 24, 24n. See also *SP* 10 (November 1850): 339, (April 1850): 100, and Incidents 2, p. 160.

26. *Diary* 1:564 (11 March 1861).

27. Ruffin, *Calcareous Manures* (2d ed.), p. v; *SA* (February 1844): 47; *SC* 1 (March 1843): 9–10; *SC* 4 (July 1846): 97–100, (August 1846): 120; *SC* 10 (August 1852): 228; *SS* 2 (January 1852): 199, (June 1852): 274–76; *SS* 4 (January 1854): 2–3, (December 1854): 360.

28. *SS* 4 (November 1854): 323.

29. *FR* 10 (June 1842): 260.

30. *RCP* (1856): 203, 211, 219.

31. *FR* 1 (June 1833): 18–19; ibid. 10 (June 1842): 280; Bruce, "Virginian Agricultural Decline Fallacy," p. 10.

32. *FR* 10 (June 1842): 280; ibid. 1 (June 1833): 18, (July 1833): 106.

33. Tuomey, *Report on the Geology of South Carolina*, p. 263.

34. See, for example, *FR* 5 (January 1838): 613; ibid. 8 (April 1840): 194.

35. *RCP* (1853): 80, 262–64; ibid. (1852): 114.

36. Kennedy, *State of Maryland*, pp. 11–14. See also *FR* 5 (January 1838): 613; *FR* 6 (April 1838): 3, (November 1838): 453–54; *FR* 8 (April 1840): 193–94.

37. *FR* 9 (March 1841): 128, (September 1841): 528–29; *FJ* 1 (April 1852): 9; *AA* 6 (September 1853): 174; *RCP* (1850): 347; *RCP* (1851): 266.

38. *FR* 5 (December 1837): 544, (April 1838): 2–3; ibid. 6 (November 1838): 453–54; ibid. 7 (March 1839): 116; *SC* 10 (May 1852): 135; *RCP* (1850): 347.

39. *FR* 5 (January 1838): 613; ibid. 9 (September 1841): 529. See also ibid. 7 (March 1839): 167; Kennedy, *State of Maryland*, pp. 12–13.

40. *FR* 9 (September 1841): 529; *RCP* (1850): 347.

41. See Gray, *History of Southern Agriculture* 2:918–19; Jordan, "The Peruvian Guano Gospel in the Old South," pp. 216–20.

42. Ruffin, *Calcareous Manures* (3d ed.), p. vii.

43. *FR* 1 (June 1833): 17–19, (July 1833): 106; ibid. 6 (October 1838): 421–22; ibid. 7 (February 1839): 108; ibid. 10 (January 1842): 40, (April 1842): 159–72, 274, 280–82, (June 1842): 179, 260; *SP* 10 (May 1850): 147: *RCA* (1868): 390; Bruce, "Virginian Agricultural Decline Fallacy," pp. 9–11.

44. *FR* 7 (February 1839): 79; ibid. 1 (July 1833): 79; ibid. 10 (April 1842): 172; ibid. 8 (February 1839): 108.

45. Ibid. 10 (June 1842): 260; ibid. 3 (September 1835): 262; ibid. 7 (August 1839): 501; ibid. 6 (June 1838): 142; ibid. 9 (February 1841): 80; *FJ* 1 (September 1852): 163; *SP* 4 (May 1844): 99; *SP* 6 (April 1846): 81; *SP* 8 (January 1848): 12; *SP* 13 (May 1853): 137.

46. The area includes Westmoreland County, already mentioned. See also remarks by "A Potomac Farmer" in *SP* 7 (April 1847): 97–98.

47. *FR* 7 (April 1839): 209; ibid. 4 (June 1836): 108; ibid. 5 (July 1837): 189, (August 1837): 219, (January 1838): 606; ibid. 7 (January 1839): 63–64; ibid. 10 (June 1842): 304; *SP* 4 (August 1844): 97–98, (December 1844): 265; *SP* 6 (February 1846): 27.

48. *SP* 13 (July 1853): 203–4; ibid. 14 (August 1854): 243–45, (December 1854): 363–64; ibid. 6 (March 1846): 49–50, (June 1846): 129–33; *FR* 9 (July 1842): 385; *FR* 1 (March 1834): 631.

49. *SP* 3 (June 1843): 130. See also ibid. 8 (February 1848): 60–61; ibid. 9 (April 1849): 113, (October 1849): 291, (May 1856): 131; ibid. 16 (March 1856): 73–74; ibid. 19 (October 1859: 612; *FR* 4 (October 1836): 376; *FR* 8 (April 1841): 205–6; *FR* 10 (August 1842): 389; *RCP* (1850): 443, *RCA* (1868): 394, (1870): 285.

50. *SP* 8 (February 1848): 59; ibid. 9 (August 1849): 246; *RCA* (1868): 394, (1870): 286; *FR* 10 (October 1842): 459.

51. *SP* 9 (August 1849): 246.

52. *FR* 1 (January 1834): 468.

53. Ibid. 7 (September 1839): 576; ibid. 8 (May 1840): 257–58; Burgwyn Papers, H. K. Burgwyn to A. H. Souter, 24 July and 25 September 1843; *AA* 2 (February 1845): 51–52; Emmons, *Survey of North Carolina*, pp. 50, 76, 162–63.

54. Greenlee Diary, 12, 13, 21 July, 10, 22 August, 4, 9 October 1854; Norfleet Diaries 2, Expenses of Plantation, 1853–54, 1856–61.

55. Gray, *History of Southern Agriculture* 1:295–97; Ruffin, *Diary* 1:564 (11 March 1851); Ruffin, *Survey of South-Carolina*, appendix, p. 9; Tuomey, *Survey of South Carolina*, p. 16; Tuomey, *Geology of South Carolina*, p. 266; *FR* 6 (November 1838): 689; *FR* 7 (September 1839): 576; *FR* 8 (March 1840): 180; *FR* 9 (May 1841): 287, (August 1841): 469–70; Hammond Papers (LC), Account Book 1849–57, lime entries 1848–50; Boykin Papers, Folders, 23 September 1853.

56. *FR* 8 (March 1840): 176–77; Tuomey, *Geology of South Carolina*, p. 266; Ruffin, *Exhausting and Fertilizing Systems*, p. 19; *SP* 10 (April 1850): 100.

57. *SP* 10 (April 1850): 100; *FR* 8 (March 1840): 176–77. In 1849 we find Charles F. Mills, a Savannah merchant, sending 175 barrels of lime up to Augusta by steamboat for sale on joint account there (Mills Account and Letter Books 5, Invoices, November 1849). It had almost certainly been imported and transhipped.

58. *SS* 2 (December 1852): 380; ibid. 5 (September 1854): 263; *SC* 11 (July 1853): 206–7.

59. *AA* 9 (September 1846): 274.

60. Ruffin, *Exhausting and Fertilizing Systems*, p. 20.

61. The year 1850 has been selected not because it is particularly helpful for any argument but because it makes sense now and then to avoid the hypnotic terminal year of 1860.

62. Craven, *Soil Exhaustion*, p. 128.

63. By 1850 slaves made up only 2.5 percent of the population in Delaware, 15.6 percent in Maryland, and 26.2 in Virginia (though percentages were generally a good deal higher in tidewater and marling counties, as shown in Tables 5 and 6). De Bow, *Statistical View*, pp. 205, 248, 320, 326.

64. Craven, *Soil Exhaustion*, pp. 129, 131–32, 153–55.

65. Ruffin, *Lower North Carolina*, pp. 295–96.

66. Ruffin Papers (UNC), Hammond Correspondence, James Hammond to Edmund Ruffin, 26 September 1847. See also Genovese, *Political Economy of Slavery*, p. 133; Lamar Plantation Book, "Crop of 1848 Planted by Jonas Smith at Domine Place, Sumpter [*sic*] (Ga.)."

Chapter Eight

1. *FR* 1 (August 1833): 5.

2. See, for example, ibid. 2 (March 1835): 636; ibid. 3 (September 1835): 311. Ruffin hired slaves in the 1820s. See *Calcareous Manures* (Sitterson ed.), pp. 187–90.

3. Phillips, *American Negro Slavery*, pp. 339, 349. See also Fogel and Engerman, *Time on the Cross* 1:223–27.

4. Genovese, *Political Economy of Slavery*, p. 43; also pp. 136–41.

5. Stampp, *Peculiar Institution*, p. 60; also pp. 336–37.

6. Gray, *History of Southern Agriculture* 1:469.

7. *FR* 1 (February 1833): 7.

8. Ibid. 10 (June 1842): 264.

9. Hammond Papers (LC), Diary 1841 to 1846, 15 May 1846.

10. *SC* 1 (March 1843): 9.

11. Edmund Ruffin Jr. Plantation Diary (aggregations on manure, greensand, and marl for 1851–59).

12. Tuomey, *Survey of South Carolina*, pp. 49, 54.

13. Ruffin, *Calcareous Manures* (Sitterson ed.), p. 152.

14. *FR* 1 (February 1833): 8.

15. Edmund Ruffin Jr. Plantation Diary, 7 March 1851.

16. Ibid., 11, 17, 22 March, 6 April 1852.

17. *SA* (June 1843): 223.

18. Ibid., p. 216.

19. *SC* 4 (July 1846): 98.

20. *FR* 10 (April 1842): 191; Ruffin Papers (UNC), Hammond correspondence, James Hammond to Edmund Ruffin, 22 July 1846.

21. *FR* 8 (November 1840): 691.

22. Ibid. 1 (February 1834): 555.

23. *SC* 4 (July 1846): 98.

24. Ruffin, *Calcareous Manures* (Sitterson ed.), pp. 152–54.

25. Ruffin, *Lower North Carolina*, pp. 294–95.

26. Ruffin, *Calcareous Manures* (Sitterson ed.), p. 157.

27. Quoted in Tuomey, *Survey of South Carolina*, pp. 54–55.

28. MFJ, 23 May 1844.

29. Ruffin, *Calcareous Manures* (Sitterson ed.), p. 157. However, he also mentions carts breaking down because of "careless driving and worse carpentry" (p. 194).

30. MFJ, introduction and 12 June, 25 July 1844.

31. Ruffin, *Calcareous Manures* (Sitterson ed.), p. 157.

32. See, for example, *FR* 1 (February 1834): 567.

33. Quoted in Ruffin, *Survey of South-Carolina*, p. 50. See also *SC* 8 (March 1850): 38.

34. MFJ, 4 May 1844.

35. Ruffin, *Calcareous Manures* (Sitterson ed.), pp. 155–56.

36. Ibid., p. 156; Ruffin, *Lower North Carolina*, pp. 293–94; Tuomey, *Survey of South Carolina*, pp. 51, 55; *SC* 4 (July 1846): 99.

37. *RCA* (1868): 391.

38. For example, *FR* 1 (October 1833): 266; *SC* 2 (September 1844): 144; MFJ, 4 April 1844; Norfleet Diaries 4 (30 December 1858).

39. *SA* (April 1844): 138. See also *RCP* (1859): 156–57, 159.

40. Norfleet Diaries 4 (11 September 1858).

41. See, for example, *SC* 1 (March 1843): 9.

42. Emmons, *Survey of North Carolina*, p. 57; *SA* (July 1838): 385.

43. *RCP* (1859): 159; *RCA* (1868): 391.

44. Emmons, *Survey of North Carolina*, p. 58.

45. *SA* (October 1844): 396.

46. Emmons, *Agriculture of North-Carolina*, 2:29.

47. Cited in Ruffin, *Calcareous Manures* (3d ed.), p. 238.

48. *SP* 10 (April 1850): 99.

49. *SA* (October 1844): 396; *AA* 4 (April 1847): 119.

50. Ruffin, *Lower North Carolina*, p. 293.

51. *SS* 2 (February 1852): 199. See also *SA* (May 1844): 179.

52. *SP* (n.s.) 3 (July 1869): 409–10.

53. *SA* (October 1844): 396.

54. Ruffin, *Lower North Carolina*, p. 294.

55. Ruffin, *Calcareous Manures* (Sitterson ed.), p. 146.

56. Tuomey, *Survey of South Carolina*, p. 324.

57. *SC* 1 (March 1843): 9.

58. *FR* 1 (August 1833): 158.

59. Ibid. 2 (March 1835): 644.

60. MFJ, 24 February 1844, 2 March 1844.

61. See, for example, Tuomey, *Survey of South Carolina*, p. 49; *AA* 8 (March 1849): 106.

62. Norfleet Diaries 4 (20 December 1858).

63. MFJ, 1 October 1844.

64. Tuomey, *Survey of South Carolina*, p. 53.

65. Ruffin, *Lower North Carolina*, pp. 293–94.

66. *FR* 1 (August 1833): 158.

67. Ibid. 3 (January 1836): 555.

68. Tuomey, *Survey of South Carolina*, p. 49.

69. *SA* (December 1838): 636.

70. MFJ, 4 April 1849.

71. Phillips, *American Negro Slavery*, p. 339.

Chapter Nine

1. *SC* 4 (July 1846): 98.
2. *SA* (October 1844): 395.
3. Emmons, *Survey of North Carolina,* pp. 45–46; *SC* 4 (July 1846): 98.
4. *SA* (October 1844): 396.
5. *SC* 4 (July 1846): 98.
6. Ibid.; *FR* 5 (July 1837): 186, (December 1837): 511; *FR* 10 (December 1842): 523; *RCA* (1868): 391.
7. Ruffin, *Survey of South-Carolina,* pp. 43–45; Emmons, *Survey of North Carolina,* pp. 44–45; *SC* 4 (July 1846): 98; *SA* (January 1844): 36–38; *FR* 8 (August 1840): 500; Norfleet Diaries 4 (7 September, 13 December 1858).
8. *SC* 4 (July 1846): 10.
9. Wrightson, *Agricultural Text-Book, Embracing Soils, Manures, Rotations of Crops, and Live Stock,* p. 116; Smith, *Manures and Fertilizers,* pp. 44–45; Genovese, *Political Economy of Slavery,* pp. 91, 94–95; Kerridge, *Agricultural Revolution,* pp. 245–46; Morton's *Cyclopedia* 7:372–73; *SC* 4 (July 1846): 98; Robinson, *Guano: A Treatise of Practical Information for Farmers,* pp. 43–56; Taylor "Commercial Fertilizers in South Carolina," p. 183. See also Lawton Papers, Plantation Diary, 11 March 1828 (cottonseed at 30 bushels per acre); Edmund Ruffin Jr. Plantation Diary, 10 October 1851 (bone dust at five bushels per acre). John Taylor of Caroline was in the habit of using one bushel of gypsum to the acre in combination with manure. Taylor, *Arator* (Bradford ed.), p. 62.
10. *FR* 9 (January 1841): 23.
11. Kennedy, *Eighth Census,* pp. 225–27, 231, 235–37, 243–45.
12. Ruffin, *Calcareous Manures* (Sitterson ed.), pp. 146, 191–98.
13. Ibid., pp. 198–99.
14. MFJ, 28 July, 14 December 1846.
15. Ibid., 17 May, 12 September 1849.
16. *FR* 1 (October 1833): 266.
17. Ibid. (February 1834): 567.
18. Ibid. 2 (March 1835): 636.
19. Ibid. 9 (May 1841): 265.
20. Edmund Ruffin Jr. Plantation Diary, sundry entries, January–April 1851, January–May 1852.
21. Hammond Papers (LC), Correspondence and Speeches, James Hammond to Edmund Ruffin, 13 November 1841.
22. *SC* 1 (March 1843): 9.
23. Ibid.
24. Hammond Papers (LC), Plantation Book, 1849–58, 1, 4 September, 10–11, 24–27 October 1849.
25. *SC* 1 (March 1843): 9.
26. *FR* 1 (February 1834): 568. See also *SP* 13 (May 1853): 141–42.
27. *FR* 1 (February 1834): 567, (March 1835): 636; ibid. 8 (November 1840): 691.

28. Ibid. 1 (February 1834): 555.

29. Ibid. 6 (June 1838): 184; ibid. 8 (August 1840): 489; ibid. 9 (January 1841): 23; ibid. 10 (June 1840): 264; Ruffin, *Lower North Carolina*, pp. 293.

30. *FR* 5 (May 1837): 5.

31. Ibid. 8 (August 1840): 489.

32. Ibid. 7 (September 1839): 575.

33. Ibid. 9 (May 1841): 267.

34. Norfleet Diaries 4, sundry entries, September, December 1858. (The figure of sixty field hands has been suggested to me by Professor William K. Scarborough.)

35. Ibid. 3 and 4, sundry entries, 1856–58.

36. *SA* (June 1843): 222.

37. Tuomey, *Survey of South Carolina*, pp. 51–55.

38. Hammond Papers (LC), Plantation Book, 1849–58, sundry entries, September, October 1849.

39. Suggested by Anderson and Gallman, "Slaves as Fixed Capital," p. 30. For slightly more modest estimates, see Ruffin, *Calcareous Manures* (Sitterson ed.), p. 169; *SP* 13 (May 1853): 141. (Ruffin suggests 257 days for women.)

40. *SC* 1 (March 1843): 9.

41. *FR* 8 (August 1840): 489.

42. For instances of similar scheduling with other "leisure" work, see Anderson, "Labor Utilization and Productivity, Diversification and Self-Sufficiency, Southern Plantations, 1800–1840," pp. 206, 220, 249.

43. Anderson and Gallman, "Slaves as Fixed Capital," p. 29. See also Genovese, *Political Economy of Slavery*, p. 49; Stampp, *Peculiar Institution*, p. 4.

44. Anderson and Gallman, "Slaves as Fixed Capital," pp. 27–39.

45. Anderson, "Labor Utilization," pp. 183–84.

46. Ibid., p. 190. See also Stampp, *Peculiar Institution*, pp. 44–49, 73–85.

47. *RCA* (1868): 39 (my italics).

48. *SP* 13 (May 1853): 138.

49. Ruffin, *Calcareous Manures* (Sitterson ed.), pp. 188–91, 195, 198.

50. Tuomey, *Survey of South Carolina*, p. 55.

51. Ibid.; Ruffin, *Calcareous Manures* (Sitterson ed.), p. 197.

52. *FR* 10 (December 1842): 523.

53. Tuomey, *Survey of South Carolina*, p. 55.

54. Hammond Papers (LC), Correspondence and Speeches, Edmund Ruffin to James Hammond, 7 September 1845.

55. *FR* 6 (August 1838): 689; ibid. 10 (October 1842): 489.

56. *SS* 5 (December 1855): 356; *AA* 6 (August 1847): 247.

57. Ruffin, *Calcareous Manures* (Sitterson ed.), pp. 195, 198.

58. *SC* 8 (March 1850): 38. The famous Northern commentator on agricultural affairs did not please his host at Silver Bluff: "Disposed to be social & even jovial, but very crass & very vain." Ruffin Papers (UNC), Hammond correspondence, James Hammond to Edmund Ruffin, 27 March 1850.

59. *FR* 6 (June 1838): 142.

60. Ibid. 5 (July 1837): 186.

61. Ibid. 10 (October 1842): 489.

62. A common application for best Peruvian guano was 200 to 250 lbs. At the peak wholesale price of $65 per ton in 1857–58, that meant around $6.50 an acre *before* dealer's profits, transport to farm, hauling, and spreading. See Genovese, *Political Economy of Slavery,* p. 94; Mathew, *The House of Gibbs and the Peruvian Guano Monopoly,* pp. 137–46, 190; Robinson, *Treatise on Guano,* pp. 43–56; Taylor, "Commercial Fertilizers," pp. 179–89; Rubin, "The Limits of Agricultural Progress in the Nineteenth-Century South," pp. 359–70; *SP* 18 (May 1858): 284. As already noted, doses of marl in Britain were larger. William Marshall estimated Norfolk costs in the late eighteenth century at around $15 per acre. Cited in Riches, *Agricultural Revolution in Norfolk,* p. 81.

63. *SC* 4 (July 1846): 99.

64. *FR* 1 (December 1833): 396.

65. *SS* 4 (November 1854): 323.

66. *SP* 9 (August 1849): 227–37.

67. *FR* 5 (July 1837): 186.

68. Ibid. 8 (August 1840): 492.

69. Ibid. 10 (October 1842): 489.

Chapter Ten

1. F. M. L. Thompson, "Second Agricultural Revolution," pp. 63–70.

2. See, for example, Lindstrom, *Economic Development in the Philadelphia Region,* pp. 100–101, 112–13, 117–19.

3. *FR* 1 (February 1834): 567; ibid. 8 (November 1840): 691; ibid. 9 (July 1841): 388.

4. Ibid. 8 (November 1840): 691; ibid. 2 (March 1835): 636; ibid. 4 (December 1837): 511.

5. Ibid. 1 (July 1833): 106, (December 1833): 396; ibid. 4 (February 1837): 623, (July 1837): 186; ibid. 9 (July 1841): 390.

6. Ibid. 9 (February 1841): 80; ibid. 5 (June 1838): 142; *SP* 6 (April 1846): 82.

7. *FR* 1 (February 1834): 535. From Connecticut the marl was sent upcountry along the Farmington Canal. Ibid. 3 (November 1836): 506.

8. Ibid. 8 (May 1840): 257; *SA* 4 (1844): 214.

9. *FR* 10 (April 1842): 191; *SC* 1 (March 1843): 9; Ruffin Papers (UNC), Hammond correspondence, James Hammond to Edmund Ruffin, 22 July 1846.

10. Rough estimate, from figures in chapter 9.

11. Segal, "Canals and Economic Development," in Goodrich, *Canals and American Economic Development,* pp. 227, 243.

12. Turner, "Railroad Service to Virginia Farmers, 1828–1860," p. 244.

13. Segal in Goodrich, *Canals,* pp. 234, 286n.

14. *FR* 7 (February 1839): 108; ibid. 10 (August 1842): 385; ibid. 8 (November 1840): 682; ibid. 10 (April 1842): 172.

15. *FJ* 1 (September 1852): 167. See also ibid. (April 1852): 9, for Edward Sta-

bler's comments on the failure of Maryland farmers to make use of their waterways for transporting marl.

16. Emmons, *Survey of North Carolina,* p. 74.

17. See also Galpin, "The Grain Trade of Alexandria, Virginia," p. 407; *FR* 9 (July 1841): 388–89.

18. *FR* 9 (July 1841): 388–89.

19. *SC* (April 1853): 105.

20. Fogel and Engerman, *Time on the Cross* 1:255. See also Fishlow, *American Railroads and the Transformation of the Antebellum Economy,* p. 9.

21. See, among others, Crittenden, "Inland Navigation in North Carolina, 1763–1789," pp. 146, 151–52; Fleetwood, *Tidecraft,* pp. 87–88. *FR* (September 1836): 296.

22. Phillips, *A History of Transportation in the Eastern Cotton Belt to 1860,* p. 10.

23. See Hinshaw, "North Carolina Canals Before 1860," p. 25; Barnard, "The South Atlantic States in 1833, as Seen by a New Englander," p. 318; *FR* 3 (December 1835): 501; Ruffin Papers (UNC), SC Diary, 15 March 1843.

24. MacGill, *History of Transportation in the United States Before 1860,* map facing p. 654 showing amount of tidewater navigation which gave less than three feet minimum depth; Jefferson, *Notes on the State of Virginia* (Peden ed.), pp. 5–7; Hart, *Southeastern United States,* p. 45; *FR* 4 (September 1836): 294; Emmons, *Survey of North Carolina,* p. 74; Savage, *River of the Carolinas,* p. 251.

25. Ruffin Papers (UNC), SC Diary, 9, 17, 19, 25 February, 15 March, 12, 13, 17 April, 27 May 1843. Savage writes of frequent floods on the Santee rivers, average flows increasing sometimes more than twentyfold. *River of the Carolinas,* p. 21. See also *SA* (August 1844): 287.

26. Gray, *History of Southern Agriculture* 2:684–85.

27. Phillips, *Transportation in the Eastern Cotton Belt,* pp. 43–44.

28. Savage, *River of the Carolinas,* p. 251. See also Phillips, *Transportation in the Eastern Cotton Belt,* pp. 75–77, 82, 128, for comment on Georgia and North Carolina.

29. Hinshaw, "North Carolina Canals," pp. 34, 36, 38; Bodichon, *An American Diary* (Reed ed.), pp. 131, 176.

30. Lytle, *Merchant Steam Vessels of the United States, 1807–1868,* passim.

31. See Mak and Walton, "Steamboats and the Great Productivity Surge in River Transportation," pp. 619–35; Hunter, *Steamboats on the Western Rivers,* passim; Haites, Mak, and Walton, *Western River Transportation,* passim.

32. Taylor, *Transportation Revolution,* pp. 56–57; Phillips, *Transportation in the Eastern Cotton Belt,* pp. 25–26, 71; Fleetwood, *Tidecraft,* pp. 81, 87, 89, 95–100.

33. Mak and Walton, "The Persistence of Old Technologies," pp. 444–49.

34. MacGill, *History of Transportation,* p. 250. Phillips writes of "the necessity of every man being in most cases his own carrier." *Transportation in the Eastern Cotton Belt,* p. 131.

35 Haites and Mak, "Ohio and Mississippi River Transportation, 1810–1860," p. 162.

36. Segal in Goodrich, *Canals,* pp. 211–13.

37. Segal in Goodrich, *Canals,* pp. 176–79, 188–89, 194, 204, 211–15, 228, 233,

240–41, 244–45; Phillips, *Transportation in the Eastern Cotton Belt*, pp. 15–16; Savage, *River of the Carolinas*, pp. 249–50; Dozier, *A History of the Atlantic Coast Line Railroad*, pp. 14–15.

38. Ruffin Papers (UNC), SC Diary, 2 February 1843.

39. Starling, "The Plank Road Movement in North Carolina," p. 173.

40. Ruffin Papers (UNC), SC Diary, 16 March, 24 April, 7, 24 June 1843. See also Fleetwood, *Tidecraft*, pp. 81, 86.

41. Ruffin, *Calcareous Manures* (Sitterson ed.), p. 147n.

42. *FR* 4 (October 1836): 370. See also Fogel, *Railroads and American Economic Growth*, p. 38.

43. From figures in Fishlow, *American Railroads*, p. 337.

44. Alavi, "India and the Colonial Mode of Production," p. 184; also p. 190. Alavi borrows the notion of disarticulation from Samir Amin's *Accumulation on a World Scale*.

45. See, for example, Eaton, *Southern Civilization*, pp. 196–220; *SC* 18 (December 1860): 370–71.

46. See Chandra, "Indian Nationalists and the Drain," pp. 103–33.

47. McColley, *Slavery and Jeffersonian Virginia*, p. 9; Cash, *The Mind of the South*, p. 53; Sitgreaves, "Letters from South Carolina, 1821–22" (Staudenraus ed.), p. 210; Eaton, *Southern Civilization*, p. 297 (see also pp. 187, 319).

48. Olmsted, *The Slave States* (Wish ed.), p. 73.

49. Ruffin Papers (UNC), Hammond correspondence, James Hammond to Edmund Ruffin, 24 October 1853. See also Faust, *Sacred Circle*, p. 43.

50. Ruffin Papers (UNC), SC Diary, passim.

51. Ibid. Closing Scenes of the Life of Thomas Cocke, 25 February 1840; ibid., Incidents 2, p. 162.

52. See Wright, *Cotton South*, pp. 109–10; Elkins and McKitrick, "A Meaning for Turner's Frontier," p. 341.

53. *FR* 8 (July 1840): 415–16.

54. Johnson, "The Ante-Bellum Town in North Carolina," p. 372.

55. Ruffin Papers (UNC), SC Diary, 25 May 1843.

56. Quoted in Eaton, *Southern Civilization*, p. 248. "The greatest and most important branch of the commerce of every nation," wrote Adam Smith, ". . . is that which is carried on between the inhabitants of the town, and those of the country." *The Wealth of Nations* 2:179.

57. Genovese, *Political Economy of Slavery*, p. 165.

58. Furtado, *Economic Growth of Brazil*, p. 53.

59. Metzer, "Rational Management, Modern Business Practices, and Economics of Scale in the Ante-Bellum Southern Plantations," pp. 127–31; Battalio and Kagel, "The Structure of Antebellum Southern Agriculture: South Carolina," pp. 33–34. On Wright, see note 61 below.

60. Genovese, *Political Economy of Slavery*, p. 49; Anderson and Gallman, "Slaves as Fixed Capital," p. 24.

61. Anderson and Gallman, "Slaves as Fixed Capital," pp. 28, 31–32, 34, 36, 42, 46. See also Gallman, "Self-Sufficiency in the Cotton Economy of the Antebellum

South," pp. 21–23. Anderson and Gallman's approach is accepted with minor caveats by Gavin Wright. He also introduces "safety-first" considerations with particular reference to smaller farms in which self-sufficiency was pursued as a low-risk objective in a market context of varying prices both for the income-generating staple and the purchased foodstuff: "using cotton as a means of meeting food requirements involved the combined risks of cotton yields, cotton prices, and corn prices." *Cotton South*, pp. 55–74.

62. Phillips, *Transportation in the Eastern Cotton Belt*, p. 8.

63. Gray, *History of Southern Agriculture* 2:940.

64. See Newby, *The South*, pp. 126–27; also note 61 above.

65. Stampp, *Peculiar Institution*, p. 280; also pp. 279–92. For further discussion, see Fogel and Engerman, *Time on the Cross* 1:109–17, and Richard Sutch in David, *Reckoning with Slavery*, pp. 231–301.

66. Parker calls the figure "a generous estimate." See "Slavery and Southern Economic Development," p. 120; also pp. 116–17.

67. Gray, *History of Southern Agriculture* 2:934.

68. Wright, *Cotton South*, p. 117.

69. Gates, *Farmer's Age*, p. 113.

70. *FR* 8 (November 1840): 686.

71. *CC* 3 (April 1857): 60. See also Bidwell and Falconer, *History of Agriculture in the Northern United States*, p. 234.

72. Schmidt, *Agriculture in New Jersey*, p. 130; also pp. 129, 131; Lindstrom, *Philadelphia Region*, pp. 100–101, 112–13, 117–19.

73. Fitzherbert, *The Boke of Husbandry*, cited in Prothero, *English Farming*, p. 10.

74. Ruffin, *Calcareous Manures* (Sitterson ed.), p. 173; *FR* 1 (November 1833): 365.

75. Robertson, *General View of the Agriculture of the County of Perth*, pp. 317–18. See also Leslie, *General View of the Agriculture of the Counties of Nairn and Moray*, p. 281.

76. Lindsay, *The Canals of Scotland*, p. 179.

77. A journey of nearly forty miles. John Smith, *General View of the Agriculture of the County of Argyle*, p. 217n. See also Samuel Smith, *General View of the Agriculture of Galloway*, pp. 45–48, 209–13.

78. Kerridge, *Agricultural Revolution*, pp. 221, 241 and passim.

79. Priestley, *Historical Account of the Navigable Rivers, Canals, and Railways of Great Britain*, passim; Holland, *General View of the Agriculture of Cheshire*, p. 312. How much marl was in fact carried on these railways and waterways, we have no means of telling. National railway returns, as Dr. T. R. Gourvish has pointed out to me, usually only distinguish "livestock," "minerals," and "general merchandise," and canal statistics are even less informative.

80. For some idea of the density, see Prince, "Norfolk Pits," pp. 20–27; also the photograph of a pitted landscape in Edlin, *East Anglian Forests*, facing p. 35.

81. Marshall, *Rural Economy of Norfolk* 1:18–22, 24–26.

82. See sketch in Woodward, *The Geology of England and Wales*, p. 287, and reproduction of John Sell Cotman's watercolor "The Marl Pit" (1808) in Prince, "Norfolk Pits," plate 4.

83. Marshall, *Rural Economy of Norfolk* 1:99.

84. Young, *General View of the Agriculture of the County of Norfolk*, pp. 406–8. Distances given are based on rough guesses for the likely routes followed.

85. Quoted in Malster, *Wherries and Waterways*, p. 72. See also Prince, "Norfolk Pits," p. 25; Trimmer, "On the Geology of Norfolk as Illustrating the Laws of the Distribution of Soils," p. 480.

86. Defoe, *A Tour Through the Whole Island of Great Britain*, pp. 99–100.

87. Vancouver, *General View of the Agriculture of the County of Essex* 1, passim.

88. Marshall, *Review of County Reports*, 3:483–84.

89. Boys, *General View of the Agriculture of the County of Kent*, p. 149. See also Prothero, *English Farming*, p. 192; Chambers and Mingay, *Agricultural Revolution*, pp. 62–63; Kerridge, *Agricultural Revolution*, p. 250.

90. T. S. Willan, *The English Coasting Trade*, passim; Willan, *The Inland Trade*, pp. 26–41; Davis, *The Rise of the English Shipping Industry in the Seventeenth and Eighteenth Century*, pp. 402–5.

91. Malster, *Wherries and Waterways*, pp. 10, 45, 112–23.

92. Ibid., pp. 112–23.

93. Davies, "The Canal System," pp. 8, 15–17, 22. See also Jackman, *The Development of Transportation in Modern England*, pp. 435–44.

94. Wilson, "The Aire and Calder Navigation" 4:5. For more general information on boats and ownership, see Willan, *River Naviation in England*, pp. 102–5, 114–17, 127–30.

Chapter Eleven

1. *SP* 13 (January 1853): 10.

2. *FR* 8 (August 1840): 486.

3. Ibid. 7 (November 1839): 658.

4. Faust, *Sacred Circle*, pp. 12–13.

5. Genovese, *World the Slaveholders Made*, pp. 123–26; Genovese, *Roll, Jordan, Roll*, pp. 296–97; Genovese, "The Slave South," in Weinstein and Gatell, *American Negro Slavery*, pp. 264–65, 272–74; Luraghi, *The Rise and Fall of the Plantation South*, pp. 47, 62, 74–75, 82, 88, 91.

6. Gray, *History of Southern Agriculture* 1:96, 450–51, 498; Craven, *Soil Exhaustion*, p. 23; Gates, *Farmer's Age*, pp. 7, 137, 154; Cash, *Mind of the South*, p. 97; Cathey, "Agricultural Implements in North Carolina," p. 135; Smith, *Old Cotton State*, pp. 84–104; Flanders, *Plantation Slavery in Georgia*, pp. 137, 225–27; Moore, *Agriculture in Ante-Bellum Mississippi*, p. 41.

7. Mathew, "Planter Entrepreneurship," pp. 207–21.

8. Conrad and Meyer, "Economics of Slavery," p. 95; Rothstein, "The Cotton Frontier of the Antebellum South," pp. 160–61; Metzer, "Rational Management," pp. 144, 147; Fogel and Engerman, *Time on the Cross* 1:86–94, 202–9, 253; *Cotton South*, pp. 140–43.

9. Gray, *History of Southern Agriculture* 1:487–500.

10. Moore, *Social Origins of Dictatorship and Democracy,* p. 331. See also pp. 356, 366; Neale, "Land Is to Rule," in Frykenberg, *Land Control and Social Structure in Indian History,* pp. 8–13; Macpherson, "Economic Development in India Under the British Crown," in Youngson, *Economic Development in the Long Run,* pp. 136–38, 149–50, 162–72.

11. Gerschenkron, *Economic Backwardness in Historical Perspective,* p. 121; Milward and Saul, *The Development of the Economies of Continental Europe,* pp. 229, 359–60.

12. Gerschenkron, *Economic Backwardness,* p. 64. See also Clapham, *The Economic Development of France and Germany,* pp. 47, 52, 202–3, 206.

13. Caird, *English Agriculture in 1850–51,* p. 490. See also pp. 124, 134–35, 145–46, 220, 331–33, 472, 488–509. "By and large," writes C. Ó Gráda, "the farmer and the landlord have been given low marks for adaptability and initiative in the mid- and late-Victorian era." "Agricultural Decline 1860–1914," in Floud and McCloskey, *The Economic History of Britain Since 1700,* p. 176. For Southern comparative comment, see *SFF* 1 (1859): 5.

14. *AF* 6 (March 1824): 5; *FR* 18 (June 1840): 343.

15. MFJ, 9 May 1851; Edmund Ruffin Jr. Plantation Diary.

16. *SC* 4 (July 1846): 99; Hammond Papers (LC), Account Book 1849–57.

17. *RCP* (1859): 159; *SC* 19 (February 1861): 49.

18. Ruffin, *Calcareous Manures* (Sitterson ed.), pp. 126–27; Ruffin, *Survey of South-Carolina,* p. 50; Tuomey, *Survey of South Carolina,* p. 35; Emmons, *Survey of North Carolina,* pp. 29–30, 78–79; *RCP* (1851): 49, (1852): 380, 388, (1856): 217, 136, (1859): 154; *FR* 1 (July 1833) 108; *FR* 2 (March 1835): 644; *FR* 3 (January 1836): 553; *FR* 5 (May 1837): 5; *FR* 8 (February 1840): 115–16, (April 1840): 253, (August 1840): 501; *FR* 10 (August 1842): 385–86; *AA* 4 (April 1845): 118, (July 1845): 220; *AA* 9 (July 1850): 221; *SP* 6 (April 1846): 82; *SP* 10 (November 1850): 388–40; *SC* (December 1850): 180; *FJ* 1 (March 1853): 381–82; *FJ* 3 (October 1854): 198.

19. *FR* 8 (August 1840): 501; *SS* 2 (January 1852): 138; Ruffin, *Lower North Carolina,* p. 85.

20. Emmons, *Survey of North Carolina,* p. 76

21. Ruffin, *Calcareous Manures* (Sitterson ed.), p. 104. See also p. 98. *FR* 1 (July 1833): 108, (February 1834): 581; ibid. 3 (August 1835): 225; ibid. 8 (August 1840): 491–96; ibid. 9 (January 1841) 28, (May 1841): 265; *SA* (January 1844): 37; Ruffin Papers (UNC), Hammond correspondence, James Hammond to Edmund Ruffin, 1 June 1847. Another adverse effect was the occasional proliferation of troublesome wire grass. See *AF* 6 (March 1824): 5.

23. *FR* 3 (January 1836): 555, (August 1835): 225; ibid. 10 (June 1842): 298; *SS* 4 (December 1854): 360.

24. Rubin, "Limits of Agricultural Progress," pp. 368, 370, 372–73.

25. Chapman and Sherman, *United States and Canada Atlas,* p. 85.

26. *SC* 11 (August 1853): 253.

27. Ibid. 3 (November 1845): 171; MFJ, 13 May 1847; Incidents 2, insert, p. 44.

28. Genovese, *Political Economy of Slavery,* p. 110 and chapter 5 passim.

29. Gray, *History of Southern Agriculture* 2:823.

30. See comment in Bonner, "Genesis of Agricultural Reform in the Cotton Belt," pp. 496–97.

31. *RCA* (1866): 576–77, (1874): 229; *RCP* (1860): 225–30.

32. Somers, *The Southern States Since the War*, pp. 70–72.

33. Hammond, *South Carolina*, p. 3.

34. Whitehead, *Virginia as She Is*, p. 19.

35. *YDA* (1903): 522–26, (1906): 193, 202–3, (1914): 266–67.

36. Stampp, *Peculiar Institution*, p. 394.

37. Metzer, "Rational Management," p. 135 (also pp. 123, 125–27); Conrad and Meyer, "Economics of Slavery," p. 95.

38. *RCD* (1852): 381. Noah B. Cloud phrased the planters' question: "How shall we best improve our land without curtailing the crop?" *SC* 6 (1848): 6.

39. Genovese, "The Slave South," p. 275; Genovese, *Political Economy of Slavery*, p. 133; Flanders, *Plantation Slavery in Georgia*, pp. 69, 225.

40. Ruffin, *Essays and Notes*, pp. 125, 128–30, 138–39, 142–45.

41. Metzer, "Rational Management," p. 145; Aufhauser, "Slavery and Scientific Management," pp. 816–17; Cairnes, *The Slave Power*, pp. 54–56, 62.

42. *FR* 3 (April 1836): 749.

43. Ruffin Papers (UNC), Hammond correspondence, James Hammond to Edmund Ruffin, 26 September 1847.

44. See *SP* 20 (February 1860): 69–76.

45. *SC* 6 (October 1848): 149–50, (December 1848): 181–82.

46. Range, *A Century of Georgia Agriculture*, p. 18; *RCA* (1874): 229; Gray, *History of Southern Agriculture* 2:823; *YDA* (1906): 202.

47. Ruffin Papers (UNC), Hammond correspondence, James Hammond to Edmund Ruffin, 4 March 1844.

48. The first edition was issued as a Belknap Press reprint in 1961, edited by J. Carlyle Sitterson.

49. Ruffin Papers (UNC), SC Diary, 1 March 1842; *FJ* 3 (October 1854): 201.

50. *FR* 9 (May 1841): 287; ibid. 8 (June 1840): 341; ibid. 1 (April 1834): 648; *DBR* 25 (July–December 1858): 395.

51. *FR* 3 (August 1835): 225. See also his observations quoted in Demaree, *American Agricultural Press*, p. 233.

52. *FR* 1 (February 1834): 574, (April 1834): 648.

53. Ruffin Papers (UNC), Hammond correspondence, James Hammond to Edmund Ruffin, 27 March 1850, and 18 March, 23 August, 6 October 1846.

54. Gray, *History of Southern Agriculture* 2:788.

55. McColley, *Slavery and Jeffersonian Virginia*, p. 57; Numbers and Numbers, "Science in the Old South," pp. 173, 177, 180, 183. See Scarborough, "Science on the Plantation," p. 34. Ronald and Janet Numbers also suggest secondary links with slavery through "wasted time and energy devoted to its defense, an antipathy toward centralized government, and a predominantly agricultural economy" (p. 171). See also p. 164.

56. *FR* 3 (August 1835): 225.

57. Ibid. 2 (February 1835): 521–22; ibid. 8 (May 1840): 274–75.

58. Ruffin Papers (UNC), Hammond correspondence, James Hammond to Edmund Ruffin, 22 July 1846.

59. Ibid., 16 June 1846.

60. *FR* 3 (April 1836): 751–52.

61. Ruffin, "Agricultural Education," pp. 6–14.

62. Ruffin Papers (UNC), Hammond correspondence, James Hammond to Edmund Ruffin, 1 February 1846; *SP* 14 (May 1854): 132; *DBR* 25 (July–December 1858): 161–63, 395. See also Cash, *Mind of the South,* pp. 117–18; Numbers and Numbers, "Science in the Old South," pp. 179–80; Barnard, "South Atlantic States," p. 376.

63. Jenkins and Jones, "Cantab. Alumni," pp. 93–116.

64. Mathew, "The Origins and Occupations of Glasgow Students," pp. 78–88.

65. Barnard, "South Atlantic States," p. 376.

66. Gray, *History of Southern Agriculture* 2:791–92.

67. Numbers and Numbers, "Science in the Old South," p. 165 and passim.

68. Scarborough, "Science on the Plantation," pp. 2–6, 10–11, 33–34.

69. *FJ* 1 (August 1852): 145.

70. *FR* 10 (July 1842): 366; ibid. 8 (July 1840): 417.

71. Ruffin Papers (UNC), Hammond correspondence, James Hammond to Edmund Ruffin, 11 March 1851.

72. See Genovese, *World the Slaveholders Made,* pp. 123, 126; Genovese "The Slave South," pp. 264–65, 272–73. See also Habib, "Economy of Mughal India," pp. 53–54, 56–60.

73. See Eaton, *Southern Civilization,* p. 15.

74. Barnard, "South Atlantic States," p. 318.

75. Ruffin Papers (UNC), SC Diary, 28 June 1843.

76. Ruffin, *Essays and Notes,* pp. 274–77.

77. *FR* 1 (February 1834): 574.

78. Ruffin, *Calcareous Manures* (Sitterson ed.), p. 163.

79. *FR* I (July 1833): 123. McDonald and McWhiney agree that there was a common aversion to labor in the South, but suggest that this had nothing to do with slavery. The exclusive cause was the Celtic cultural heritage of Southerners above tidewater. Their focus is on "plain folk" and their "opulently easy society." The argument, however, is unpersuasive, as the authors fail to resolve a number of elementary problems.

1. How does one determine the certain existence of a universal and persisting cultural trait—in this instance, laziness—for widespread communities in the British Isles and subsequently for widespread communities in North America? Sources must be treated with great caution, especially when the culture in question was linguistically, religiously, economically, and politically marginalized in Britain, attracting the contempt and ethnic stereotyping of the materially superior, yet insecure, Anglo-Saxon neighbors and their local collaborators. The quoted sources in this instance are too few and too tendentiously sweeping.

2. How does one limit the culture entity itself to a fairly homogeneous body of

people? McDonald and McWhiney acknowledge very loosely that the "Celt" was *genetically* diverse in the relevant areas: Scotland, Northern Ireland, Wales, and the so-called Celtic frontier regions of western and northern England. They might have added that there are very few people of genuine Celtic ancestry anywhere in Britain. This is no problem, of course, for a purely social argument if, as the authors assert, all the people in question "shared a common cultural heritage." Unfortunately, this suggestion is nonsensical, and the offered alternative concept of "non-English" is only of service if it can be shown that the very exclusion from Englishness was itself culturally unifying. The authors make the elementary error of including under the Celtic label Scottish Lowlanders and their emigré Scotch-Irish kinfolk in Ulster—Anglo-Saxons, English speakers, Gael-fighters, and, in the case of the Scotch-Irish, occupying Irish land as part of a "planting" exercise to help London control the indigenous Celts (whose circumstances, incidentally, usually precluded any resort to laziness). For these Presbyterian people, the stereotype (largely self-invented, rather than contrived from without) was that of the God-fearing, providential, thrifty man, playing a sober but active role in the affairs of church and state, enjoying the highest educational aspirations for himself and his family, and proud of the practical and intellectual achievements of the society around him. Effort and success were virtues. Laziness was among the very worst of vices.

3. How to find an economic basis for an alleged culture trait? McDonald and Mc-Whiney allege that the laziness came from "a long-standing tradition of open-range pastoralism and an accompanying disdain for tillage agriculture." Medieval evidence is produced and its later relevance is established by the Celts being described as "amazingly resistant to changing their ways." The point is utterly remote from the facts of industrialization and agricultural advance in the Scottish Lowlands, South Wales, and the Belfast area—vigorous, capitalistic activity, dating in the main from the mid-eighteenth century. But, of course, such areas should never have been part of the culture zone to begin with. Even if one reduces the numbers rather drastically, by counting only the Gaels, the characterization still does not fit. The authors have to acknowledge potato cultivation. As for the Scottish Clearances, these were not some attack on backward herders by improvers eager to maximize returns from the land by modern methods; they were an assault on small-scale, low-renting, mixed farmers by moneyed, "pastoralist," Anglo-Saxon sheep men, exercising (to transfer the McDonald and McWhiney phraseology) a quite ruthless "disdain for tillage agriculture."

The issue, then, is not closed. It might be very difficult to mount a case relating Southern entrepreneurial defects to the possession of slaves, but the possibility of there being some significant relationship between the two is hardly precluded by any externally derived cultural propensities of white men. McDonald and McWhiney, "The South from Self-Sufficiency to Peonage," pp. 1103–1108. See also Rowland Berthoff's remarks in the *Journal of Southern History* (and a response from McDonald and McWhiney) which have recently come to my attention. I am happy to see that I have reached conclusions very much in line with Professor Berthoff's informed and careful analysis—though not always with the same specifics and logic. Berthoff, "Celtic Mist Over the South," pp. 523–50).

80. *SS* 4 (April 1854): 170.

81. Incidents 2, p. 139; Incidents 3, p. 258.

82. *FR* 4 (March 1837): 696.

83. *SC* 14 (March 1956): 84. Some movement was still possible within it, especially to northern and western Georgia. For the most part, however, the Old South frontier had been reached by the Civil War and Georgia itself had become a major source of emigrants. See Gray, *History of Southern Agriculture* 2: 899; Flanders, *Plantation Slavery in Georgia*, p. 77; Bonner, *Georgia Agriculture*, pp. 61–65, 71–72.

84. *FR* 3 (August 1835): 236, (April 1836): 753–54; *SA* (January 1842): 20.

85. Ruffin, *Calcareous Manures* (Sitterson ed.), p. 140.

86. *FR* 3 (August 1835): 236–37; Gray, *Southern Agriculture* 1:450–51; *RCA* (1866): 572.

87. *FR* 9 (July 1841): 414; ibid. 3 (April 1836): 751. See also *SS* 4 (January 1854): 3.

88. *FJ* 1 (April 1852): 30.

89. Emmons, *Agriculture of North-Carolina*, 2:84.

90. Craven, *Soil Exhaustion*, p. 23; Moore, *Agriculture in Mississippi*, p. 41; Cash, *Mind of the South*, p. 97.

91. Ruffin, *Calcareous Manures* (Sitterson ed.), p. 133; *SA* (July 1844): 246; Ruffin Papers (UNC), SC Diary, 22 March; Ruffin Papers (LC), *Diary* 14, 16, 17, 18 June 1865).

92. Ruffin Papers (UNC), Hammond correspondence, Hammond to Ruffin, 5 February 1843, 7 July 1844, 20 July 1851.

Chapter Twelve

1. Craven, foreword to Ruffin, *Diary* 1:xiii; Craven, *Ruffin*, p. 64; Sitterson, introduction to Ruffin, *Calcareous Manures*, p. ix (also p. vii for reference to Ruffin's "transformation of the economy of the upper South from poverty to agricultural prosperity"); Bruce, "Virginian Agricultural Decline Fallacy," p. 3.

2. Eaton, *Southern Civilization*, p. 179.

3. Scarborough, introduction to Ruffin, *Diary* 1:xvi. See also chapter entitled "A Time of Triumph" in Mitchell, *Ruffin*, pp. 77–91.

4. For interesting comment here, see Allmendinger, "Early Career of Ruffin," passim.

5. Ruffin, *Exhausting and Fertilizing Systems*, p. 26.

6. Race rather than class considerations have been stressed in this study, reflecting Ruffin's clear emphasis. For additional comment on institutional preoccupations, see Faust, "The Rhetoric and Ritual of Agriculture in Antebellum South Carolina," pp. 558–60.

7. *FR* 3 (September 1835): 310–12.

8. Genovese, *Political Economy of Slavery*, pp. 43–61, 110–13, 131–44.

9. Genovese acknowledges this. Ibid., p. 139.

10. Rubin, "Limits of Agricultural Progress," pp. 369–70.

11. Genovese, *Political Economy of Slavery,* p. 93, referring to Taylor, "Commercial Fertilizers in the South Atlantic States," and Jordan, "Peruvian Guano Gospel."

12. Gates, *Farmer's Age,* p. 327; Mathew, *Peruvian Guano Monopoly,* pp. 168, 190–91; Jordan, "Peruvian Guano Gospel," pp. 216–17; *SP* 8 (October 1857): 592–93.

13. Mathew, *Peruvian Guano Monopoly,* p. 252.

14. Allowing a conservative 224 lbs. to the acre (cf. Genovese, *Political Economy of Slavery,* pp. 94–95) and assuming that, for the most part, farmers did not try to use it (like marl) as a permanent improvement.

15. Taylor "Commercial Fertilizers," pp. 180–82. See also Cooper, "The Cotton Crisis in the Antebellum South," pp. 386, 390, for suggestions that the issue of labor skills was probably an irrelevance in fertilizer application (squaring with our findings on marling).

16. Genovese, *Political Economy of Slavery,* p. 94.

17. *SC* 11 (April 1853).

18. *Thomas Ruffin Papers* 4:52 (Edmund Ruffin to George Watt, 7 November 1859).

19. Moore, *Agriculture in Mississippi,* pp. 37–38.

20. The notion of widespread success here is questioned in Wright, *Cotton South,* pp. 74–87.

21. Mathew, "Planter Entrepreneurship," p. 217.

22. Numbers and Numbers, "Science in the Old South," p. 171.

23. This theme of rural-urban conflict is prominent in Mathew, "Demise of the *Farmers' Register,*" passim.

24. For a handy survey of Southern abolitionism and manumission practice, see Collins, *White Society,* chapter 4. Collins shows that the proportion of blacks in the upper South classified as free rose from 10.4 percent in 1810 to only 12.8 percent in 1860. Over the same half-century in the lower South, the percentage fell, from 3.9 to 1.5 (p. 54).

25. The most inescapable modern example of the unreformable tyranny, pulling together elements of both slavery and imperialism, is South African apartheid. It should not be forgotten, of course, that slavery and imperialism were also historically related in the Americas.

26. Basically, cleared land in arable or pastoral use.

27. County figures have been taken from the 1850 census. Correlation coefficients are as follows:

1. *Percentage population change, 1840–50, on slave percentage*

Tidewater	−0.16
Maryland	−0.42
Virginia	0.61
South Carolina	−0.06

2. *Percentage improved farmland, 1850, on slave percentage*

Tidewater	−0.26
Maryland	−0.06
Virginia	0.61
South Carolina	−0.06

3. *Land values, 1850, on slave percentage*
Tidewater   −0.27
Maryland   −0.44
Virginia   0.02
South Carolina 0.48

28. Ruffin, "Exhausting and Fertilizing Systems," pp. 12–13.

29. Poinsett, "Agricultural Address," p. 253.

30. Smith, *Wealth of Nations* 1:362.

31. Genovese, *Political Economy of Slavery,* p. 159.

32. Prothero, *English Farming,* p. 330. See also Caird, *English Agriculture,* pp. 515–16; Hunt, "Labour Productivity in English Agriculture," pp. 284–88, 290; and county-by-county evaluations in Haggard, *Rural England.*

33. Hindess and Hirst, *Pre-Capitalist Modes of Production,* p. 167.

34. Bowser, *The African Slave in Colonial Peru,* chapter 4, 6.

35. Wright, *Cotton South,* pp. 107–27.

36. Parker, "Slavery and Southern Economic Development," pp. 115–25.

37. Landes, *The Unbound Prometheus,* p. 21.

38. Genovese, *Political Economy of Slavery,* pp. 125, 144.

39. Fogel and Engerman, *Time on the Cross* 1:5 and passim.

40. Ibid., p. 9 (my emphasis).

Bibliography

Abbott, Martin. "The First Shot at Fort Sumter." *Civil War History* 3 (1957).

Adams, James Truslow. "The Dilemma of Edmund Ruffin." *Virginia Quarterly Review* 10 (1934).

Akehurst. B. C. *Tobacco*. London: Longmans, 1968.

Alavi, Hamza. "India and the Colonial Mode of Production." *Socialist Register* (1975).

Allmendinger, David F., Jr. "The Early Career of Edmund Ruffin, 1810–1840." *Virginia Magazine of History and Biography* 93 (1985).

Amin, Samir. *Accumulation on a World Scale*. New York: Monthly Review Press, 1974.

Anderson, Ralph V. "Labor Utilization and Productivity, Diversification and Self-Sufficiency, Southern Plantations, 1800–1840." Doctoral dissertation, University of North Carolina at Chapel Hill, 1974.

Anderson, Ralph V., and Robert E. Gallman. "Slaves as Fixed Capital: Slave Labor and Southern Economic Development." *Journal of American History* 64 (1977).

Arbuckle, W. F. "The Gowrie Conspiracy," parts 1 and 2. *Scottish Historical Review* 36 (1957).

Ashley, Sir William. *The Bread of Our Forefathers*. Oxford: Clarendon Press, 1928.

Åslander, Alfred. "Standard Fertilization and Liming as Factors in Maintaining Soil Productivity." *Soil Science* 74 (1952).

Aufhauser, R. Keith. "Slavery and Scientific Management." *Journal of Economic History* 33 (1973).

Bachman, John. *The Doctrine of the Unity of the Human Race*. Charleston: Canning, 1850.

Barbé, Louis A. *The Tragedy of Gowrie House*. Paisley, London: Alexander Gardner, 1887.

Barnard, Henry. "The South Atlantic States in 1833, as Seen by a New Englander." Edited by Bernard C. Stemer. *Maryland Historical Magazine* 13 (1918).

Battalio, Raymond C., and John Kagel. "The Structure of Antebellum Southern Agriculture: South Carolina, A Case Study." *Agricultural History* 44 (1970).

Batten, James W., and J. Sullivan Gibson. *Soils: Their Nature, Classes, Distribution, Uses, and Care.* University, Ala.: University of Alabama Press, 1977.

Baumol, William J., "Entrepreneurship in Economic Theory." *American Economic Review* 58 (1968).

Bear, Firman Edward. *Chemistry of the Soil.* New York: Rheinhold, 1955.

Berlin, Ira. *Slaves Without Masters.* New York: Vintage Books, 1976.

Berthoff, Rowland. "Celtic Mist Over the South." *Journal of Southern History* 52 (1986).

Bidwell, Percy Wells, and John Ironside Falconer. *History of Agriculture in the Northern United States, 1620–1860.* Clifton, N.J.: Kelley, 1973. (First published 1925)

Black, Charles Allen. *Soil-Plant Relationships.* New York: Wiley, 1960.

Black, George F. *The Surnames of Scotland.* New York: New York Public Library, 1962.

Boatner, Mark M. *Cassell's Biographical Dictionary of the American Civil War, 1861–1865.* London: Cassell, 1973.

Bodichon, Barbara Leigh Smith. *An American Diary, 1857–8.* Edited by Joseph W. Reed, Jr. London: Routledge & Kegan Paul, 1972.

Bonner, James C. "Genesis of Agricultural Reform in the Cotton Belt." *Journal of Southern History* 9 (1943).

———. "Advancing Trends in Southern Agriculture." *Agricultural History* 21 (1947).

———. *A History of Georgia Agriculture, 1731–1860.* Athens: University of Georgia Press, 1964.

Bowser, Frederick P. *The African Slave in Colonial Peru, 1524–1650.* Stanford: Stanford University Press, 1974.

Boys, John. *General View of the Agriculture of the County of Kent.* London: Sherwood, Neely, 1813.

Brady, Nyle C. *The Nature and Properties of Soils.* New York, London: Macmillan, 1974.

Bridges, E. M. *World Soils.* Cambridge: Cambridge University Press, 1970.

Bruce, John. *Papers Relating to William, First Earl of Gowrie, and Patrick Ruthven.* London: J. E. Taylor, 1867.

Bruce, Kathleen. "Virginian Agricultural Decline to 1860: A Fallacy." *Agricultural History* 6 (1932).

Bunting, Brian T. *The Geography of Soil.* London: Hutchinson, 1967.

Buol, S. W., F. D. Hole, and F. J. McCracken. *Soil Genesis and Classification.* Ames: Iowa State University Press, 1973.

Burnet, Bishop Gilbert. *History of His Own Time.* Oxford: Oxford University Press, 1833. (First published 1724, 1734)

Cabell, N. F. *Early History of Agriculture in Virginia.* Washington: 1915.

Caird, James. *English Agriculture in 1850–51.* London: Longman, Brown, Green, and Longmans, 1852.

Cairnes, John Elliott. *The Slave Power.* London: Parker & Bourn, 1862.

Cash, W. J. *The Mind of the South.* Harmondsworth, Middlesex: Penguin Books, 1973. (First published 1941)

Cathey, Cornelius Oliver. "Agricultural Implements in North Carolina, 1783–1860." *Agricultural History* 25 (1951).

———. *Agricultural Developments in North Carolina, 1783–1860.* Chapel Hill: University of North Carolina Press, 1956.

Chambers, J. D., and G. E. Mingay. *The Agricultural Revolution.* London: B. T. Batsford, 1966.

Chandra, Bipan. "Indian Nationalists and the Drain, 1880–1905." *Indian Economic and Social History Review* 2 (1965).

Channing, Steven A. *Crisis of Fear: Secession in South Carolina.* New York: W. W. Norton, 1970.

Chapman, John D., and John C. Sherman, advisory eds. *Oxford Regional Economic Atlas: United States and Canada.* Oxford: Clarendon Press, 1973.

Chernov, V. A. *The Nature of Soil Acidity.* Madison: Soil Science Society of America, 1964.

Clapham, J. H. *The Economic Development of France and Germany.* Cambridge: Cambridge University Press, 1955.

Clay, James W., Douglas M. Orr, and Alfred W. Stuart. *North Carolina Atlas.* Chapel Hill: University of North Carolina Press, 1975.

Cokayne, George E. *The Complete Peerage.* Vols. 5 and 9. London: St. Catherine Press, 1926, 1936.

Cole, Arthur H. "An Approach to the Study of Entrepreneurship." In *Enterprise and Secular Change,* edited by Frederick C. Lane and Jelle C. Riemersma. London: Allen and Unwin, 1953.

Collings, Gilbert H. *Commercial Fertilizers.* London: H. K. Lewis, 1947.

Collins, Bruce. *White Society in the Antebellum South.* London and New York: Longman, 1985.

Conrad, Alfred H., and John E. Meyer. "The Economics of Slavery in the Ante Bellum South." In *Slavery and the Southern Economy,* edited by Harold Woodman. New York: Harcourt Brace, 1966.

Cooke, G. W. *The Control of Soil Fertility.* London: Crosby Lockwood, 1967.

Cooper, William J. "The Cotton Crisis in the Antebellum South: Another Look." *Agricultural History* 49 (1975).

Craven, Avery O. *Soil Exhaustion as a Factor in the Agricultural History of Virginia and Maryland, 1606–1860.* Urbana: University of Illinois Press, 1926.

———. "The Agricultural Reformers of the Ante-Bellum South." *American Historical Review* 33 (1927–28).

———. "John Taylor and Southern Agriculture." *Journal of Southern History* 4 (1938).

———. *Edmund Ruffin, Southerner.* Baton Rouge: Louisiana State University Press, 1966. (First Published 1932)

Crittenden, Charles Christopher. "Inland Navigation in North Carolina, 1763–1789." *North Carolina Historical Review* 8 (1931).

Cromerty, George, Earl of. *An Historical Account of the Conspiracies by the Earls of Gowry and Robert Logan of Restalrig Against King James VI.* Edinburgh: J. Watson, 1713.

Cummings, Ralph A. "Agronomic Problems in the Agricultural Reconversion of the South." *Proceedings of the Soil Science Society of America* 10 (1945).

Darby, H. C., ed. *A New Historical Geography of England.* Cambridge: Cambridge University Press, 1973.

David, Paul A., et al. *Reckoning with Slavery.* New York: Oxford University Press, 1976.

Davies, Chris. "The Canal System: The Competitive Challenge, 1830–44." Transport History Group Conference Paper, Polytechnic of Central London (1977).

Davis, Ralph. *The Rise of the English Shipping Industry in the Seventeenth and Eighteenth Century.* Newton Abbott: David & Charles, 1962.

Davy, Sir Humphry. *Elements of Agricultural Chemistry.* Edinburgh, London: Constable et al., 1813.

De Bow, J. D. B. *Statistical View of the United States . . . Being a Compendium of the Seventh Census.* Washington: A. O. P. Nicholson, 1854.

Defoe, Daniel. *A Tour Through the Whole Island of Great Britain.* London: P. Davies, 1927. (First published 1724)

Demaree, Albert Lowther. *The American Agricultural Press, 1819–1860.* New York: Columbia University Press, 1941.

Dickson, David, and James M. Smith. *David Dickson's and James M. Smith's Farming.* Edited by G. F. Hunnicutt. Atlanta: Cultivator, 1910.

Donahue, Roy L., John C. Shickluna, and Lynn S. Robertson. *Soils.* Englewood Cliffs, N.J.: Prentice-Hall, 1971.

Donaldson, Gordon. *Scottish Historical Documents.* Edinburgh: Scottish Academic Press, 1970.

Dozier, Howard Douglas. *A History of the Atlantic Coast Line Railroad.* Boston, New York: Hart, Schaffner, Marx, 1920.

Eaton, Clement. *The Growth of Southern Civilization, 1790–1860.* New York: Harper Torchbooks, 1963.

Edlin, Herbert L., ed. *East Anglian Forests.* London: H. M. Stationery Office, 1972.

Elkins, Stanley, and Eric McKitrick. "A Meaning for Turner's Frontier." *Political Science Quarterly* 89 (1954).

———. *Slavery: A Problem in American Institutional and Intellectual Life.* 2d ed. Chicago: University of Chicago Press, 1968.

Elliott, William. *Address Delivered by Special Request Before the St. Paul's Agricultural Society.* Charleston: Walker & James, 1850.

Emmons, Ebenezer. *Report of Professor Emmons on His Geological Survey of North Carolina.* Raleigh: Seaton Gales, 1852.

———. *Agriculture of North-Carolina, Part 2.* Raleigh: W. W. Holden, 1860.

Ewen, C. L'Estrange. *A History of Surnames of the British Isles.* London: Kegan Paul, Trench, Trubner, 1931.

Faust, Drew Gilpin. *A Sacred Circle.* Baltimore: Johns Hopkins University Press, 1977.

———. "The Rhetoric and Ritual of Agriculture in Antebellum South Carolina." *Journal of Southern History* 45 (1979).

———. *James Henry Hammond and the Old South: A Design for Mastery.* Baton Rouge: Louisiana State University Press, 1982.

Fergus, E. N., Carsie Hammonds, and Hayden Rogers. *Southern Field Crops Management.* Chicago: J. B. Lippincott, 1944.

Fippin, Elmer O. *Address Delivered at the Summer Meeting of the Agricultural Society of South Carolina, July 14, Nineteen-fifteen.* Charleston: Walker, Evans and Cogswell, 1915.

Fishlow, Albert. *American Railroads and the Transformation of the Antebellum Economy.* Cambridge, Mass.: Harvard University Press, 1965.

Fitzherbert, John. *The Boke of Husbandry.* London: Thomas Berthelet, c. 1540.

Fitzhugh, George. *Sociology for the South: or, The Failure of Free Society.* Edited by Harvey Wish. New York: B. Franklin, 1965. First published by A. Morris (Richmond, Va., 1854).

———. *Cannibals All! or, Slaves Without Masters.* Edited by C. Vann Woodward. Cambridge, Mass.: Harvard University Press, Belknap Press, 1960. First published by A. Morris (Richmond, Va., 1857).

Flanders, Ralph Betts. *Plantation Slavery in Georgia.* Cos Cob, Conn.: John E. Edwards, 1967. (First published 1933)

Fleetwood, Rusty. *Tidecraft: The Boats of Lower South Carolina and Georgia.* Savannah: Coastal Heritage Society, 1982.

Floud, Roderick, and Donald McCloskey, eds. *The Economic History of Britain Since 1700.* Vol. 2, *1860 to the 1970s.* Cambridge: Cambridge University Press, 1981.

Fogel, Robert William. *Railroads and American Economic Growth.* Baltimore: Johns Hopkins University Press, 1964.

Fogel, Robert William, and Stanley L. Engerman. *Time on the Cross.* 2 vols. Boston: Little, Brown, 1974.

———. "Explaining the Relative Efficiency of Slave Agriculture in the Antebellum South." *American Economic Review* 67 (1977).

Foth, H. D., and J. W. Schafer. *Soil Geography and Land Use.* New York: 1980.

Fox-Genovese, Elizabeth, and Eugene D. Genovese. *Fruits of Merchant Capital: Slavery and Bourgeois Property in the Rise and Expansion of Capitalism.* New York: Oxford University Press, 1983.

Franklin, John Hope. *The Militant South, 1800–1861.* Cambridge, Mass.: Belknap Press of Harvard University Press, 1966.

Frykenberg, Robert Eric, ed. *Land Control and Social Structure in Indian History.* Madison: University of Wisconsin Press, 1969.

Furtado, Celso. *The Economic Growth of Brazil.* Berkeley and Los Angeles: University of California Press, 1968.

Fussell, G. E. "Crop Nutrition in Tudor and Early Stuart England." *Agricultural History Review* 3 (1955).

Gallman, Robert E. "Self-Sufficiency in the Cotton Economy of the Antebellum South." *Agricultural History* 44 (1970).

Galpin, W. Freeman. "The Grain Trade of Alexandria, Virginia, 1801–1815." *North Carolina Historical Review* 4 (1927).

Gardner, H. W., and H. V. Garner. *The Use of Lime in British Agriculture.* London: Farmer & Stock-Breeder Publications, 1953.

Gates, Paul W. *The Farmer's Age: Agriculture, 1815–1860.* New York: Harper Torchbooks, 1961.

Genovese, Eugene D. *The Political Economy of Slavery.* New York: Vintage Books, 1967.

———. *The World the Slaveholders Made.* New York: Vintage Books, 1971.

———. *In Red and Black.* New York: Vintage Books, 1972.

———. "The Slave South: An Interpretation." In *American Negro Slavery,* edited by

Allen Weinstein and Frank Otto Gatell. New York: Oxford University Press, 1973.

————. *Roll, Jordon, Roll.* New York: Vintage Books, 1976.

Gerschenkron, Alexander. *Economic Backwardness in Historical Perspective.* Cambridge, Mass.: Belknap Press of Harvard University Press, 1962.

Golden, L. B., N. Gammon, and R. P. Thomas. "A Comparison of Methods of Determining the Exhangeable Cations and the Exchange Capacity of Maryland Soils." *Proceedings of the Soil Science Society of America* 7 (1943).

Goodrich, Carter, et al. *Canals and American Economic Development.* New York: Columbia University Press, 1961.

Gras, Norman S. *History of Agriculture in Europe and America.* New York: F. S. Crofts and Co., 1925.

Gray, Lewis Cecil. *History of Agriculture in the Southern United States to 1860.* 2 vols. Gloucester, Mass.: Peter Smith, 1958. (First published 1933)

Grigg, David. *The Agricultural Revolution in South Lincolnshire.* Cambridge: Cambridge University Press, 1966.

Habib, Irfan. "Potentialities of Capitalistic Development in the Economy of Mughal India." *Journal of Economic History* 29 (1969).

Haggard, H. Rider. *Rural England, Being an Account of Agricultural and Social Researches Carried Out in the Years 1901 and 1902.* London: Longmans Green, 1902.

Haites, Eric F., and James Mak. "Ohio and Mississippi River Transportation, 1810–1860." *Explorations in Economic History* 8 (1970–71).

Haites, Eric F., James Mak, and Gary M. Walton. *Western River Transportation, 1810–1860.* Baltimore: Johns Hopkins University Press, 1975.

Hallock, Judith Lee. "The Agricultural Apostle and His Bible: Edmund Ruffin and the *Farmers' Register." Southern Studies* 23 (1986).

Hammond, Harry. *South Carolina.* Spartanburg: Reprint Company, 1972. (First published 1883)

Harston, C. B., and W. A. Albrecht. "Plant Nutrition and Hydrogen Ion: IV. Soil Acidity for Improved Nutrient Delivery and Nitrogen Fixation." *Proceedings of the Soil Science Society of America* 8 (1943).

Hart, John Fraser. *The Southeastern United States.* Princeton: D. Van Nostrand, 1967.

Haystead, Ladd, and Gilbert C. Fite. *The Agricultural Regions of the United States.* Norman: University of Oklahoma Press, 1955.

Helper, Hinton Rowan. *The Impending Crisis of the South: How to Meet It.* New York: A. B. Burdick, 1860.

Henderson, J. R. *The Soils of Florida.* University of Florida Agricultural Experiment Station Bulletin 334 (1939).

Hindess, Barry, and Paul Q. Hirst. *Pre-Capitalist Modes of Production.* London: Routledge & Kegan Paul, 1975.

Hinshaw, Clifford Reginald. "North Carolina Canals Before 1860." *North Carolina Historical Review* 25 (1948).

Holland, Henry. *General View of the Agriculture of Cheshire.* London: Sherwood, Neely, 1808.

Hunt, E. H. "Labour Productivity in English Agriculture, 1850–1914." *Economic History Review,* 2d ser. 20 (1967).

Hunter, Louis C. *Steamboats on the Western Rivers.* Cambridge, Mass.: Harvard University Press, 1969.

Hurd-Karrer, Annie M. "Relation of Soil Reaction to Toxicity and Persistence of Some Herbicides in Greenhouse Plots." *United States Department of Agriculture Technical Bulletin 911* (1946).

Inman, Joseph F., and Isobel B. Inman. *Hanover County, Virginia: 1850 United States Census.* Richmond: 1974.

Jackman, W. T. *The Development of Transportation in Modern England.* London: Cass, 1962.

Jefferson, Thomas. *Notes on the State of Virginia.* Edited by William Peden. New York: W. W. Norton, 1954. (First published 1787)

Jenkins, Hester, and D. Caradog Jones. "Social Class of Cantab. Alumni of the 18th and 19th Centuries." *British Journal of Sociology* 1 (1950).

Johnson, Guion Griffis. "The Ante-Bellum Town in North Carolina." *North Carolina Historical Review* 5 (1928).

Johnstone, James B. *Place-Names of Scotland.* Edinburgh: S. R. Publishers, 1970. (First published Edinburgh: David Douglas, 1892.)

Jones, E. L., ed. *Agriculture and Economic Growth in England, 1650–1815.* London: Methuen, 1967.

Jones, Joseph. *First Report to the Cotton Planters' Convention of Georgia on the Agricultural Resources of Georgia.* Augusta: Chronicle & Sentinel, 1860.

Jones, L. I. Rodwell, and P. W. Bryan. *North America: An Historical, Economic and Regional Geography.* London: Methuen, 1948.

Jordan, Weymouth T. "The Peruvian Guano Gospel in the Old South." *Agricultural History* 24 (1950).

Kennedy, Joseph. *History and Statistics of the State of Maryland According to the Returns of the Seventh Census of the United States, 1850.* Washington: Gideon, 1852.

———. *Agriculture of the United States in 1860; Compiled from the Original Returns of the Eighth Census.* Washington: Government Printing Office, 1864.

Kerridge, Eric. *The Agricultural Revolution.* London: Allen & Unwin, 1967.

Kilby, Peter. "Hunting the Heffalump." In *Entrepreneurship and Economic Development,* edited by Peter Kilby. New York: Free Press, 1971.

Kirzner, Israel M. *Perception, Opportunity, and Profit: Studies in the Theory of Entrepreneurship.* Chicago: University of Chicago Press, 1979.

Knight, Frank. *Risk, Uncertainty and Profit.* Boston and New York: Houghton Mifflin, 1921.

Landes, David. *The Unbound Prometheus.* Cambridge: Cambridge University Press, 1969.

Lane, Frederic C. and Jelle Riermersma, eds. *Enterprise and Secular Change.* London: Allen and Unwin, 1953.

Lang, Andrew. *James VI and the Gowrie Mystery.* London: Longmans, Green, 1902.

Lee, General Stephen D. "Who Fired the First Gun at Sumter?" *Southern Historical Society Papers* 24 [with reply from Julian M. Ruffin].

Leslie, William. *General View of the Agriculture of the Counties of Nairn and Moray.* London: Sherwood, Neely, 1813.

Lewis, David W. *Transactions of the South Central Agricultural Society.* Macon: Benjamin F. Griffin, 1852.

Liebig, Justus von. *The Natural Laws of Husbandry.* Edited by John Blyth. London: Walton & Maberley, 1863.

Lindsay, Jean. *The Canals of Scotland.* Newton Abbott: David & Charles, 1968.

Lindstrom, Diane. *Economic Development in the Philadelphia Region, 1810–1850.* New York: Columbia University Press, 1978.

Luraghi, Raimondo. *The Rise and Fall of the Plantation South.* New York: New Viewpoints, 1978.

Lyell, Sir Charles. *A Second Visit to the United States of North America.* London: J. Murray, 1849.

Lytle, William M. *Merchant Steam Vessels of the United States, 1807–1868.* Edited by Forrest R. Holdcamper. Mystic, Conn.: Steamship Historical Society of America, 1952. (First published 1931)

McCardell, John. *The Idea of a Southern Nation.* New York: W. W. Norton, 1979.

McColley, Robert. *Slavery and Jeffersonian Virginia.* Urbana: University of Illinois Press, 1973.

McDonald, Forrest, and Grady McWhiney. "The South from Self-Sufficiency to Peonage: An Interpretation. *American Historical Review* 85 (1980).

MacGill, Caroline E. *History of Transportation in the United States Before 1860.* Washington: Carnegie Institution, 1917.

McKitrick, Eric L., ed. *Slavery Defended: The Views of the Old South.* Englewood Cliffs, N.J.: Spectrum Books, 1963.

Macpherson, W. J. "Economic Development in India Under the British Crown, 1858–1947." In *Economic Development in the Long Run,* edited by A. J. Youngson. London: Allen & Unwin, 1972.

Magistad, O. C. "The Aluminum Content of the Soil Solution and Its Relation to Soil Reaction and Plant Growth." *Soil Science* 20 (1925).

Mak, James, and Gary M. Walton. "Steamboats and the Great Productivity Surge in River Transportation." *Journal of Economic History* 32 (1972).

———. "The Persistence of Old Technologies: The Case of Flatboats." *Journal of Economic History* 33 (1973).

Malherbe, I. de V. *Soil Fertility.* Cape Town: Oxford University Press, 1964.

Malster, Robert. *Wherries and Waterways.* Lavenham, Suffolk: Terence Dalton, 1971.

Marshall, William. *The Rural Economy of Norfolk.* London: T. Cadell, 1787.

———. *The Review and Abstract of the County Reports to the Board of Agriculture.* Vol. 3, Eastern Department. London: Longman, Hurst, 1818.

Mathew, David. *James I.* London: Eyre & Spottiswoode, 1967.

Mathew, W. M. "The Origins and Occupations of Glasgow Students, 1740–1839." *Past and Present* 33 (1966).

———. *The House of Gibbs and the Peruvian Guano Monopoly.* London: Royal Historical Society, 1981.

———. "Planter Entrepreneurship and the Ruffin Reforms in the Old South, 1820–60." *Business History* 27 (1985).

———. "Edmund Ruffin and the Demise of the *Farmers' Register.*" *Virginia Magazine of History and Biography* 94 (1986).

————. "Agricultural Adaptation and Race Control in the American South: The Failure of the Ruffin Reforms." *Slaverv & Abolition* 7 (1986).

————. "Slave Skills, Plantation Schedules, and Net Returns in Southern Marling, 1830–60." *Plantation Society in the Americas* 2 (1986).

Meredith, Roy. *Storm Over Sumter.* New York: Simon and Schuster, 1957.

Merrens, H. Roy. "A View of Coastal South Carolina in 1778: The Journal of Ebenezer Hazard." *South Carolina Historical and Genealogical Magazine* 63 (1972).

Merritt, Elizabeth. *James Henry Hammond, 1807–1864.* Baltimore: Johns Hopkins University Press, 1923.

Metzer, Jacob. "Rational Management, Modern Business Practices, and Economies of Scale in the Ante-Bellum Southern Plantations." *Explorations in Economic History* 12 (1975).

Midgely, A. R. "Lime—Its Importance and Efficient Use in Soils." *Proceedings of the Soil Science Society of America* 8 (1943).

Millar, C. E., L. M. Turk, and H. D. Foth. *Fundamentals of Soil Science.* New York: John Wiley, 1965.

Milward, A., and S. B. Saul. *The Development of the Economies of Continental Europe, 1850–1914.* London: Allen & Unwin, 1977.

Mingay, G. E., ed. *Arthur Young and His Times.* London: Macmillan, 1975.

Mitchell, Betty. *Edmund Ruffin: A Biography.* Bloomington: Indiana University Press, 1981.

Moore, Barrington. *Social Origins of Dictatorship and Democracy.* Harmondsworth, Middlesex: Penguin University Books, 1974.

Moore, John Hebron. *Agriculture in Ante-Bellum Mississippi.* New York: Bookman, 1958.

Morton, John C., ed. *Morton's Cyclopedia of Agriculture.* Edinburgh and London: Blackie, 1855.

Moser, Frank. "Calcium Nutrition at Respective pH Levels," *Proceedings of the Soil Science Society of America* 7 (1942).

Neale, Walter C. "Land Is to Rule." In *Land Control and Social Structure in Indian History,* edited by Robert Eric Frykenberg. Madison: University of Wisconsin Press, 1969.

Newby, I. A. *The South: A History.* New York: Holt, Rinehart and Winston, 1978.

Numbers, Ronald L., and Janet S. Numbers. "Science in the Old South: A Reappraisal." *Journal of Southern History* 48 (1982).

Oakes, James. *The Ruling Race.* New York: Alfred A. Knopf, 1982.

Ogg, W. G. "The Revival of Liming." *Scottish Journal of Agriculture* (1942).

Ó Gráda, C. "Agricultural Decline 1860–1914." In *The Economic History of Britain Since 1700.* Vol. 2, *1860 to the 1970s,* edited by Roderick Floud and Donald McCloskey. Cambridge: Cambridge University Press, 1981.

Olmsted, Frederick Law. *The Slave States.* Edited by Harvey Wish. New York: Capricorn Books, 1959. (First editions of original books, 1856, 1857, 1860, 1861).

Otto, John Solomon. "Southern 'Plain Folk' Agriculture: A Reconsideration." *Plantation Society* 11 (1983).

Paden, W. R., and W. H. Garman. "Yield and Composition of Cotton and Kobe

Lespedeza Grown at Different pH Levels." *Proceedings of the Soil Science Society of America* 11 (1947).

Parker, William N. "Slavery and Southern Economic Development: An Hypothesis and Some Evidence." *Agricultural History* 44 (1970).

Pearson, Robert W., and Fred Adams, eds. *Soil Acidity and Liming.* Madison: American Society of Agronomy, 1967.

Phillips, Ulrich Bonnell. *A History of Transportation in the Eastern Cotton Belt to 1860.* New York: Columbia University Press, 1908.

———. *American Negro Slavery.* Baton Rouge: Louisiana State University Press, 1966. (First published 1918)

Pierre, W. H. "Hydrogen-Ion Concentration, Aluminum Concentration in the Soil Solution, and Percentage Base Saturation as Factors Affecting Plant Growth in Acid Soils." *Soil Science* 31 (1931).

Pindell, Richard. "The Unrepentant Rebel." *Civil War Times* 24 (1985).

Poinsett, Joel. *An Agricultural Address Delivered Before the State Agricultural Society, 27th Nov. 1845.* Columbia: Summer & Carroll, 1846.

Priestly, Joseph. *Historical Account of the Navigable Rivers, Canals, and Railways of Great Britain.* London: Longmans, Rees, 1831.

Prince, H. C. "The Origins of Pits and Depressions in Norfolk." *Geography* 49 (1964).

Proceedings of the Agricultural Convention and of the State Agricultural Society of South Carolina, from 1839 to 1845. Columbia: Summer & Carroll, 1846.

Prothero, R. E. *English Farming, Past and Present.* London: Longmans, Green, 1936.

Range, Willard. *A Century of Georgia Agriculture, 1850–1950.* Athens: University of Georgia Press, 1954.

Rawick, George P. *The American Slave: A Composite Autobiography,* Vol. 1, *From Sundown to Sunup.* Westport, Conn.: Greenwood, 1972.

Reports and Resolutions of the General Assembly of South-Carolina, Passed at Its Regular Session of 1843. Columbia: A. H. Pemberton, 1844.

Riches, Naomi. *The Agricultural Revolution in Norfolk.* London: Cass, 1967.

Roark, James. *Masters Without Slaves.* New York: W. W. Norton, 1977.

Robertson, James. *General View of the Agriculture of the County of Perth.* Perth: Morison, 1813.

Robinson, Solon. *Guano: A Treatise of Practical Information for Farmers.* New York: Solon Robinson, 1853.

Rothstein, Morton. "The Cotton Frontier of the Antebellum South: A Methodological Battleground." *Agricultural History* 44 (1970).

Rubin, Julius. "The Limits of Agricultural Progress in the Nineteenth-Century South." *Agricultural History* 49 (1975).

Ruffin, Edmund. *An Essay on Calcareous Manures.* Edited by J. Carlyle Sitterson. Cambridge, Mass.: Belknap Press of Harvard University Press, 1961. (First edition Petersburg, 1832; fifth and last edition Richmond, 1852)

———. *Desultory Observations on the Abuses of the Banking System.* Petersburg: Edmund & Julian C. Ruffin, 1841.

———. *Report of the Commencement and Progress of the Agricultural Survey of South-Carolina, for 1843.* Columbia: A. H. Pemberton, 1843.

————. *An Address on the Opposite Results of Exhausting and Fertilizing Systems of Agriculture.* Charleston: Walker and James, 1853.

————. *Premium Essay on Agricultural Education.* Richmond: J. W. Randolph, 1853.

————. *Address to the Virginia State Agricultural Society on the Effects of Domestic Slavery on the Manners, Habits and Welfare of the Agricultural Population of the Southern States.* Richmond: J. W. Randolph (?), 1853. [Reproduction in *Southern Planter* 13 (1853): 8–16, used here]

————. *Essays and Notes on Agriculture.* Richmond: J. W. Randolph, 1855.

————. *The Political Economy of Slavery.* Washington: n.p., 1857. (First published 1852)

————. *Slavery and Free Labor Described and Compared.* N.p.: 1859.

————. *African Colonization Unveiled.* Washington: L. Towers, 1859.

————. *Notes on the Cane-Brake Lands, or the Cretaceous Region of Alabama.* Richmond: J. W. Randolph, 1860.

————. "The Free Negro Nuisance and How to Abate It." Reprinted in *The Diary of Edmund Ruffin,* Vol. 1, edited by William Kauffman Scarborough. Baton Rouge: Louisiana State University Press, 1972.

————. *Sketches of Lower North Carolina and the Similar Adjacent Lands.* Raleigh: Institution for the Deaf & Dumb & the Blind, 1861.

————. *The Diary of Edmund Ruffin.* Vol. 1, *Toward Independence, October 1856–April 1861.* Vol. 2, *The Years of Hope, April 1861–June 1863.* Edited by William Kauffman Scarborough. Baton Rouge: Louisiana State University Press, 1972, 1976.

————. *Agriculture, Geology, and Society in Antebellum South Carolina: The Private Diary of Edmund Ruffin, 1843.* Edited by William M. Mathew (Forthcoming).

Ruffin, Edmund, Jr. "Death of Edmund Ruffin." *Tyler's Quarterly Historical and Genealogical Magazine* 5 (1924).

Russell, Sir E. John. *Soils and Manures.* Cambridge: Cambridge University Press, 1946.

————. *The World of the Soil.* London: Collins, 1963.

Savage, Henry. *River of the Carolinas: The Santee.* New York: Rinehart, 1956.

Scarborough, William Kauffman. "Science on the Plantation." (Presented at the first Barnard-Millington Symposium on Southern Science and Medicine, Oxford, Mississippi, 1982; cited by kind permission of the author).

Schmidt, Hubert G. *Agriculture in New Jersey: A Three-Hundred-Year History.* New Brunswick, N.J.: Rutgers University Press, 1973.

Segal, Harvey H. "Canals and Economic Development." In *Canals and American Economic Development,* edited by Carter Goodrich. New York: Columbia University Press, 1961.

Shackle, George. *Epistemics and Economics.* Cambridge: Cambridge University Press, 1972.

Sharp, James Roger. *The Jacksonians versus the Banks.* New York: Columbia University Press, 1970.

Sitgreaves, Samuel. "Letters from South Carolina, 1821–22." Edited by P. J. Staudenraus. *South Carolina Historical and Genealogical Magazine* 58 (1957).

Smith, A. M. *Manures and Fertilizers*. London and New York: Thomas Nelson, 1958.

Smith, Adam. *The Wealth of Nations*. London: J. M. Dent & Sons, 1950. (First published 1776–78)

Smith, Alfred Glaze, Jr. *Economic Readjustment of an Old Cotton State: South Carolina, 1820–1860*. Columbia: University of South Carolina Press, 1958.

Smith, J. Russell, and M. Ogden Phillips. *North America*. New York: Harcourt Brace, 1942.

Smith, John. *General View of the Agriculture of the County of Argyle*. London: Sherwood, Neely, 1813.

Smith, Samuel. *General View of the Agriculture of Galloway*. London: Sherwood, Neely, 1913.

Soltow, James H. "The Entrepreneur in Economic History." *American Economic Review* 58 (1968).

Somers, Robert. *The Southern States Since the War*. London and New York: Macmillan, 1871.

Stampp, Kenneth M. *The Peculiar Institution*. New York: Vintage Books, 1956.

———. *The Imperiled Union*. New York: Oxford University Press, 1980.

Starling, Robert J. "The Plank Road Movement in North Carolina," parts 1 and 2. *North Carolina Historical Review* 16 (1939).

Stuck, W. M. *Soil Survey of Beaufort and Jasper Counties, South Carolina*. Washington: U.S. Department of Agriculture, 1973.

Sutch, Richard. "The Care and Feeding of Slaves." In *Reckoning with Slavery*, by Paul David et al. New York: Oxford University Press, 1976.

Taylor, George Rogers. *The Transportation Revolution, 1815–1860*. New York: Holt, Rinehart, 1964.

Taylor, John. *Arator: Being a Series of Agricultural Essays, Practical and Political, in Sixty-Four Numbers*. Edited by M. E. Bradford. Indianapolis: Liberty Classics, 1977. (First published 1813)

Taylor, Rosser H. *Slaveholding in North Carolina: An Economic View*. Chapel Hill: University of North Carolina Press, 1926.

———. "Commercial Fertilizers in South Carolina." *South Atlantic Quarterly* 29 (1930).

———. "The Sale and Application of Commercial Fertilizers in the South Atlantic States to 1900." *Agricultural History* 21 (1947).

Taylor, William Robert. *Cavalier and Yankee: The Old South and the American National Character*. New York: Braziller, 1961.

Thirsk, Joan, ed. *The Agrarian History of England and Wales*. Vol. 4, *1500–1640*. Cambridge: Cambridge University Press, 1967.

Thompson, F. M. L. "The Second Agricultural Revolution," *Economic History Review* 2, no. 21 (1968).

Thompson, Louis M. *Soils and Soil Fertility*. New York: McGraw-Hill, 1957.

Thomson, George Malcolm. *A Kind of Justice: Two Studies in Treason*. London: Hutchinson, 1970.

Thorpe, Earl E. *Eros and Freedom in Southern Life and Thought*. Westport, Conn.: Greenwood Press, 1979.

Trimmer, Joshua. "On the Geology of Norfolk as Illustrating the Laws of the Distribution of Soils." *Journal of the Royal Agricultural Society of England* 7 (1846).

Truog, Emil. "Lime in Relation to Availability of Plant Nutrients." *Soil Science* 65 (1949).

Tuomey, M. *Report on the Geological and Agricultural Survey of the State of South Carolina: 1844.* Columbia: A. S. Johnston, 1844.

———. *Report on the Geology of South Carolina.* Columbia: A. J. Johnston, 1848.

Turner, Charles W. "Railroad Service to Virginia Farmers, 1828–1860." *Agricultural History* 21 (1947).

United States Census. *Reports* and *Abstracts* for 1830, 1840, 1860. (For 1850, and partly for 1860 as well, material was taken from De Bow and Kennedy; see above.)

Vancouver, Charles. *General View of the Agriculture of the County of Essex.* London: W. Smith, 1975.

Von Hayek, Friedrich. "Economics and Knowledge." *Economica* 4 (1937).

Von Mises, Ludwig. *Human Action: A Treatise on Economies.* London: Hodge, 1949.

Walker, M. E., and A. W. White. "Effects of Liming on Crop Yields and Chemical Properties of Tifton and Greenville Soils." *Georgia Agricultural Experiment Stations Bulletin,* n.s. 108 (1963).

Weinstein, Allen, and Frank Otto Gatell, eds. *American Negro Slavery.* New York: Oxford University Press, 1973.

White, K. D. *Roman Farming.* London: Thames & Hudson, 1970.

White, Laura A. *Robert Barnwell Rhett: Father of Secession.* New York: Century Company, 1931.

Whitehead, Thomas, ed. *Virginia, as She Is.* Richmond: State Board of Agriculture, 1889.

Wilcox, Arthur M., and Warren Ripley. *The Civil War at Charleston.* Charleston: News & Courier and Evening Post, 1984.

Willan, T. S. *River Nagivation in England, 1600–1750.* London: Oxford University Press, 1936.

———. *The English Coasting Trade, 1600–1750.* Manchester: Manchester University Press, 1938.

———. *The Inland Trade.* Manchester: Manchester University Press, 1976.

Williamson, Arthur E. *Scottish National Consciousness in the Age of James VI.* Edinburgh: Donald, 1979.

Willson, David H. *James VI and I.* London: Cape, 1962.

Wilson, R. G. "The Aire and Calder Navigation. Part 4. The Navigation in the First Half of the Nineteenth Century." *Bradford Antiquary,* n.s. 45 (1971).

Woodman, Harold D., ed. *Slavery and the Southern Economy.* New York: Harcourt Brace, 1966.

Woodward, C. Vann. *The Burden of Southern History.* Baton Rouge: Louisiana State University Press, 1960.

Woodward, Horace B. *The Geology of England and Wales.* London: Longmans, Green, 1876.

Wright, Gavin. "Prosperity, Progress, and American Slavery," in *Reckoning with Slavery,* by Paul David et al. New York: Oxford University Press, 1976.

————. *The Political Economy of the Cotton South.* New York: W. W. Norton, 1978.

Wrightson, John. *Agricultural Text-Book, Embracing Soils, Manures, Rotations of Crops, and Live Stock.* Glasgow: William Collins, 1872.

Young, Arthur. *General View of the Agriculture of the County of Norfolk.* London: Phillips, 1804.

Youngson, A. J., ed. *Economic Development in the Long Run.* London: Allen & Unwin, 1972.

Index

References to Edmund Ruffin (ER) in chapters 4–12 have been indexed selectively. Of the many counties and districts cited in the text, only Prince George County, Virginia, and Edgecombe County, North Carolina, appear as index entries.

Lyell, Sir Charles, 88
Lytle, William M., 159

McColley, Robert, 162, 184
McCord, David, 38
McCord, Louisa, 38
McCracken, F. J., 13
McDonald, Forrest (with Grady
    McWhiney): "Celtic" cultural heritage,
    251 (n. 79)
MacGill, Caroline, 160
McLenahan (scientist), 87
McWhiney, Grady. *See* McDonald, Forrest
Macon, Ga., 45
Maine: lime exports to Southeast, 118,
    120, 121, 122
Mak, James, 159
Malherbe, I. de V., 82
Manassas Gap Junction, Va., 52
Manning, John, 188
Manure, farm, 22, 43, 72, 74, 75, 83, 93,
    94, 103, 104, 114, 117, 119, 123, 125,
    136, 138, 141, 145, 147, 175, 176, 182,
    242 (n. 9)
Manuring, Green, 175
Marks, Edward, 96, 99
Marks, John, 96, 99
Marl. *See* Marling
Marlbourne plantation (Va.), 53, 95, 98,
    134, 135, 143, 198; purchase made on
    ER's behalf by eldest son, 40; ER moves
    in, 41; drainage, 41; machinery, 41;
    livestock, 41; overseer, 41; slave families
    split, 41; marling, 41, 42, 86, 231
    (n. 20); price, 41, 43; acreage, 41, 43;
    labor, 41, 43; ER farm journal, 42;
    foreman, 42; lacks marl, 42, 225 (n. 72);
    crops and rotations, 43; profits, 43, 105,
    151; secluded, 43, 161, 196
Marling, 74, 93–94, 109, 126, 129, 140,
    183, 189, 200, 201, 209; organic needs,
    12, 140–41, 175–77; main subject of
    Farmers' Register, 24; extent in Virginia,
    24, 41–43, 47, 111–14, 117, 199; extent
    in South Carolina, 32, 40, 115–16, 117;
    effects in Virginia, 43, 94, 95–96, 98–99,
    100–101, 103–9, 151; plantation costs
    and returns, 43, 148–52, 165, 167, 174,
    175, 190, 220 (n. 31), 244 (n. 62);

meaning, differing between United States
and Britain, 75–76, 77; and soil texture,
75–76, 77, 104, 111; British, 75–76, 77,
150, 165–68; preparation, 76–77;
resources, 76–77, 84–89, 110, 111, 115,
136, 153; constitution, 77, 87, 88, 111;
effects on corn, 93, 94, 95–97, 100–104,
151; effects on crops, 93–94, 104, 149,
151, 175–77, 200; effects in South
Carolina, 94, 97, 102–6, 108; effects on
cotton, 94, 102–4; effects in North
Carolina, 97, 103–5, 107–9; effects on
wheat, 98–99, 101–4, 151; effects in
Maryland, 100, 103; effects on clovers,
grasses, potatoes, oats, rye, tobacco, 103;
effects on legumes, 103, 104; effects on
forage, 104; doses, 104, 140–41, 150,
174, 175, 176, 177, 243 (n. 57), 254
(n. 14); effects on animal and human
health, 105; effects on sorrel, 105; effects
on farm incomes, 105–6, 148–152;
effects on land values, 106–8, 149, 151;
demographic effects, 107–9; statistics
lacking, 110; extent in Delaware, 110;
extent in Maryland, 110–11, 117; extent
in North Carolina, 114–15; 117, 237
(n. 19); attended to mainly by large
planters, 114, 116, 183, 188, 189, 199,
209; effects in Georgia, 117; digging,
131, 132–34, 142–43, 145–46, 148–50,
154–56, 161, 163, 173, 174; transport,
131, 133, 134–36, 142–50, 173, 174,
175, 240 (n. 12), 244 (n. 10) 245 (n. 17),
246 (n. 60), spreading, 131, 137–39,
142, 144–46, 148, 174, 175; laborious,
131, 139, 172–74, 185, 191, 201;
inundation of pits, 132–34, 175; use of
children, 135, 137, 142, 143, 149;
preparing for fields, 136–37; composting,
136–7; use of women, 137, 138, 142,
149, 243 (n. 39); plowing under, 138,
163, 174; labor specialization hardly
resorted to, 141–48; flexible plantation
schedule, 141–49, 152, 174, 178; some
hired labor, 144, 149, 240 (n. 2);
secondary activity on plantation, 148,
163; preliminary and concomitant work,
173–77; badly conducted, 175–77; marl
burn, 176–77; different from liming,